Cultural Studies of Modern Germany

History, Representation, and Nationhood

Russell A. Berman

THE UNIVERSITY OF WISCONSIN PRESS

The University of Wisconsin Press
114 North Murray Street
Madison, Wisconsin 53715

3 Henrietta Street
London WC2E 8LU, England

Library of Congress Cataloging-in-Publication Data
Berman, Russell A., 1950–
    Cultural studies of modern Germany: history,
representation, and nationhood / Russell A. Berman.
       236 p.   cm.
    Includes bibliographical references and index.
    ISBN 0-299-14010-5   ISBN 0-299-14014-8 (pbk.)
    1. Germany—Civilization—20th century—Philosophy.
2. Germany—Intellectual life. 3. National characteristics, German.
4. Nationalism—Germany. 5. Politics and literature—Germany.
6. German literature—20th century—Political aspects. I. Title.
DD67.B47   1993
943.087—dc20   93-9987

Contents

Preface

The essays collected in this volume are concerned with Germany, from the beginning of the nineteenth century to the end of the twentieth, from the emergence of nationalism in the Napoleonic Wars to the debate over the Gulf War, the first foreign policy challenge of reunified Germany. The underlying theme of the essays is the representation of nationhood in aesthetic culture, where the vagaries of national identity intersect with the complexities of art. Understanding that political units, like nations, are culturally mediated and not simply natural is an initial step in the project of cultural studies. Simultaneously culture is assumed to have a double character, following its own internal and formal logic, while framing a terrain on which political and social contests are played out.

Many of these essays have been published previously. Chapter 2 is reprinted from *Heinrich Heine and the Occident*, edited by Peter Uwe Hohendahl and Sander L. Gilman, by permission of the University of Nebraska Press, copyright © 1991 by the University of Nebraska Press. Chapters 4 and 11 appeared in *Telos*, and parts of Chapter 5 appeared in *Theory, Culture & Society*, and are reprinted with permission. Chapter 6 is reprinted from *Fascism, Aesthetics, and Culture*, edited by Richard Golsan, 1992 by University Press of New England, by permission of University Press of New England. Chapter 7 is from "A Solidarity of Repression" in *The Films of G. W. Pabst: An Extraterritorial Cinema*, edited by Eric Rentschler, copyright © 1990 by Rutgers, the State University and is reprinted by permission of Rutgers University Press. Chapter 8 appeared in *Our Faust? Roots and Ramifications of a Modern German Myth*, edited by Reinhold Grimm and Jost Hermand, © 1987 Board of Regents of the University of Wisconsin System, and is reprinted with permission of the University of Wisconsin Press. Chapter 9 was published in *Germanic Review*, Vol. 66, no. 4, Fall 1991, pp. 155-160; reprinted with permission of the Helen Dwight Reid Educational Foundation, published by Heldref Publications, 1319 Eighteenth Street NW, Washington, D.C. 20077-6117, copyright © 1991. "The Return of the Jewish Volunteer" is reproduced with permission of the Jewish Museum, New York, and Art Resource.

vii

To acknowledge all the colleagues individually whose suggestions, encouragements, and rebukes have contributed to these essays would be a lengthy undertaking indeed. I thank them again for those discussions. I dedicate this book, with gratitude for all their help and support, to my parents, Herbert and Evelyn Berman.

Cultural Studies of Modern Germany

Introduction

Marking Time

The proliferation of *post* formulations—postmodern, postmarxist, postpolitical, posthistory—points to a changed experience of time, as if we felt always too late, always after the fact, always already marking time. This confession of perpetual epigonism might betray an exaggerated cathexis of the past to which we feel never equal, but it certainly has a simultaneously debilitating and exculpatory function in the present. The problem with time is that there is never enough, which is of course the perfect and constant excuse for every omission. Instead of acting, we wait or are condemned to wait for the sign that never arrives: "Hey Mister Postman, look and see, is there a letter in your bag for me?"

Such posthistorical enervation is odd indeed. On the individual level, new technologies give growing strata of the population access to an electronically mediated, global network of information that implies a sort of universal simultaneity. On the global level, the past years have hardly been devoid of what might be regarded as historical, indeed world-historical events. Not everyone has been marking time, and certainly not in Germany, the classic case of the belated nation. Indeed the pronouncements that history has come to an end or that the master narratives of history have collapsed are an indication more of various conservative wishes—the wish that time would stand still and nothing more change—than of any real reorganization of temporality, at least for the political and social systems.[1] Marking time has another meaning, however: not only the conservative freeze on progress but also the time of marking, the time of writing, scarring, inscribing, and distinguishing. Leaving traces makes a difference. History imagined as a caricature of Hegel, an ineluctable, monodirectional flow leading mechanically toward a goal—such history has indeed ceased to have much of a following. However, history as the temporal field in which identities are constructed, contested, and revised, as the time it takes to mark and remark and initiate meaning and expressivity: this history continues to witness the constant reinvention of identities, especially collective ones, through signs of distinction. And the central project of the contempo-

3

rary humanities has become the exploration and deciphering of cultural identities, in all their agonistic complexities, rather than the fetishized cultivation
of inherited canons.

Yet these identities are problematic because they are always the site of oppo-
sitions, marginalizations, minorities, and secessions, i.e., they are very complex texts. An adequate approach to this terrain would, at the very least, defer
taking sides for the course of the inquiry, and neither advocate cohesive identity nor celebrate the marginal as somehow heroically oppositional. It would
be prudent to withhold affirming the received opinion that alterity disrupts
the normative and hegemonic and upsets encrusted identity formations. It is,
so the standard story goes, the locus of the different, the original, and the innovative, and therefore a threat and challenge to the structures of stability and
hierarchy. But what if the process is more complex: what if innovation and stability are not incompatible but always interwoven. Then subversion might be
productive, marginality a prerequisite for centering, and the mark in time not
a mutilation of a perfect expanse but the action that constitutes history.

Still, the contemporary critical scene imagines difference as oppositional,
and with such an adversarial profile, it is not surprising to encounter a political drama framing the issue: on the right, cultural conservatives denounce
alterity as subversive of the symbols of national identity that provide coherence to the community, while, on the left, the defenders of minority positions
presumably cite precisely the same grounds in order to mobilize alterity against
the putatively oppressive symbolic material of master narratives and hegemonic
discourse. In other words, the alternative judgments share the evaluation that
alterity is essentially progressive and a threat to a status quo, whether one wants
to preserve or transform it. How tenable is that sort of unanimous claim? The
point is that when opponents share the same ground—which they regard as
a battlefield—they may also be sharing a misconception, in this case, the presumption that difference makes a difference.

Inquiring into the resonances of alterity, I want to suggest in the briefest
of terms two theoretical problems pertinent to the claim of adversariality and
then explore at greater length a third issue. The first problem might be designated as culturalism, a feature associated with both neoconservatism and discourse theory, i.e., the claim that value structures or rhetorics or narratives—culture—are the primary source of identity formation. The attribution
of an inordinate importance to cultural identity on the part of scholars of culture is a likely expression of professional interest. When it is coupled with a
political claim, the misapprehension becomes more significant, since it implies an objective consequence; yet it is by no means obvious that cultural alterity has any consequence at all or, to put it polemically, that integrating the literary curriculum really integrates the classroom, the university, society, or
anything except, of course, the photocopied curriculum. Getting rid of the elite

canon does not get rid of the elite. At the very least, therefore, the democratizing claims associated with alterity need some greater substantiation.

In fact, despite conservative anxieties and poststructuralist aspirations, the genealogy of alterity as a theoretical concept is such that a linkage between it and a diminished democracy is more plausible than its opposite, the suggested affinity of alterity and democratic politics. On the level of political theory, one does well to take account of the Schmittian opposition of democracy as majoritarian and therefore homogeneous to liberalism as the paradigmatic expression of minority, i.e., elite interests. More germane, however, is the articulation of alterity, understood as an alternative to universalism and abstract egalitarianism, precisely in the context of the Reaganite 1980s with its hierarchical reassertion of inequality and difference.[2] Let me make the provocation clear: multiculturalism and Reaganomics are two simultaneous institutionalizations of difference, two disruptions of universalizing schemes—one in the cultural, the other in the socio-economic realm, one along a horizontal, the other along a vertical axis, but both clearly implicated in a valorization of alterity rather than identity. That is to say, if a slippage can be registered between horizontal and vertical versions of alterity, then alterity per se is not at all necessarily a safely progressive alternative to identity.

The ambiguous implications of alterity are even more apparent, however, with regard to a third matter, the decisionistic problem of distinguishing among particular differences. Any theory of alterity will turn out to be inadequate if it cannot go beyond the mere determination of the fact of difference and provide instead some guidance among competing and competingly differential options. Yet making such a choice would entail wagering that one difference may be preferable to another, suggesting in turn a hierarchical thought structure, i.e., precisely the problem that the politics of alterity claimed to want to escape. How to adjudicate among different differences: the problem goes to the heart of any consideration of alterity, and not only in the all-too-familiar version of playing categories such as race, class, and gender off against each other. More dramatically, because disruptive of conventional political understandings, the valorization of difference that leads to a celebration of, say, minority discourse as oppositional to national identity is, surprisingly enough, equally available to nationalist discourse. In other words, an argument for alterity can lead, with equal cogency, to multicultural and to nationalist results, especially when one is operating with German material: is the German difference the difference within Germany (the minority status) or Germany as itself the different, the qualitatively different nation, whose *Sonderweg* distinguishes it from normative models of national development?

The answer is, of course, both, and this oscillation within alterity can be explicated with regard to three sorts of materials. It is, first, a mirror image of the dialectic of nationalism: a democratic term when understood inclusively, but more frequently a term of belligerence, counterposing one nation to another. In the abstract, the "nation" is as empty a category as the different; indeed, it may not be very different at all, suggesting that alterity may ultimately just be the contemporary heir to nationhood. Second, the counterintuitive overlap between minoritarian difference and nationalist difference is, as I have argued elsewhere, precisely indicative of West German counterhegemonic discourse in the early and mid-1980s, where a left cultural agenda could coexist with a rearticulation of a discourse of national interest in the context of the Euromissiles debates.[3] Finally the duplicity of alterity was staged in the 1989 metamorphosis of revolutionary slogans from "Wir sind das Volk" (different from the elite) to "Wir sind ein Volk" (internally nondifferentiated but therefore different from the others): from democracy to unification to nationalism, where national identity has become the crucial difference.

The play of difference with regard to national identity can lead in various directions; I want to explore this range with two examples treating the Polish border—the site, guaranteed by international law, of national difference—which has held particular significance in the process leading to unification. In Peter Schneider's "Reise durch das deutsche Nationalgefühl," included in his collection *Extreme Mittellage* (1990), the author explores expressions of German nationalism on the part of the German minority in Poland. Clearly the choice of this material, rather than, say, the question of the Turkish minority in Germany, leads to a radically different inflection of the question of minority discourse. Schneider proceeds by conceding as much.

> One has to ask what is bubbling up forty-five years after the end of the Second World War. . . . I want to explore this through the perhaps most difficult question, the German minority in Poland. This project can only elicit disgust from every halfway enlightened German. For the provocation of "Germans in Silesia" immediately brings to mind Silesian regional organizations, the Association of Exiles and its President Herbert Czaja. . . . But does this incorrigible truly speak for the Germans in Poland?[4]

Precisely this inquiry into the validity of minority representation, i.e., the representatives of the minority, structures the text, leading the author into Poland in order to discover an ethnographically authentic voice. The strategy allows for a separation between a threatening misleadership and an endearingly innocent populace: "The further I traveled to the east, the more moderate I found the Germans. Instead of finding the fortress of revanchism, I found modest two-family homes, in which modest people pursued modest goals."[5] The point is that the threat of difference, the image of reactionary ethnic Germans calling into question the Oder-Neisse border—and borders are after all the geographic manifestation of difference—is defused: not by dissolving difference into a universalist internationalism but by magnifying difference, so that the individual member of the minority is played off against the self-appointed leadership of the minority group, who is therefore repositioned as a hegemonic, and therefore weakened, voice. This logic of difference unfolds through a multicultural defense of minority rights into an even greater differentiation, displacing the advocates of group rights by the vocalization of individual speakers. It is poised therefore precisely in between the entitlement of protected groups and the critique of the rhetoric of victimization associated with such entitlement policies.

If the tendency of Schneider's liberalism is to atomize the border, Hans Jürgen Syberberg spiritualizes it in his polemical *Vom Unglück und Glück der Kunst in Deutschland nach dem letzten Kriege* (1990). I won't belabor Syberberg's explicitly reactionary positions; the provocative point is rather that precisely as a reactionary he is perhaps the most consistent thinker of alterity, i.e., Germany as different from the West, a stance which is thoroughly compatible with the conservative appreciation of difference as hierarchy. For Syberberg insists that in the "reunification meant by the heart,"[6] a spiritual rather than political reconciliation with Poland is crucial, owing to the centrality of the German-Polish connection for cultural identity: "Without the Poles, no Prussia; but without Germany, no Christian Poland. . . . It is not a matter of moving the borders, that old shifting of the administrative competencies of the changing managers, but of that which lies beyond the borders, the unification of hearts of common European presumptions."[7] Yet in the manner of traditional German conservatism's eastern orientation, it is this spiritual reencounter with Poland which allows for both an alternative to the capitalist West and the transfiguration of traditionalist social models:

> We will have to see if there is still hope to escape those new laws of business and intellectual arguments along with the imperialism of the new invaders, or to see whether anyone is hungry. . . . We will see if the faces and costumes look alike and whether the houses are tempting or threatened; we will see if they can stand on free soil in a brief moment of solidarity, their hands full of work and with a head that guides these hands. These are the key auxiliary tools, rather than compulsory slavery to business, where life was a direct gift from nature and not banished from her, and where weaknesses turn into virtues.[8]

Poland is therefore the guarantor of German difference from the reifying logic of equalization; in this sense, I spoke of Syberberg's spiritualizing the border, as an expression of his romantic anticapitalism, while Schneider dissolves the problem by pursuing difference differently: from the minority as the objectification of difference to the individual as the difference within the minority.

That the anticapitalist voice, so pronounced in the conservative Syberberg, is all but absent in Schneider is a telling commentary on the vicissitudes of German political culture after 1989. In both, however, a specifically political sphere is undermined: in Schneider through the subversion of claims to political representation, in Syberberg through the dismissive marginalization of the state in the interest of higher cultural values. Is that weakening of the political sphere evidence of the resilience of the older, unpolitical German? Alternatively, one could argue that it is not German particularity but rather precisely the discourse of alterity—in both its liberal and conservative variants—that retreats somehow from political institutions, especially majoritarian ones, and therefore contributes to the emergence of postpolitical structures.

This commentary on alterity and on the debate over German identity is symptomatic of the sorts of issues pursued in this book. The central question is the production of identity through distinction, the potentials of and threats to communitarian cohesion. The central thesis is that shared histories and narratives depend on the practices of marking, differentiation, and distance. The answers given in the body of the book derive from the ongoing theory discussion with no pure allegiance, although the overriding influences have been from the Frankfurt School and from cultural studies. Both legacies lead, of course, away from an exclusive concentration on literary texts, but in very different ways. For all of its insistence on the importance of particularity, the Frankfurt School preserved some considerable indebtedness to classical Marxist economics and neo-Hegelian historico-philosophy. For all of its own insistence on the working class, British cultural studies has cultivated a sort of insularity that could easily be read as nationalistic: the international proletariat may not have a home, but the English worker certainly does, on English territory and, more important, within English culture. If critical theory universalizes the particular by dissolving concrete instances into the categories of neo-Hegelianism, cultural studies particularizes the universal: culture, if not socialism, in one country.

The first chapter explores some interrelations between these two interpretive paradigms, Frankfurt and Birmingham. Their juxtaposition highlights the lability of the concept of context, even though both schools tend to take it as a given. Yet instead of merely presuming particularity as an alternative to the tyranny of the Enlightenment, as critical theory might, or to capitalism, in the manner of British cultural studies, it is crucial to understand that context, too, is made; particularity is not a blindly inherited legacy but the concretization of active experience; and community is the consequence of practices of self-constitution. Politics is the terrain of struggle among competing practices for the always provisional definition of shared culture. This process of self-constitution betrays the political component in culture, an issue that is particularly relevant to the reading of a certain class of authors whose texts appear to have—or are understood to have—a particularly strong implication for nationhood and national literary history. This issue is broached in the second chapter on Heine and Whitman. The third chapter too treats the limits of nationhood by looking closely at a key document of German-Jewish emancipation, the painting by Moritz Oppenheim entitled *Return of the Volunteer to His Family Still Living According to the Old Customs*. The topic of nationhood is explored again in the fourth chapter by examining a unique set of material: documentation, from the era of German unification, of the German perception of Italian unification. The discursive doubling highlights the process of invention, which in turn implies the contingency of national coherence. When diversity challenges monolithic identity, politics turn to regionalism or federalism.

In Chapter 5, I return to a primarily theoretical material, the debate over deconstruction. The issue has a special relevance to the study of German culture, given the material of the debate: de Man's collaboration with the Nazis in occupied Belgium and the legacy of Heidegger in Derrida's work. The chapter is devoted mainly to deconstruction and the problem of history, as it emerges from de Man's reading of Rousseau's Second Discourse, as well as to the possibility of literary history: is history anything more than just another fiction? Can scholarship make truth claims? These questions become particularly urgent at the political edges of deconstruction, especially the South Africa debate. These politics themselves interlock with German cultural material through the issue of race, and the theoretical issues fit into the competition between critical theory and cultural studies.

The next three chapters explore visual culture, collective identity formation, and mass culture: what marks circumscribe experience and produce cohesion? what marks are traces of a repression that destabilizes community? Chapter 6 is devoted to the vicissitudes of the painter Emil Nolde, his primitivism and its relation to fascist aesthetics; Chapter 7 analyzes G. W. Pabst's celebration of proletarian solidarity in his film *Kameradschaft*; Chapter 8 surveys cinematic renderings of the Faust myth.

War and peace as registers of community unify the last three chapters, in which the topic is again literature or literary intellectuals. Chapter 9 discusses war in a famous short story by Heinrich Böll and how the critique of Nazi militarism simultaneously entails a revision of a classical Western scene, the battle of Thermopylae: the confrontation with Asia. It is also an investigation of a scene of writing that is simultaneously a staging of fascism. Nearly the same problematic concerns Peter Handke in his novel *Across*, discussed in Chapter 10: marking as neo-Nazi graffiti, history as the possibility of narration, and narration as the guarantor of peace. The concluding Chapter 11 is, like the earlier discussion of Heine and Whitman, emphatically comparative and is also very much involved with the question of nationality: the Gulf War as a dramatic deployment of loyalties and citizenship and the differential responses of intellectuals in Germany and the United States, particularly with regard to questions of national culture, local histories, and popularity.

Cultural studies is the examination of the symbolic orders in which inter-subjective meanings and social practices are constituted and contested, and this pertains to literary works, to other artistic materials, and to nonartistic, but nevertheless symbolic materials, e.g., modes of political representation, the organization of private and public spaces, and codes of gender distinction. The essays collected in this volume range across this spectrum: some are decid-edly literary, others look at the visual arts, and some focus on explicitly polit-ical texts. They point, however, to an overriding concern with the construction of collective identities precisely as such identities are modulated by difference and particularity. Culture is therefore understood to be necessarily plural, always coexisting with other cultures and always internally diversified. Con-sequently, no matter how theoretical cultural studies may be, it has as its empir-ical object material that is always multiple and differential. If a rigorous study of literature qua literature might focus on abstract form, and if traditional lit-erary history is trapped in the pure linearity of individual canons, cultural studies inquires into the fabrication of shared meanings, understood to be always in competition, internally and externally, with other codes of mean-ings. The result is not so much "cultural relativism" as the recognition that multiplicity is the inescapable, and hence universal, condition of culture. Yet this multiplicity can just as well be celebrated as repressed, and all sorts of options in between: minority emancipations, local regionalisms, class-based collectivism, populist nationalism, one-dimensional normalizations, to name some of the models relevant to the empirical cases examined in this book. If they are examined with reference to the question of nationhood, it is not because of any essential identification of culture with nation, but because for cultural studies the nation is one particularly intriguing site at which symbolic orders are distinguished, established, and questioned. For the representation of the nation is the historical practice of instituting a shared distinction: marking time.

Chapter 1

Cultural Criticism and Cultural Studies

Reconsidering the Frankfurt School

If the questions that cultural theory addresses are significant, then the answers are likely to be contested and the terrain of cultural-theoretical analysis therefore implies a multiplicity of voices. Appropriately enough, one should add, since the material of study, culture, equally implies a plurality of participants. Culture is never individual, but individuality may be a cultural phenomenon. Yet that cultural plurality is often described with terms that impute cohesion—community, nation—and disguise contestation. One project of cultural theory is the recovery of the plural in the singular.

That seemingly minor shift is of course not minor at all, indicating a refusal to impute a uniform character to what is in fact a multiplicity of interventions in that complex discursive formation, itself always multidimensional and dynamic, too quickly reduced and reified by the label "literary theory." That old problem with labels: for a moment one is even tempted to wish for an imaginary language that would allow us to transpose each term into a plural form and thereby avoid the violence that every abstraction performs on its referent. No matter how much intellectual labor depends on the process of clarification through conceptual formulations, that same conceptual clarity is also an eclipse that casts an impenetrable shadow on the material, separating the subject from its object once it has been reduced to a mere object, susceptible to manipulation, appropriation, and control. Hence the melancholy at the conclusion of Hegel's *Phenomenology* when the mind, at the end of its arduous novel of development, finds itself at the Golgotha of the spirit. It is this same neo-Hegelian pessimism that achieves its definitive expression in the classical text of the Frankfurt School, the *Dialectic of Enlightenment*: the Enlightenment begins as the project to overcome the violence of brute nature by reason but, in an imitation of nature, reproduces that violence in an exponentially heightened form. The trajectory of a logocentric Western civilization leads inexorably to a rationalism gone amok, an irrational rationalism in which total administration and total destruction become totally indistinguishable from one another: Auschwitz, Hiroshima, the Gulag.

That was admittedly a very quick transition, from a comment on methods in cultural theory to the major catastrophes of the twentieth century. Perhaps it was even a very German performance: too quick, too deep, and too morose. An appropriate response to that reaction would investigate the relationship between American culture, in which the recognition of plurality is almost a matter of course, and some very different experiences, intellectual and historical, in Germany. What the spirit of tolerance and formal courtesy inherent in pluralism might miss, however, includes a possibly strong relationship between the conceptually separable dimensions of culture and society, aesthetic judgment and practical reason. Characteristic for the Frankfurt School, especially for the aesthetic criticism of Theodor Adorno, is that this relationship is always taut and hyperbolic, linking the radical microstructures of the cultural object to a historical narrative of civilization that is both pessimistic and nearly inescapable. It is a dialectic that embraces the exaggerated extremes and abjures the comfort of the middle. And it is with a rhetoric more characteristic of the Frankfurt School that I have tried to begin this reconsideration of the Frankfurt School.

Recognizing the multiplicity of theory is salutary, and not only from the standpoint of the critique of the Enlightenment but with regard to our own institutional setting as well. During the past decade of intense literary-theoretical debates, one has all too often heard theoretical altercations posed as conflicts between something called "German theory" and an equally uniform opponent dubbed "French theory." As if the Rhine were a philosophical argument, as if national identity grounded the conceptual imagination! This passport approach to intellectual life necessarily tends to ignore the importance of, say, Freud, Husserl, and Heidegger for Merleau-Ponty, Sartre, and Lacan, just as it misses the indebtedness of an heir apparent of the Frankfurt School, Jürgen Habermas, to Anglo-American philosophy and social theory. This national reduction of theoretical debate has arguably been symptomatic of the political-cultural mood of the past conservative decade, marked by a reassertion of nationalist sentiment on both sides of the Atlantic. The plurality of theory happily subverts the articulation of any monolithic "German" account and at least opens the way to a recognition that what is at stake in this theory is least of all its "Germanness." How historically ironic, indeed wrongheaded a distortion it would be to treat as characteristically German the work of intellectuals forced to leave Germany and to find a home in the United States; for some, like Leo Lowenthal and Herbert Marcuse, that American home became permanent; and for Max Horkheimer and Adorno, central texts, like the *Dialectic of Enlightenment* and *Minima Moralia*, are best understood as theoretical accounts of American, not German, society. Precisely that negativity of historical displacement becomes the topic of theoretical reflection: "Heimat ist Entronnensein"—home is the state of having escaped. The natural home is naturally uncanny, *unheimlich*, as brutal as blind nature; a genuine home would never entail a return but only the product of social labor and, equally, a graceful fortune: the "humanized nature" of the young Marx tempered by a modernist sense of lucky accident.

If it is inappropriate to categorize the Frankfurt School under the rubric of a "German theory," there is a further incongruity if it is located naively within the academic province of German departments. Of course, it is perfectly appropriate for German departments to include Frankfurt School material in their curricula; my point is that this has not been the case, until very recently, and it is important to explain why. The discipline of German studies in the United States has its own past to come to grips with, its own "Vergangenheit zu bewältigen." The phrase refers to a political and cultural project of postwar West German intellectuals who, especially during the 1960s, attempted to thematize the devastation of the Nazi era and to raise questions regarding its consequences for the Federal Republic. Even a brief account of that terrain, stretching from Günter Grass's *Tin Drum* of 1959 or Rolf Hochhuth's *Deputy* of 1963 to the grand reversals of Bitburg or the recent historians' debate would lead too far afield. What was the field of German departments in the United States after 1933 and what accounts of National Socialism did they provide after 1945? Much research has yet to be done regarding this institutional history, but it is fair to say that they were not, by and large, hotbeds of anti-fascism. More typical, I believe, is the following anecdote from my own university. When, in the mid-thirties, a young emigré Germanist arrived in California and inquired about a possible teaching position, he was told, in perhaps uniquely frank terms, that a scholar out of favor with the new regime in Germany would not be welcome in the department; that the rejected applicant later became one of the leading lights of postwar *Germanistik* only adds a bitter twist to the story. While it would be wrong to extrapolate from this case and impute a hard-core *völkisch* line to German departments fifty years ago, it would be equally wrong to repress it and ignore the subsequent bias in the curricula. The theoretical contributions of the German emigrés of the Frankfurt School have had an impact on American intellectual life through other channels—sociology, political science, and the popular culture of the New Left— much more than through German departments. A reconsideration of the Frankfurt School will have to ask the question why it has taken so long to consider the Frankfurt School in the first place.

Misunderstood as somehow emphatically German and never truly welcome in German departments, the Frankfurt School furthermore resists classification as one of several contributions to literary theory, if by that latter phrase is meant the systematic methodological self-clarification of the academic study of literature. From Walter Benjamin's failed university career in the 1920s and the marginality of the original Institute for Social Research at the University of Frankfurt through the exile years to the outsider status of Horkheimer and Adorno in West German intellectual life and more recent controversies regarding Habermas' university appointment, the members of the Frankfurt School have tended to stand at odds with the established university hierarchy (a status shared, by the way, by some other anti-academic academics who have become crucial for literary theory, Freud and Nietzsche, although of course not Heidegger). The negativity of this position resonates with the substance of the philosophical claims. "Nothing in aesthetic theory can still be taken for granted," Adorno writes in his *Aesthetic Theory*, "not even the existence of art."[1] Or in the *Philosophy of Modern Music*: "The only works of art that still count are those which are no longer works."[2] These are hardly auspicious grounds for the foundation of a systematic literary theory or the establishment of a methodological school, in the normal sense of the term. No church will stand on this rock. Consequently the last thing one would want to do in an account of the Frankfurt School that claims to be more than descriptive intellectual history would be to generate a set of dogmas that would constitute a reproducible method for the automatic processing of literary texts. In terms of its substance and its sociology, the Frankfurt School, despite its academic setting, has less in common with established academic orthodoxies like hermeneutics or deconstruction, with their hierarchies of masters and acolytes, and more with movements of radical cultural criticism like surrealism or situationism. The distillation of a basic method of Frankfurt School criticism would distort the legacy, just as the advocacy of some imaginable Frankfurt orthodoxy would run counter to the school's principled heterodoxy. A filial, that is, epigonic loyalty to some patriarchal teachings would necessarily betray the insistence on autonomy and likely lead to the sort of embarrassing piety that has characterized many of the recent apologies in the de Man affair, especially Derrida's.

Not German, not Germanist, not academic: introducing the Frankfurt School in this way, I am imitating the negativity of its own argumentative forms that commence by calling the question into question or asserting the dubiousness of a chosen topic (a *creatio ex negativo*.) Only through the retraction of the origin does the argument get under way, since a positive continuation from any arbitrary origin would only amount to an extrapolation, constantly reproducing an eternal return of the given. The possibility of achieving the qualitatively new, that is, a genuine progress that is more than more of the same, depends on the enfigurement of an antideterminist freedom at the outset. Listen to the beginning of Adorno's "Cultural Criticism and Society," the first essay in *Prisms*: "To anyone in the habit of thinking with his ears, the words 'cultural criticism' [*Kulturkritik*] must have an offensive ring, not merely because, like 'automobile,' they are pieced together from Latin and Greek."[3] The highbrow gesture implicit in the etymological gloss is no doubt part of a hidden agenda, a parody of Heidegger's pseudo-etymological mode of argument, and is therefore subject to syntactic relativization. "He speaks as if he represented either unadulterated nature or a higher historical stage. Yet he is necessarily of the same essence as that to which he fancies himself superior." Cultural criticism turns out to be a self-contradiction, a logical impossibility, but instead of consequently collapsing, this self-negation sets in motion an open dialectic, with no positive beginning and certainly with no synthetic closure. The shape of the argument is the serial chiasmus, a perpetual pacing back and forth in the Weberian iron cage imposed by a frozen history, and the essay concludes within the same spatial structure of confinement: "To write poetry after Auschwitz is barbaric,"[4] i.e., an escape into an aestheticist culture has become incompatible with the human project of culture itself, but even this profoundly cultural insight has become impossible, as he continues: "And this corrodes even the knowledge of why it has become impossible to write poetry today."[5] Again the prose traces a repetitive criss-cross and self-negation that constantly subverts the position of the author. Yet it is precisely the recognition of the limits that permits in the final sentence a shimmer of transcendence, an imagination of what a dialectic of progress might entail: "Critical intelligence cannot be equal to this challenge as long as it confines itself to self-satisfied contemplation."[6]

The same argumentative shape recurs in the seminal essay "Poetry and Society." An initial refusal of any positive relationship between lyric verse and social structure turns into the assertion that poetry is social precisely as a vehicle of negation of a reified society, and at its most self-referential, where it appears to withdraw most fully from any realist correspondence, it suggests a transcendence, a radical revolution, and the no longer alienated language of an emancipated humanity. Aside from any of the specific claims regarding the character of criticism or the substance of verse, I have chosen these examples to demonstrate the negative dialectics of the argument: the refusal of a positive beginning; the strategy of self-subversion, reversal, and repetition; the postponement of a nevertheless intimated closure. This is not a criticism that generates narratives about traditions, good or bad, nor is it one that attempts to found traditions, Western or otherwise. The rhetoric is rather one of self-marginalization, a grand refusal of all grand systems: a principled position of *nicht mitmachen* in the culture of empire building, the accumulative imperialism of economies or categories, in which the notion of culture, understood in an emphatically utopian sense, is surely out of place.

A full understanding of this dialectical criticism depends both on an internal reconstruction of the project, such as I have already tried to offer, and on a recognition of the external setting. For Adorno, this insight is a matter of the simultaneity of what he calls immanent and transcendent criticism; in more familiar terms, an oscillation between close reading and contextualization. The Frankfurt School draws on several modern cultural currents, reviewed from the standpoint of a catastrophic twentieth-century history. Foremost among them is the Enlightenment legacy, especially the Kantian discourse of autonomy or *Mündigkeit*. It is there that the project of a self-setting individuality, freed from any heteronomous order by the Copernican turn, finds its clearest articulation. Especially in some pedagogical comments from the postwar period, Kantian autonomy is mobilized as an alternative to various contemporary concepts of education based on authoritarian notions such as social integration or successful adaptation. The Kantian perspective is modified, however, in at least two important ways. Hegel's criticism that a recognition of limits, including the Kantian constructions of reason and the tripartite structure of the critiques, already implies a position beyond the limits, which are therefore sublated and surpassed—*aufgehoben*—introduces a discourse of totality and the dialectic of the part and the whole. True, Adorno's philosophy is never as utopian or apocalyptic as its source, the neo-Hegelianism of the young Lukács, but autonomy is henceforth inseparable from considerations of totalsocial—*gesamtgesellschaftlich*—mediation. Furthermore, the Kantian formula of autonomy is treated not only as a utopian desideratum but also as a moment in the dialectic of Enlightenment: radical individualism and consistent rationalism slip via de Sade and Nietzsche into an aristocratic ethics of brutality, just as a disinterested aesthetic autonomy turns into the Trojan horse of apathetic cruelty: "The Absolute turned into absolute horror."[7]

In addition, the Frankfurt School draws on and develops certain aspects of Marxism. A maverick Marxism is self-evident in central texts of Benjamin, as are some social-democratic allegiances for Habermas. More interesting, because less obvious, is the latent Marxism in the least engaged of the group, Adorno. Lukács again is the intellectual-historical lynchpin, since his theory of reification from *History and Class Consciousness* is adopted by Adorno as a key to his analysis of advanced capitalist culture. Yet where Lukács retains an orientation toward the plausibility of a more or less imminent revolution, Adorno and the Frankfurt School are more properly understood as representatives of a so-called Western Marxism, the central question of which is not how to make a revolution but why the revolution has failed, i.e., the apparent stability of alienated society. It is, so to speak, a Marxism that has withdrawn its charge to the proletariat as a central agent of history. Consequently greater interest is directed toward material that orthodox Marxism tended to marginalize: personality forms, family structures, cultural objects. The radical revolution is displaced onto a distant horizon, a locus of utopian hopes. Needless to say, dialectical materialism and socialist realism are rejected as Soviet versions of the same anti-emancipatory authoritarianism inherent in Heideggerian ontology or American behaviorism.

Finally, the Frankfurt School draws on key aspects of the self-understanding of modern art, both the antirealism inherent in the aesthetics of abstraction and the avant-gardism that claimed a pivotal role for artistic innovation in the transformation of bourgeois society. Both of these aspects are profoundly modified when read through neo-Hegelianism and neo-Marxism, each of which, in turn, was nuanced by Max Weber's accounts of rationalization and bureaucracy. At the end of this complex process, however, an account emerged that placed central importance on the work of art. In some cases, such as Benjamin's, this entailed crediting a transformed aesthetic object with being an active agent of social change; in others, such as Adorno's, the work of art took on the passive role of the "sundial of history," a textual record of reified society which at the same time, as a locus of negation, served as a vehicle for criticism and a vessel of emancipatory projects effectively suppressed elsewhere.[8] In other words, the work of art is simultaneously a historical expression and a utopian enclave, Hegelian and Kantian, and therefore both object and subject. As a subject-object unity, however, it is also the heir to the Lukácsian construction of the revolutionary proletariat; art becomes the revolution in exile.

These three sources—German idealism, Marxism, and aesthetic modernism—undergo further transformations when they are lodged in the following account of twentieth-century social change, a paradigm most characteristic for Adorno and Horkheimer, somewhat less so for Lowenthal and Marcuse, and least of all for Benjamin. At stake is the transition from the free-market era of laissez-faire capitalism to various models of massive state intervention in the economy: Stalinism, fascism, and the New Deal. Traditional Marxism might speak of the establishment of a monopoly capitalism, but the phenomenon is equally describable within the terms of Keynesian economics. For the Frankfurt School, the process brings to a definitive end the culture and society of the liberal bourgeoisie: not only its economic viability, but its whole way of life. The patriarchal nuclear family, certainly criticized as a site of gender inequality, is nevertheless viewed in retrospect as a structure of socialization capable of producing an autonomous individuality with the ability to question authority. The gradual erosion of the family through state intervention and the penetration of mass media tends to produce instead an authoritarian personality that integrates itself with minimal resistance into the prevailing postindividual conformism: instead of entrepreneurial individuals, team players and corporation men. Aesthetic culture submits to a related, though not quite parallel, transformation. The Enlightenment effectively suppresses residues of traditional popular culture, which are replaced by a commercially produced entertainment, the so-called culture industry, which is viewed as a solely manipulative instrument. Meanwhile authentic art, which gives genuine expression to criticism and utopia, recedes into an ever more hermetic formalism, largely inaccessible to the lay public. The Enlightenment project of mas-

tering nature through the abstraction of conceptual thought comes to a bad teleological conclusion in the twentieth century, where all spheres of life are subsumed into the categories of the administrative control of the "authoritarian
state." The terror of the dictatorships and the conformism of the democracies
are, despite empirical differences, at one in their proscription of individuality and qualitative particularity. Society becomes, in Adorno's words, a *Freiluft-
gefängnis*, an open-air prison.[9]

Given this account of totalitarian uniformity, idealism appears in a very particular light. As a dimension of relatively autonomous theoretical activity not
immediately reducible to positive facts or practical programs, it is defended
as an at least weak alternative to the bad facticity of the merely given. Hence
the bitter tensions between the Frankfurt School and an activist New Left, eager
to move quickly from theory to practice. For Adorno, a unity of theory and
practice was at best a counterfactual norm, and by no means an empirical possibility, in a society marked by the universal separation of subject and object.
For precisely this reason, Adorno waged an extended polemic against the
Lukács of socialist realism, whom he could accuse of an "extorted reconciliation," i.e., a violent suppression of the antinomies of the dialectic which history had not brought to completion.[10] The idealist discourse of autonomy
becomes the philosophical locus of anticonformism, and the Hegelian legacy
of totality remains only a conceptual tool, perhaps a deferred telos, but by no
means a description of the status quo in the spirit of traditional right-wing
Hegelian apologetics. Thus Adorno contra Hegel: "The Whole is the Untruth."
The consequence for aesthetic theory, especially in his literary-critical and
musicological writings, is a sharpened attention for the moments of fragmentation and contradiction, seismographic registrations of a divided society,
which are therefore privileged in the readings and are by no means dissolved
into the complete sense which a conservative hermeneutics might attempt to
impute.

As already indicated, the Frankfurt School's relationship to Marxism is
complex. As an instrumental theory of revolution it is of no interest; as a correspondence theory of truth, it is retrograde. However, the insistence on the
interrelatedness of all spheres of social activity, notably economy and culture,
is maintained by the Frankfurt School, as are the closely related critiques
of alienation and ideology. Given the Frankfurt School's nightmarish vision of
epidemic conformism, Marxism moreover yields up an important account
of the obliteration of particularity. The theory of capitalist development is
stripped of the economistic residues—the falling rate of profit and the apocalyptic optimism of crises—and turns into a description of the occlusion of use
value by the universal abstraction of exchange mechanisms. All concrete qualities, the sensuous being of the natural object, are transformed by the market
into the universal quality of having no qualities at all, but only the quantitative
worth of cash value.

The only object that resists this universal imperative of exchange is the work of art. It too is certainly mediated by the market, but the autonomy of the object remains relatively impervious to the process of commodification. In a moment I will suggest that this heroization of the work of art may be obsolete and therefore a point where a reconsideration of the Frankfurt School might commence. The point here, however, is that art takes on this privileged role as an exception to the logic of administration through a conflation of two separate positions: the bohemian, artistic attack on bourgeois philistinism and the Marxist critique of the bourgeois economy.

The paradigm of Frankfurt School concerns that I have elaborated so far runs the risk of overgeneralization, obscuring theoretical shifts that took place in different historical contexts and, especially, ignoring significant points of disagreement among the various critics. Nevertheless, the account by and large holds, at least as a description of the theoretical terrain within which the Frankfurt School developed. In order to foreground the heterogeneity of positions, however, I want to point out some divergent ramifications of this account with special regard to the implications for literary theory. While this is not the place for even an extremely abbreviated sketch of representative figures, it may be useful to comment on several distinct directions that the Frankfurt School proposes for aesthetic criticism.

The paradigmatic assertion of two historical settings—a bygone liberal era and a contemporary age of total administration—is echoed, but with new contents, in Benjamin's seminal essay "The Work of Art in the Age of Mechanical Reproduction." The narrative describes a biphasic trajectory of the social status of art: once characterized by the uniqueness of the original, in the present it is increasingly reproducible, as in photography and film, where the notion of the original object has no or little significance when compared with the stature of, say, an original Rembrandt. At times the essay seems to approach a technological determinism, suggesting that a directly causal relationship prevails between the mechanical conditions of aesthetic production and wider claims regarding political culture. Elsewhere there are indications that this strict argument is couched in a larger distinction between an earlier, essentially premodern setting and the modern, industrialized, and urbanized society. In both versions, however, Benjamin tells a story about secularization with profound consequences for the production, reception, and substance of the work of art. Art is originally the object of cultic veneration that thrives on its animistic uniqueness in a numinous here and now. Its magic power is its aura which demands respectful submission from the contemplative recipient. Even after the emancipation of art from ecclesiastical institutions, i.e., in postmedieval Europe, the auratic work is embedded in a set of covertly religious assumptions, and its isolation from social life is, if anything, heightened; in the prevailing paradigm, individual artists produce unique and organic, i.e., naturelike, works for privatized recipients. In the age of mechanical reproduc-

tion, however, the individual artist-as-genius is replaced by figures of technical competence—journalists, photographers—and, even more, by the collective production mechanism of the film industry. The representative mode of
reception is no longer the isolation of the reader of novels, sequestered in a
private sphere, but the public community of the cinema audience. Furthermore,
the new work of art no longer attempts to conceal its fabricated character in
an aesthetics of harmonious reconciliation but rather flaunts its artificiality,
especially through montage and jump cuts. In this new setting of simulacral
iteration, Benjamin imagines the likelihood of a new public which, vis-à-vis
the postauratic work, rejects the passivity of the erstwhile contemplative viewer
and can instead engage actively in a critical discussion.

There are plenty of untenable points in Benjamin's argument, beginning
with the broad-brush account of the social history of art. Peter Bürger provides a constructive commentary on this issue in his *Theory of the Avant-Garde*.
Nevertheless, there are also some extremely fertile contributions in the essay
which need mentioning. What is at stake for Benjamin is not simply the investigation of a series of works but the examination of the processes of production and reception within which these works are lodged. The suggestion is that
the study of literature, to the extent that it focuses exclusively on the meaning
of the privileged text, is trapped in a premodern and presecular habit and would
do well to address the norms and practices in the various historical institutions
of literature. It follows then that not only the authorized texts of an approved
canon are fair objects of study—a restriction of study to these texts has no intellectual grounding—but also texts of popular culture and nonbelletristic writing, as well as film. In contrast to Adorno, Benjamin draws attention to putatively emancipatory tendencies in mass culture; whether or not one shares his
optimism, it is evident that the texts and practices of mass culture cannot be
excluded from literary-theoretical consideration or critical study.

Yet the crucial term in Benjamin is the aura that dwindles in the age of
mechanical reproduction. Or does it dwindle? There is an ambivalence in the
essay which raises questions regarding secularization, rationalization, fetishism, and spectacularity in capitalist culture. As the work of art becomes less
like an idol, it may become more like a commodity which, pace Benjamin,
carries an aura of its own; or, conversely, the end of the auratic work of art
may usher in the auraticization of fetishized social relations and therefore a
universal pacification of society transfixed by the commodity spectacle.

This negative outcome of the history of secularization appears at the conclusion of Benjamin's essay. If the politicization of art, i.e., its thorough secularization in tandem with the vocalization of a critical public, if that Enlightenment project should fail, the alternative is the aestheticization of politics,
which Benjamin defines as fascism. Yet if the sensationalist label is left aside,
the concluding passage of the essay and its argument regarding the vicissitudes

of aura suggest, at the least, that the eye of the aesthetic critic has to take in much more than the certified works of art. The notion of an "aestheticization of politics" may be less useful for the study of fascism than for the critique of postwar consumerism and the politics—or postpolitics—of scopophilia.

In contrast to Benjamin's optimism, at least in this essay, the early Habermas outlines a narrative much more in line with the pessimistic teleology of the classical Frankfurt School. The key term here is the public sphere or *Öffentlichkeit*, a realm of collective discussion and debate that develops in the seventeenth and eighteenth centuries as a new social space wedged between a private sphere of family life and economy and, on the other side, the absolutist state. That is, it is a realm of social activity outside the state and, equally, outside private identity, and the discussion that transpires within it is consequently characterized by a proscription of consideration of private status or governmental office: the interlocutors engage in a discussion as equals, no matter what discrepancies may exist among them outside the public sphere. The public sphere, which initially takes form in coffeehouses, salons, and reading societies, consequently generates a counterfactual norm of universal equality which is harmless enough as long as it is restricted to its original topic, the discussion of literature. When it becomes politicized, however, it turns into the slogan of bourgeois democracy against the absolutist state and, after the revolution, is institutionalized in parliament and suffrage.

Habermas' early work *The Structural Transformation of the Public Sphere* describes the collapse of this institution of bourgeois liberalism in classical Frankfurt School terms. The intervention of the state in the economy, i.e., the conflation of the private and political spheres, robs the *Öffentlichkeit* of its autonomous and mediating status; it is replaced by the culture industry and a solely acclamatory politics of media spectacles. Whether or not this pessimism is appropriate, the important ramification for literary theory is the identification of the public sphere as a realm of literary activity or, rather, the identification of literary life as a function of the public sphere. One consequence that has produced fruitful research is the insistence on the importance of a history of literary criticism, not as a chronology of individual aesthetic judgments on literary texts but as an account of the transformation of the institutional settings and discursive structures of literary debate. As with Benjamin, the privileged text ceases to be the canonic work, but while Benjamin tends to displace it with film and similar objects of popular culture, the Habermasian suggestion underscores the importance of critical prose, literary journalism, feuilleton, and intellectual life in the mass media. Why does the salon become the *Bildzeitung*, how does the *Spectator* become *USA Today*? The overriding concern becomes the possibility of establishing, maintaining, or recovering a public sphere in which a critical and rational discussion is possible, as an emancipatory alternative to the manipulation of the culture industry.

The projects of both Benjamin and Habermas are directed toward an emancipation from restrictive social and cultural structures. Yet the difference between Benjamin's postauratic popular culture and Habermas' public sphere corresponds to the alternative between the former's messianic notion of redemption and the latter's valorization of a more sober rationalism, or, in political terms, Benjamin's call for a "politicization of aesthetics," which he regards as the substance of what he calls "communism," versus Habermas' construction of a public political culture as a liberal corrective to the authoritarian tendency of executive power. This corresponds perhaps to a difference in temperament and, certainly, to the alternative contexts of the mid-thirties for Benjamin and the early sixties for Habermas. In any case, the link between this early Habermas and his more mature work is the effort to conceptualize and defend the structures of modernity, especially the norm of rational discourse and the Kantian separation of the spheres of science, ethics, and art. In contrast to Horkheimer and Adorno, who claim that it is Enlightenment reason *tout court* that reverts to violence and myth, Habermas directs his critique toward the colonizing expansionism of the single modality of instrumental reason throughout other social spheres; and he would like to see this process of technological-administrative control—appropriate in its own limited domain—balanced by a public sphere of what he calls the "life-world" of local communities and an autonomous citizenry engaged in discussions guided by the norm of consensus formation and not decisionism or violent authority. It is therefore absolutely off the mark when Jean-François Lyotard, from the standpoint of a postmodern political theory, accuses Habermas of totalizing or even totalitarian inclinations because of his valorization of consensus. On the contrary, the fact that the project of consensus and a lord-only-knows modified equality provoke such accusations indicates how much Lyotard's postmodern condition shares with a traditional conservatism, for which, since Burke, reason and equality have always been the harbingers of terror and Jacobin dictatorship.

Defending the differentiated logics of modernity, Habermas also defends the autonomy of art: against realism, against avant-gardist projects to sublate life and art, and against any postauratic reductions. On this point, he concurs with Adorno, the Frankfurt School's avatar of aesthetic modernism filtered through a neo-Hegelian neo-Marxism. Precisely the difference between art and quotidian concerns imbues art with a critical potential. Precisely the uselessness of art in a utilitarian society, where the worst crime is to be good-for-nothing, turns the work of art into a cipher of a good life. The function of art is to have none and thereby counteract the imperatives of functionality: not effectively, not as the communicative vehicle of some message, but as a placeholder of a negativity, the substitute for the potential of a radical alternative. The successful work becomes all the more hermetic, the more social relations become reified; the objective contradictions of society are not mirrored but echoed ephemerally in the formal contradictions of the work, the "sundial of history" mentioned earlier. Instead of locating the meaning of the work, Adorno insists on its brokenness and enigmatic quality; hence his distance from traditional hermeneutics. But the alienation and fragmentation which the work records are neither ontological nor a consequence of a necessarily mendacious language, but rather—for the neo-Marxist—historical and social; hence the distance from Heidegger and de Manian deconstruction. For the possibility of an emancipated humanity remains the horizon of criticism. The refusal inherent in the nonidentity of autonomous art is the sole challenge to the bad identification of its binary opposite, the kitsch of the culture industry, the message of which is, according to Adorno, always adapt, submit, and conform. Aura, public sphere, nonidentity and autonomy: even though these ramifications of the Frankfurt School for literary theory share certain philosophical and historical assumptions, they are extraordinarily divergent and lead to dissimilar intellectual agendas. This only reflects the multiplicity within the Frankfurt School, which, however, makes the reconsideration of the school all the more difficult. Nevertheless, I want to suggest how a rethinking of three basic premises of the school might nuance the project: in the sense of not a retraction but a *Weiterdenken*, a thinking-further of critical theory.

My first point regards the binary model of aesthetic culture. For Adorno, autonomous art and the culture industry are "torn halves of an integral whole to which however they do not add up."[11] To a certain extent, his privileging of a set of high-cultural texts reflects the cultural-conservative predilections of a German mandarin and is therefore an idiosyncratic moment, which a consistent reformulation of the theory would want to revise. Yet that very dichotomous structure that counterposes high culture to a popular dimension is probably no longer useful: not because popular culture turns out to be the unexpected locus of resistance, subversion, or polyphony but, on the contrary, because of the obsolescence of the heroization of art as a vehicle of emancipation. Whatever validity that claim may have had in the past, it has lost its plausibility in the age of corporate art and the integration of the avant-garde into the hegemonic canon. That does not mean that one should turn a blind eye toward critical moments in either art or popular culture; one should recognize them wherever they occur, but there is no reason to assume that they are more likely in commodified aesthetics than anywhere else in commodified society. The relevant legacy of classical critical theory is therefore neither in the aesthetics of hermetic modernism nor in a postauratic popular culture but in the recognition of the aesthetic dimension as a medium of domination, the "aestheticization of politics." Adorno himself suggests as much when, in "Cultural Criticism and Society," he writes, "Cultural criticism must become social physiognomy."[12]

Second, the social description of total administration desperately needs considerable revision. Even for cultural pessimists, fascism (if the term is to retain any useful specificity) is not arguably the likely outcome of Western rationality, and, in the age of perestroika, the apparatus of socialist domination may turn out to be capable of considerable reform. Closer to home, the model of the bureaucratic welfare state and state intervention in the economy appears increasingly to be a historical relic. That is to say that the account of universal administration articulated by the Frankfurt School was not wrong but neither was it a conclusive fate; rather it described the fundamental logic of a transitional stage of capitalist modernization which has by now taken on a new shape. The ruse of reason has finally caught up with neo-Hegelianism, since the particularity which critical theory imagined itself to be defending against the totalizing logic of the Enlightenment turns out to be precisely the same substance that the regimes in the major Western states are desperately trying to foster—initiative, creativity, innovation, opposition—in order to revitalize the administered societies, otherwise tending to stagnate: the stability of contemporary society depends on the generation of an artificial negativity, not its eradication. This reversal probably explains why critical theory, so long marginalized in the academy, has been rediscovered. More generally, the historic role of the new literary theory may be considerably less radical than its defenders often claim, since it contributes so effectively to the development of a cultural discourse adequate to the needs of a postindustrial information society.

If the theorem of the "aestheticization of politics" is tenable and aesthetic processes of representation are as evident in all social activities as in works of art proper; and if the logic of administration has been modified by the exigency of an artificial negativity; then the critical theory of the Frankfurt School could well reexplore a theoretical direction which it blocked in its earliest years: the phenomenological investigation of everyday life as a locus of creativity, resistance, and emancipatory hopes. Because of the drift of much of German vitalism, *Lebensphilosophie*, toward a prefascist irrationalism and, especially, because of Heidegger's enthusiasm for National Socialism, Adorno closed himself off from this line of thought, although occasionally an inkling of the importance of preconceptual quotidian experience survives his austere dialectics. The case is somewhat different for Heidegger's student Marcuse for whom, however, phenomenological moments were eventually displaced by a scientistic appropriation of the psychoanalytic theory of a libidinal economy. As already mentioned, Habermas thematizes the "life-world," but he means by that community organizations, grassroots democracy, and *Bürgerinitiativen*, corresponding to the political project of the new social movements. The theoretical project of the Frankfurt School, however, requires a better grounding in an account, probably Husserlian in nature, of everyday experience as a critical counterpoint to the reified structures of society and science.

Reconsidering the Frankfurt School, one comes up with a prescription to expand the set of texts beyond autonomous art and high modernism; to reconsider the empirical possibilities of social negativity and de facto contestation in a not thoroughly administered world; and to turn critical attention to processes of representation, conflict, and creativity in everyday experience. This agenda, derived from the immanent problematics of critical theory itself, approximates the agenda of a critical current in contemporary cultural theory that goes by the name of cultural studies. The programs are by no means identical, and the background to cultural studies is clearly a different one: anthropology, Althusserian Marxism, and British radicalism are some of its key sources. More important, however, are the significant overlaps: the revision of the canon, the sense for contradiction, and the attention to everyday life. With this common agenda, cultural criticism and cultural studies represent an alternative to the various programs, hermeneutic and deconstructive, to preserve aesthetic autonomy, cultural authority, and an auratic construction of literature. The differences between these camps will fuel the debates in literary theory for some time to come.

Chapter 2

Poetry for the Republic

Heine and Whitman

It was a tricky situation in which Thomas Mann found himself in October of 1922. Addressing a conservative audience hostile to the young Weimar Republic, the reknowned author, whose wartime support for the German Empire against the Western democracies had won him acclaim in nationalist circles, now undertook the onerous task of convincing his listeners of the worthiness of democracy. Avoiding the easy path of pragmatic realism—democracy as the result of the military defeat of the empire in 1918 or as an ideological demand of the emergent American hegemony—he attempted instead to demonstrate the compatibility of democratic principles with fundamental aspects of German culture in order to defend the counterintuitive proposition that the notion of a "German Republic" was not itself a contradiction in terms.

The literary formula that Mann selected to make his case was Novalis plus Whitman, i.e., the presumed affinity between the emblem of German aesthetic culture and the representative poet of American democracy. With a series of quotations he did in fact suggest that German culture at its most romantic—and for the public, that meant at its most German moment—was not at all hostile to the political thought of enlightened modernity. Thus, glossing a Novalis citation on international law, Mann comments, "That is political enlightenment, it is indisputably democracy—from the mouth of a knight of the blue flower, who was moreover a born Junker from whom one would expect a medieval sense of battle or a love of honor in a suit of mail rather than these modernisms."[1] The clincher then follows with the link to Whitman. For if Junker and Yankee are at one in their enthusiasm for democracy, then the conservative *Bildungsbürgertum* would do best to follow Novalis' lead by rallying around the new republic, German to its core, and not—as the antirepublican right claimed—a foreign form dictated by the victors at Versailles and imposed on an essentially undemocratic German *Volk*.

So far, so good, at least as far as Mann's intentions go, and this speech, "Von deutscher Republik," can be treated as a literary counterpart to the Weimar

26

constitution, two of the founding documents of republican culture in Germany. That is, however, a very ambivalent praise, implying that Mann's speech and its formula, Novalis plus Whitman, may have been as flawed as the republic and its constitution. For scrutinizing the text, one cannot but wonder if Mann has not conceded too much to his opponents or if the attempt to make the republic palatable to its opponents has not already eviscerated it. In fact, it seems as if Mann's efforts to assert the identity of a German republic keep running aground on the resilience of the oxymoron he is trying to repress. Does the text, then, in current parlance, subvert itself?

One might note, for example, that the very project of a "German Republic"—Mann stresses the adjective—is not without a nationalist ring, for it is distinguished emphatically from alternative, more radical versions, the individualism of what he calls nefariously "a certain West," and the "political mysticism" of, even more ominously, "*Slawentum*," the Slavic East; hence a sort of two-front war in the competition of political forms.[2] In addition, the articulation of the republic as a romantic (and therefore acceptable) possibility is achieved only at the price of adopting the romantic critique of the Enlightenment state, i.e., Novalis' attack on Friderician Prussia. Yet that critique is directed not at all against the authoritarian substance of enlightened despotism but only at its putatively mechanical character, which, according to Novalis, might be overcome with more religion, more enthusiasm, and, particularly trenchant, more uniforms.

Mann's rhetorical strategy may be working backward: instead of convincing conservatives to support the republic, he transforms democracy into a program acceptable to conservatives because it has been robbed of its radical substance, a democracy so to speak without a democratic revolution. This reading of "the German Republic" as a covertly antidemocratic program despite the author's intentions might be confirmed by an examination of the introduction, a laudatio to Gerhart Hauptmann on his sixtieth birthday. Assiduously avoiding any of the likely images of republicanism, such as popular sovereignty or civic virtue or heroic rebellion, Mann opts instead for a prescription that could hardly offend his recalcitrant public—royal legitimacy and patriarchal authority—whereby it is now the playwright Hauptmann who plays the role of a glorious *Volkskönig*, while the *Reichspräsident* is endearingly invoked as an irresistible Mr. Niceguy, good old "Vater Ebert." The cast of characters chosen by Mann clearly suggests a political orientation toward a centrist support for the new regime; Hauptmann's social dramas of the 1890s are invoked piously, and, in any case, Mann affirms his loyalty to the Social-Democratic head of state. Nevertheless, the organization of this state of affairs is one in which traditional structures of authority have been retained with only a minor shuffling of the players. Royalty and paternity are the terms which pervade the opening passages of the speech, the logic of power has clearly not been interrupted, the state has not been refashioned by a revolutionary process, and it is therefore only consistent for Mann, the self-described conservative, to suggest that conservatives would do themselves a better service by participating in the political processes of the Weimar Republic than by opposing it from without.

If the really-existing Weimar Republic was indeed represented by the pair Hauptmann plus Ebert, themselves representing the rather unrepublican constellation of king plus father, then something was evidently amiss with the democratic claims of the "German Republic," and the error may well lie in the formula for democracy that Mann has proposed. Is Novalis plus Whitman a literary Article 48 of the cultural constitution of the Weimar Republic? Should ever Whitmanesque democracy threaten to go too far, conservatives might count on Novalis for a romantic tradition to preserve law and order: faith and love instead of parliament and popular suffrage.

My point here is not to suggest that romantic political philosophy is necessarily conservative but that Mann, for obviously tactical reasons, makes this equation in order to mount the following argument: Novalis is a conservative; Novalis is a democrat; therefore conservatives may be democrats, and democracy may be conservative. The weakness of that model, which could quickly transmute Hauptmann and Ebert into Ebert and Noske, Noske and von Seeckt, Ludendorff, Hindenburg, Hitler—the congenital lability of the Weimar Republic—derives from Mann's definition of the republic as thoroughly inoffensive to the antirepublican right. The response of right-wing political theory, such as that of Carl Schmitt, would be to claim that "the crisis of parliamentary democracy" is inescapable, that mass democracies are always logically impossible, and that, to the extent that a state asserts its sovereignty, it will eventually take the form of a dictatorship, despite the illusions of a bourgeois liberalism ignorant of the exigencies of power. Less cynically and with an eye to the possibility of a democratic culture, one must ask if the problem is inherent not in the emancipation project but rather in its specific formulation and historical manifestation, i.e., the inadequacy of the German Republic at its inception. If "Novalis plus Whitman" was not enough, was an alternative definition imaginable?

One can answer this question without unrolling the political history of the early twenties. It will suffice to unravel the speech because an alternative formula, an alternative to "Novalis plus Whitman," is inscribed in this founding text of the republic itself. While Mann's liberal undertaking undermines itself the more it attempts to sublate the self-marginalization of the conservatives by incorporating them into the republican body politic, the text is simultaneously marked by a second vector which locates an outside to the same conservatism which Mann is attempting to recuperate. For in order to exhort his audience to participate in the democratic process, he must also scare them by suggesting the consequences of their continued boycott, i.e., a more radical republic. The republic, that is, may well remain substantively German, a vessel for all the blue-flowered values represented by the reassuring figure of Novalis, but only if the romantic conservatives take hold of it and do not surrender it to threatening antagonists, whose generic name is revealed in Mann's anxious plea: "I beseech you again: don't be shy. There is no reason in the world to regard the republic as a matter for smart Jewboys [scharfe Judenjungen]. Don't leave it to them! As the popular political phrase goes, take 'the wind out of their sails'—the republican wind!"[3]

This is surely a difficult passage. For the moment, Mann is evidently adopting the anti-Semitic rhetoric of the conservative right: in the semantic value of the pejorative designation *Judenjunge*, in the adjective, and in the exclusionary politics of the exhortation. Yet later in the speech, when the same *Judenjungen* make a second cameo appearance, Mann suggests that they too are an integral part of the German tradition. Nevertheless, even that moderating gloss, bordering on apologetics, pales when one grasps that the phrase presumably refers to the foreign minister, Walter Rathenau, victim of a recent right-wing assassination, and that Mann in this same speech has noted bitterly that the assassins, despite their opposition to the republic, have de facto recognized the actuality of republican culture, since, as he puts it, "shooting ministers is a superbly republican mode of action."[4] For it implies the priority of public and political virtue over a solely private sphere of aesthetic culture.

Of course Mann's intention is neither to advocate political violence nor to foster anti-Semitism, but that initial imperative, the plea to seize the republic from the smart Jewboys, is a crucial moment in the text and ought not to be dissolved too quickly into the dialectic of the full argument or the vicissitudes of Mann's subsequent career. My concern here is, after all, not Thomas Mann's intentions, and my goal is even less a harmonious reconciliation of the material in a conservative hermeneutic circle. The point is rather that the cultural formula for the republic that would fail—Novalis plus Whitman—is itself hopelessly flawed because of a repression that comes to the fore in the exclusionary admonition. Yet the very articulation of that repression leaves symptomatic traces of the alternative, the road not taken, a more radical republic not dependent on the marginalization of the Jewboys, smart or otherwise. Translated into literary-historical terms, that would have implied a revision of the cultural formula: instead of Novalis might Mann have proposed "Heine plus Whitman"? What more appropriate symbol of a German democratic tradition than Heine? Still one might object that this imaginary proposal is absurd, and not only because of the irrelevance of retrospective wishful thinking. For a century, Heine reception had been marked by vitriolic opposition from conservatives: from the initial persecution and censorship of the pre-1848 period through the battles regarding a monument at the turn of the century. Heine was an overdetermined figure, representing all that the right wing rejected: political radical, left Hegelian, Jew, Parisian exile, sensualist, materialist, internationalist, and so on—hardly a figure to inspire confidence among conservatives in the desirability of the republic, and obviously an impossible choice. That, however, is precisely the point. Opting for Novalis, Mann opted for a conservative constitution of the republic: Heine's absence from the "German Republic" is ultimately another chapter in Heine's repression, a negative reception history. He appears only as the unnamed object of negation, and it is that exclusion built into the 1922 formula of the republic that cripples the enterprise from the start. Even Thomas Mann must have come to a similar recognition less than a decade later when he recast the political project with a more radical formula—Hölderlin and Marx—but by then his topic was itself considerably more radical: instead of a German Republic, culture and socialism.

To identify the smart Jewboy as Heine is an intentional misreading that flushes out the limits of liberal culture at the outset of the Weimar Republic by measuring that culture against its repressed *Doppelgänger*, the democratic potential of a forgotten nineteenth-century legacy. Now I want to direct some closer consideration to the odd couple Mann could not name, Heine and Whitman, and their significance for a poetry for a republic. At stake is not a positivistic documentation of literary influences or borrowings. The first edition of *Leaves of Grass* appeared in 1855, the year before Heine's death, and it is not likely that Heine's verse contributed significantly to the formulation of Whitman's lyric project. The closest intellectual-historical connection that might be argued is the shared indebtedness to German idealist philosophy of the two Hegelian cousins: Heine's relationship to Hegel is rich and well known, while Whitman's familiarity was presumably only secondhand, part of the extensive mid-century American reception of idealism. The connection is interesting but, ultimately, somewhat beside the point, since Heine's work—like that of Marx—is better understood as a critical break with Hegel than as a continuation, and for Whitman, in any case, other experiences and endeavors had a considerably more formative impact than the watered-down philosophical lineage. So while a comparison of Heine and Whitman as post-Hegelian poets would not be without some historicist value, the connection would be a strained one, missing moreover the much more profound similarity, of which the shared idealism was no doubt a noteworthy characteristic, i.e., the pivotal role of the two poets in their respective literary traditions, both deeply engaged in the construction of a democratic culture, and both committed to the transformation of the prevailing institution of lyric verse in such a way as to explore the possibility of a genuine poetry for the republic. Not that their solutions look very much alike on paper: nothing in Heine resembles Whitman's long lines, and little in Whitman approaches Heine's irony. Perhaps, however, Whitman's expansive verse and Heine's ironic demolition of romanticism represent homologous innovations in the tentative construction of a new culture. The success of their experiments and the failures that the poets encounter at their limits can tell us something about the social-historical substance embedded in nineteenth-century verse as well as the utopian challenge of a democratic literature. I want to pursue these matters through parallel readings of Heine and Whitman, with regard to three issues in particular: (1) the public voice of poetry; (2) tradition and revolution; and (3) the critique of modernity.

The Public Voice of Poetry

To speak of the "pivotal role" of Heine and Whitman, as I did a moment ago, is somewhat of an overstatement, since it suggests that they were more successful in the establishment of a literary legacy than their respective poetic traditions in fact let them be (although certainly Heine encountered more opposition than Whitman). Nevertheless the pivoting which each undertook amounted to the same effort to transform the institutionalized character of lyric verse and to develop a language adequate to a democratic modernity. Both attempted to dismantle aspects of what can be coarsely labeled bourgeois-aristocratic culture, characterized by aesthetic autonomy, social elitism, and a strictly vertical hierarchy of cultural organization. For Whitman, this necessitated a painful critique of Emerson, to whom he was in fact deeply indebted, and for Heine a parallel distancing from Goethe. In both cases a new literary language had to be constructed that would incorporate aspects of everyday life and politics, public concerns mediated, again in both cases, by influential experiences in journalism.

Despite the surfeit of landscape imagery in Whitman's verse and his constant self-identification with the American topography, his "usual diction is," as F. O. Matthiessen noted in *American Renaissance*, "clearly not that of a countryman but of what he called himself, 'a jour printer,' " i.e., a journalist. This is a key point for Matthiessen, since he has to counteract a simplistic tendency, common among the first generations of Whitman's admirers, to accept the poet's self-equation with the geography of the New World.

> His speech did not spring primarily from contact with the soil, for though his father was a descendant of Long Island farmers, he was also a citizen of the age of reason, an acquaintance and admirer of Tom Paine. [Whitman] was attracted by the wider sweep of the city, and though his language is a natural product, it is the natural product of a Brooklyn journalist in the eighteen-forties who had previously been a country schoolteacher and a carpenter's helper, and who had finally felt an irresistible impulse to be a poet.[5]

Yet Matthiessen's insistence on the journalistic and not agrarian derivation of Whitman's language is more than a reaction against naturalistic reductions of the poet. This emphasis on the journalist Whitman is hardly a matter of praise. On the contrary, the critic proceeds to review Tocqueville's account of the corruption of language in democracy as an adequate sociology of Whitman's faulty diction. Whitman's introduction of journalistic experience into literary language is consequently, in Matthiessen's eyes, implicitly a falling off from the intellectual heights of Emerson's "cold intellectuality," to which the mere journalist, carpenter, and country schoolteacher could never aspire.

> In its curious amalgamation of homely and simple usage with half-remembered terms he read once somewhere, and with casual inventions of the moment, he often gives the impression of using a language not quite his own. In his determination to strike up for a new world, he deliberately rids himself of foreign models. But, so far as his speech was concerned, this was only very partially possible, and consequently Whitman reveals the peculiarly American combination of a childish freshness with a mechanical and desiccated repetition of book terms that had significance for the more complex civilization in which they had had their roots and growth. The freshness has come, as it did to Huck Finn, through instinctive rejection of the authority of those terms, in Whitman's reaction against what he called Emerson's cold intellectuality: "Suppose his books becoming absorb'd, the permanent chyle of American general and particular character—what a well-wash'd and grammatical, but bloodless and helpless race we should turn out!"[6]

Hearing Matthiessen's judgment on the plebeian journalist Whitman, one cannot help but recall similarly derogatory accounts of Heine. Indeed, just as Matthiessen measures Whitman against Emerson and, more broadly, American democracy against "more complex civilizations," so Karl Kraus plays off Heine against Goethe. Moreover, Adorno, drawing on Kraus, accounts for the inadequacy of Heine's language by suggesting that he came from a background not quite at home in German—"Heine's mother, whom he loved, was not quite fluent in German"—not far from Matthiessen's "impression of [Whitman] using a language not quite his own."[7] Yet this cultural conservatism (in the case of Adorno, certainly, a conservatism of the canon that stands at odds with his negative dialectics) mistakes for a failure the social practice of the texts, the effort to articulate a public language less exclusionary than Emerson's or Goethe's, a democratic alternative to the bourgeois-aristocratic culture of criticism and literature in the early nineteenth century. Whitman's distance from Emerson is a direct corollary to the sentiment expressed in Heine's poem "To a Former Goethean":

Hast du wirklich dich erhoben
Aus dem müßig kalten Dunstkreis,
Womit einst der kluge Kunstgreis
Dich von Weimar aus umwoben?

[Have you really gotten free
From the chilly, vapory cage
In which once the Weimar sage
Had you cooped unwittingly?][8]

The rejection of Goethean classicism and Emerson's "cold intellectuality" might have plausibly led to versions of romantic irony, a hypostatization of the impossibility of any communicative language as a superficially radical critique of the established language of the cultural elite. Heine definitively closes off that option with his judgment on "die romantische Schule"; for the younger Whitman it was never quite as strong a temptation. His poetic attitude stood, as Matthiessen put it, "in strong contrast to much European romanticism, to the pattern of qualities that Madame de Stael had seen in the emerging new literatures, 'the sorrowful sentiment of the incompleteness of human destiny, melancholy, reverie, mysticism, the sense of the enigma of life.'"[9] This distance from the romantic option is evidenced especially in his evaluation of Poe whom he ultimately found "almost without the first sign of moral principle, or of the concrete or its heroisms, or the simpler affections of the heart." Despite his appreciation for Poe's "intense faculty for technical and abstract beauty," Whitman concludes by ranking him "among the electric lights of imaginative literature, brilliant and dazzling but with no heat."[10] Poe's brilliance with no heat, Emerson's cold intellectuality, the "kalter Dunstkreis" of the "kluger Kunstgreis," the romantics with all their magic warts—the counterprograms of Heine and Whitman are parallel in their efforts to expand the participation in cultural life, to give away the esoteric secrets (*ausplaudern*), to strip away the restrictive aura of established art, and to develop a secular and nonauthoritarian literary language. Emerson viewed *Leaves of Grass* as a mixture of the *Bhagavad Gita* and the *New York Tribune*.[11]

That secularization was certainly never complete or thoroughly consistent; Whitman could write that "the priest departs, the divine literatus comes."[12] Yet the tendency remains one of deauraticization, the social-historical process that links the two poetic projects in the search for a public voice. The subsequent reaction against this loss of aura, be it in *l'art pour l'art* or George's symbolism or some of early Anglo-American modernism, indicates the resistance the modernization of culture encountered. Whitman understood this resistance and its social base—he calls it feudalism—when he writes in "Democratic Vistas":

with the priceless value of our political institutions, general suffrage, . . .
I say that, far deeper than these, what finally and only is to make our Western world a nationality superior to any hither known, and outtopping the
past, must be vigorous, yet unsuspected Literatures, perfect personalities
and sociologies, original, transcendental, and expressing (what, in the high-
est sense, are not yet expressed at all) democracy and the modern. . . . For
feudalism, caste, the ecclesiastic traditions, though palpably retreating from
political institutions, still hold essentially, by their spirit, even in this country, entire possession of the more important fields, indeed the very subsoil,
of education, and of social standards and literature.[13]

For Whitman the cultural revolution was still in the making; beyond the
rejection of the models represented by Emerson and Poe, it demanded the positive development of new literary forms. As with Heine, this literary project
was grounded in the struggle against "feudalism, caste, the ecclesiastic tradition," and it unfolded within a structural feature of the *longue durée* of modernity, the unresolved tension between cultural elitism and what might be termed
an emancipation project of a vernacular liberalism. At important points in the
oeuvre of the two writers, each explores the problematic of a public language
in an exemplary poem: "Beat! Beat! Drums!" from the "Drum-Taps" section
of *Leaves of Grass* of 1861 and "Doktrin," the first of the "Zeitgedichte" in
the *Neue Gedichte* of 1844. Despite the seventeen years which seem to separate them, they are in a substantive sense contemporary, since each is deeply
imbued with the political urgency of the moment: the outbreak of the American Civil War and the rapid radicalization on the eve of the 1848 revolution.
It is that shared political urgency that explains why these two programmatic
poems both commence with nearly identical imperatives of military and acoustic force: "Beat! Beat! Drums!—blow! bugles! blow!" "Schlage die Trommel
und fürchte dich nicht"[14] ("Beat on the drum and don't be afraid").
    In each case the text grounds the possibility of a new poetic language by
insisting on the demise of an earlier social order. All established relationships
break down and are swept into a whirlwind of radical reorganization:

> burst like a ruthless force
> Into the solemn church, and scatter the congregation,
> Into the school where the scholar is studying;
> Leave not the bridegroom quiet—no happiness must
>   he have now with his bride,
> Nor the peaceful farmer any peace, ploughing his
>   field or gathering his grain.

Heine's account is tighter but fundamentally compatible: "Trommle die Leute
aus dem Schlaf" ("Drum the people out of bed"). A new poetry is imagined

that can participate in the dismantling of an enervated past, sleepy, private, and, above all, quiet. The new poetry, in contrast, is loud and decidedly public, a vehicle of mass mobilization. Yet the programmatic exhortation is, despite the sense of emergency, never linked to a particular political crisis. Whitman eschews any reference to slavery or secession, and Heine, who otherwise delights in the inclusion of contextual allusions, mentions no new abuse in Berlin or Munich. These are, therefore, not political poems or protest poems in the manner of a *Tendenzgedicht*. On the contrary, they are explorations of the possibility of an innovative poetic language geared to a democratic public sphere, a new literary institution described as an acoustic realm of collective activity and counterposed to the muffled interiorities of Whitman's "school" and "solemn church" and to the indolence of Heine's sleepy readers.

Whitman suggests that this new public sphere will undermine established notions of acquisitive individualism and the market economy: "No bargainers' bargains by day—no brokers or speculators—would they continue?" Moreover, if established social structures and business as usual have grown obsolete, so have established forms of speech and culture:

> Would the talkers be talking? would the singer
>   attempt to sing?
> Would the lawyer rise in the court to state his
>   case before the judge?
> Then rattle quicker, heavier drums—you bugles
>   wilder blow.

In this new public organization of sound, even the familiar figure of the singer, the traditional poet, becomes an anachronism. In the high speed of modernity, where "all that is solid melts into air," hegemonic culture is stripped of its aura, and a new postauratic culture presumably becomes possible. Heine provides the corollary to the end of Whitman's singer, insofar as "Doktrin" asserts that the new activism is the consequence and genuine content and therefore the conclusion of idealist philosophy, which has only interpreted the world.

> Das ist die Hegelsche Philosophie,
> Das ist der Bücher tiefster Sinn.
>
> [That's Hegel's philosophy in short,
> That's the deepest wisdom books bestow!]

These lines are not merely a left-wing interpretation of Hegel; they clearly also indicate a supersession, since the dimension of books and scholarship is displaced, as much as is Whitman's singer, by the fearless beating of the drum. That is, both Whitman and Heine indicate the termination of a worn-out orga-

nization of culture, in the place of which a postauratic culture model, still unnamed, is taking shape.

Yet when Whitman silences his singer, one cannot but hear a deep sense
of anxiety and ambivalence. He is not yet the new poet—if he were, the imperatives would be out of place; has he discovered the possibility of his own
demise? Both poems modify their programmatic exuberance with some considerable doubts and fears regarding the possible consequences of the democratic poetry which they nevertheless invoke. At the end of the first stanza,
Whitman's drums are fierce and the bugles shrill, but the third stanza concludes
the poem on an ominous note. This is not an unbroken paean to cultural
modernization:

> Mind not the old man beseeching the young man,
> Let not the child's voice be heard, nor the
>   mother's entreaties,
> Make even the trestles to shake the dead where
>   they lie awaiting the hearses,
> So strong you thump O terrible drums—so loud
>   you bugles blow.

This is the violence of modernity: what began with the obliteration of mori-
bund cultural forms, the "solemn church" as a cipher of "feudalism," ends
with the uncanny silencing of all human relations. The dialectic of Enlightenment entails a dialectic of political poetry, in which the galvanizing acoustics
of the *levée en masse* turns into the cacophony of "terrible drums," breaking
all social bonds. It is the same ambiguity with which "Doktrin" concludes,
although Heine expresses it in the less overwhelming register of his characteristic irony:

> Das ist die Hegelsche Philosophie
> Das ist der Bücher tiefster Sinn!
> Ich hab sie begriffen, weil ich gescheit
> Und weil ich ein guter Tambour bin.
>
> [That's Hegel's philosophy in short,
> That's the deepest wisdom books bestow!
> I understand it, because I'm smart,
> I'm a good drummer boy myself, I know.][15]

It was Börne who labeled Heine "le tambour-major du libéralisme," and Heine
himself elsewhere seems to feel comfortable with such political-military self-
identification: "I was a good soldier in the liberation war of humanity," he

writes, in the *Reisebilder*. Nevertheless the concluding point of "Doktrin" indicates a dissatisfaction with a potential reduction of poetry to a mere instrument of political tendency. That sort of reduction might be labeled, in the language of critical theory, a false sublation of life and art, the bad outcome of the process of deauraticization. Heine is as aware of it as is Whitman. The two programmatic poems for a democratic literature understand that, after "feudalism," the vicissitudes of cultural modernity are by no means certain; hence the ambivalence inscribed in the text, symptomatic of the liminal status of the modern poet, poised between auratic seclusiveness and public discourse.

Tradition and Revolution

If that liminality is a consequence of the historical setting of the poetic projects—both poets stand, so to speak, with one foot still in the past of the ancien régime, and both, moreover, understand the foreboding future of aesthetic modernization—historicity is not only a matter of external contexts. On the contrary, inscribed in the poetic projects themselves is an imagined past which traps the necessarily belated writing in a present of neurotic repetition. In other words, the melancholic recollection of a traumatic event located at some distance in the past but from which the writer has not yet achieved full critical distance both determines the possibility of writing and sets a limit to the potential innovation. Poetic secularization cannot proceed untroubled along a linear path of progressive optimism. The texts are haunted by an unmastered past; their content is an incomplete *Durcharbeiten*.

My point now is not to psychoanalyze Heine and Whitman but to explore the internal temporality of their verse with the help of psychoanalysis properly understood as a theory of history. For in the two perhaps best known poems, the original deed which casts its shadow on subsequent writing is recognized as a death, the texts belie a distorted experience of guilt, and the prominent ambivalence turns out to be a matter of remorse. If "O Captain! My Captain!" records the death of Lincoln, it also locates the poet in a complicitous proximity to oedipal murder, catching him red-handed. Privy to the knowledge of death, he is consequently set apart from "the swaying mass, their eager faces turning," awaiting the victorious leader. While public life goes on elsewhere, the isolated poet is condemned to a repetitive cadence, serving the same sentence he is writing:

> Exult O shores and ring O bells!
> But I with mournful tread,
> Walk the deck my Captain lies,
> Fallen cold and dead.

Passing over water toward the erotic object on shore, the Captain is killed; the same primal scene structures the "Lorelei," and the poet flaunts or feigns his mourning for the anonymous sailor early: "daß ich so traurig bin" ("that I am so sadly inclined").[16] Yet if the accusation in the final fingerpointing lines ("Und das hat mit ihrem Singen / Die Lorelei getan" ["And this the fate that follows / the song of the Lorelei"]) is supposed to solve the crime and answer the initial question of signification ("was soll es bedeuten" ["I do not know what it means"]), the text is equally a hopelessly incriminating confessions. For if it was singing that killed cock robin, then the poet stands condemned. As long as blame is projected onto the imaginary figure, i.e., as long as the poet does not come to grips with his past, his past grips him, progressive history is prohibited, and an adequate cognition of the present is prevented by permanent ideology: "Ein Märchen aus alten Zeiten / Das kommt mir nicht aus dem Sinn" ("There is an old tale and its scenes that / will not depart from my mind").

The parricide in the wake of which poetry takes place is the radical revolution which necessarily entails the murder of the leader. It is not an empirical revolution which matters here, certainly not the American Revolution or the absent German revolution but the imagined revolutions, the violent breaks with a prior order in which Heine and Whitman both take part vicariously. Yet no matter how fictional, the affective valence of the murderous wish is as great as that of any fantasized trauma of imaginary seduction, "die wahre Gewalt." The identification with the revolution implies a complicity in death:

> Did we think victory great?
> So it is—but now it seems to me, when it cannot
>   be help'd, that defeat is great,
> And that death and dismay are great.[17]

Thus Whitman's closing lines in 1856 "To a Foil'd European Revolutionaire," and within less than a decade the experience of death takes on an American character: the Civil War and Lincoln's assassination. Whitman's representative mourning for Lincoln is homologous to Heine's commemorations of Napoleon as well as his fantasies of revolution and regicide: Charles I, Marie Antoinette, or the guillotine passage in the "Wintermärchen." The primal murder liberates and burdens simultaneously: the king is dead, long live the king.

If this poetry is always in the wake of a revolution, or better, of a revolutionary wish, then the theme of death, even in its most romantic guises, is always the trace of political violence for which the guilty poet does penance. In the case of Heine and Whitman both an anterior act of violence is a condition of possibility of verse. Yet here a crucial distinction must be made that may account for the alternative institutionalizations of poetry in the two cultures. In the seventh section of the "Wintermärchen," the poet walks with death, his writing is a bloody scrawl, and it is the gesture of the poet that unleashes the regicidal force:

Da sah ich furchtbar blinken
Des Stummen Begleiters furchtbares Beil—
Und er verstand mein Winken.

[The fearsome ax shining brightly I saw
In my mute companion's fearsome hands—
And he read my signals rightly.][18]

Yet the death of the king is, so the text implies, also the poet's death—
"Blutströme schossen aus meiner Brust" ("And spurts of blood shot from my breast"). The revolutionary poet is still deeply implicated in the old order, and, presumably, revolutionary poetry has not broken cleanly with the categories of hegemonic culture. Whitman too sets death at the origin of poetry in the crucial "When Lilacs Last in the Dooryard Bloom'd." Yet while Heine stages the struggle within the oppressive and lugubrious confines of a feudal-ecclesiastic interior, Whitman has Lincoln's coffin pass through the expanse of the American landscape, replete with imagery of vibrant nature and vigorous society. The poet can survive the murdered leader without an onerous legacy or an internalized guilt, and an effective public voice is achieved, as the deceased is lain to rest:

Passing I leave thee lilac with heart-shaped leaves,
I leave thee there in the door-yard, blooming,
	returning with the spring.[19]

Heine never reaches a similar reconciliation, and a similarly consoling leavetaking is withheld. For the melancholic Heine, the dead are not yet buried; Whitman can mourn and describe the funeral procession. In the terms of literary history, Whitman takes leave of the literary past more effectively than Heine; the desire for the death of the leader, as both a political and a literary revolution, induces a guilt which impedes the secularization of German poetry. After Heine, and despite Heine, the power of tradition and classic-romantic aesthetics remained considerably greater than was the case in the wake of Whitman; hence the *Sonderweg* of German lyric verse in which a subversive countertradition, say from Heine to Brecht, has always remained secondary to the authoritative canon from Goethe to George.

The Critique of Modernity

If the death of the father, in literature and politics, burdens the two writers, they can equally appropriate it for their project for a public poetry by redirecting it into a vehicle for public criticism. The remorse for the radical rupture makes the poetry all the more sensitive to the failures of the revolution and a bad modernity: was the break with tradition in vain? was all the violence for nought? Allowing death to march arrogantly through their poetic visions constitutes a radical critique of a developing bourgeois society that denies identity only a split second after promising its fulfillment: everyday life is capital punishment. This is not the aestheticist cult of death that Mann ascribed to a Whitman read beside Novalis, death as some weird source of creativity. On the contrary, it is a precise naming of the fatal character of the modern social condition, a night of the living dead, and it simultaneously expresses a challenge and a utopian hope: better dead than reduced to this reality. Hence the death wish at the end of the third of the *Heimkehr* poems:

Mein Herz, mein Herz ist traurig,
Doch lustig leuchtet der Mai;
Ich stehe, gelehnt an der Linde,
Hoch auf der alten Bastei.

Da drunten fließt der blaue
Stadtgraben in stiller Ruh;
Ein Knabe fährt im Kahne
Und angelt und pfeift dazu.

Jenseits erheben sich freundlich,
In winziger, bunter Gestalt,
Lusthäuser und Gärten und Menschen,
Und Ochsen und Wiesen und Wald.

Die Mägde bleichen Wäsche
Und springen im Gras herum:
Das Mühlrad stäubt Diamanten,
Ich höre sein fernes Gesumm.

Am alten grauen Turme
Ein Schilderhäuschen steht;
Ein rotgeröckter Bursche
Dort auf und nieder geht.

Er spielt mit seiner Flinte,
Die funkelt im Sonnenrot,
Er präsentiert und schultert—
Ich wollt, er schösse mich tot.

[My heart, my heart is heavy,
Though May shines bright on all,
I stand and lean on the linden
High on the bastion wall.

Below me the moat is flowing
In the still afternoon;
A boy is rowing a boat and
Fishing and whistling a tune.

Beyond in colored patches
So tiny below, one sees
Villas and gardens and people
And oxen and meadows and trees.

The girls bleach clothes on the meadow
And merrily go and come;
The mill wheel scatters diamonds—
I hear its distant hum.

On top of the old grey tower
A sentry looks over the town,
A young red-coated lad there
Is marching up and down.

He handles his shining rifle,
It gleams in the sunlight's red,
He shoulders arms, presents arms—
I wish he would shoot me dead.][20]

"Ich wollt, er schösse mich tot." The pastoral idyll of a cheerful springtime, the fisherboy, the healthy servant girls, and the glistening mill wheel—a postcard picture of Old Germany, that turns out to be a nightmare, always about to flip over into the brutality that lurks in the heart of *Gemütlichkeit*. The poet in fact invokes the catastrophe, he calls for the shooting to begin: in order to unmask the structural horror and, as victim, in order to escape. Heine's contemporary Eichendorff too could invoke violence and destruction in his verse, but it appeared as a romantic sublime counterposed to a beautiful bourgeois order; ergo a conservative apologetics for the order. Heine's text indicates that it is the order itself which is always the site of catastrophe: there's no place like home.

This concern, early in the *Buch der Lieder*, antedates by two decades the "Zeitgedichte"; for Whitman, the insistence on the presence of death as a critique of a bad life can be traced in the Calamus poems, before the Civil War. That is to say that for both, the social-critical substance of the theme is established before any explicit politicization of the verse. Nevertheless it is again in "Lilacs" that Whitman comes closest to Heine in articulating the morbidity of the social order:

> Then with the knowledge of death as walking one side of me,
> And the thought of death close-walking the other side of me,
> And I in the middle with companions, and as holding
>   the hands of companions,
> I fled forth to the hiding receiving night that talks
>   not. . . .[21]

There he discovers the possibility of an appropriate incantation, "the carol of the bird," and then "with my comrades there in the night," he has an apocalyptic battlefield vision from the war:

> I saw battle-corpses, myriads of them,
> And the white skeletons of young men, I saw them,
> I saw the debris and debris of all the slain soldiers
>   of the war. . . .[22]

Yet even more poignant than the discovery of poetry or the recognition of the carnage of the war is the very constitution of the seeing subject through "the knowledge of death": a universal negativity that is the substance of the social contract among soi-disant "companions." The poet can comprehend the sorrow and bereavement dictated by history only by understanding that bereavement has become the principle of social organization of the failed community. The pseudo-identity of the most intimate relations is susceptible to destruction in the context of total reification; unproblematic self-identity is relegated to a distant and mythic past: Whitman's "Manhatta" or Heine's "Hammonia." For the present, however, not even the radical poem can achieve that sovereign freedom: Heine's free thought rarely approaching free verse, and Whitman's open lines condemned to a syntactic eternal return and a repetitive periodic structure. The limits of social emancipation are enfigured in the limits of formal innovation; the emancipation of poetry is blocked by the failure of the revolution that has engendered a failed modernity.

What links Heine and Whitman, then, is the attempt to secularize poetry and to transform it into a public medium; the insight into the dialectics of engaged literature; the exploration of the revolution against tradition and its consequences for democratic culture; the critique of modernity inherent in the thematics of death. It is a shared project, deeply interwoven with the democratic culture of the nineteenth century and presumably too radical for Mann in his 1922 address. The failure of the "German Republic" is a measure of the repression of Heine and of a Whitman understood differently.

Coda

The name of the failure of the republic was fascism. Heine and Whitman in fact play an important role in the formation of fascist aesthetics, as objects of negation. They are not merely repressed and marginalized; rather, their insistence on the publicity of poetry is simultaneously denounced and appropriated from the standpoint of a self-described superior poetics: the aestheticization of politics. Bartels rants and raves against Heine the political radical in order to formulate the program for a reactionary literature, devoted to the extremely political project of an illusory national regeneration. Hamsun's early denunciation of Whitman's crudity is still an aestheticist gesture, colored by his lifelong hostility to democracy. Pound's reception of Whitman is more to the point: he is eager to take on the mantle of the great American poet but insists on subjecting Whitman's backwoods boorishness to the imperatives of modernist rigor.[23] The democratic public, Whitman's subject, turns into the national community, subject to imperatives. The acoustic revolution of the beating drums, addressed by Whitman, gives way to the authorial counterrevolution of Pound addressing American troops on Italian radio: this is the poetic history of the structural transformation of the public sphere.

An inquiry into the role of the negativity of Heine and Whitman in the construction of a fascist aesthetics—that is a project which I have only outlined in a preliminary fashion. A topic of more immediate concern, however, is a consideration, from the standpoint of republican poetry, of the repercussions of fascism today; the relevance of a poetry suppressed by fascism to our most self-assuredly postfascist criticism; and in this context most germane, the discourse on fascism and literary criticism that has developed in the wake of the discovery of the early writings of Paul de Man. There is, in my opinion, little reason to spend time demonstrating the self-evident incompatibility of the democratic lyric project of Heine and Whitman with the texts de Man published in the collaborationist press of occupied Belgium. Those texts, usually confused and often egregious, do not provide a conclusive answer to the *Gretch-*

frage of deconstructive criticism: Wie steht es mit der Politik? The answer can be sought rather, ironically enough, in the prose that has been mobilized in de Man's defense, a vigorously political prose that simultaneously denounces de Man's critics for pursuing a political agenda:

> Ich weiß, sie tranken heimlich Wein
> Und predigten öffentlich Wasser.

> [I know how in secret they guzzle wine
> and in public preach water-drinking.][24]

This sort of paradox and the corollary contempt for a public culture indicate the continuity of a hierarchical structure of institutionalized culture that Whitman lambasted in "Democratic Vistas":

> Literature, strictly considered, has never recognized the People, and whatever may be said, does not today. . . . It seems as if, so far, there were some natural repugnance between a literary and professional life, and the rude rank spirit of the democracies. . . . I know nothing more rare, even in this country, than a fit scientific estimation and reverent appreciation of the People . . . their entire reliability in emergencies, and a certain breadth of historic grandeur, of peace or war, far surpassing all the vaunted samples of book-heroes, or any *haut ton* coteries, in all the records of the world.[25]

Precisely this conflict between the "*haut ton*" and a "rude rank spirit" is the backdrop to the effort of Heine and Whitman to develop a democratic literature in which belletristic and journalistic languages are mixed in order to construct a postauratic public voice. This conflict is also the backdrop for de Man's apologists, who denounce the rude journalistic intervention into a sphere of high literary theory allegedly inappropriate for public scrutiny, according to the coterie's motto: close the border, stop the gap. Thus in a letter published in a prestigious literary journal in April of 1988, one could read the following comment from a well-respected critic: "When [de Man] resumed writing about literature [after the war], as a graduate student at Harvard, it was to initiate the critique of organicist and narrative figures through which he had sought to master literature for journalistic purposes."[26] Note that according to this account the young de Man had no political and certainly no fascist purposes, but only journalistic ones, as if the error of the 1940s was only a generic peccadillo, his willingness to engage in journalism at all, and not the substance or the location of that particular journalism. How fortunate then—this is the apparent suggestion of the letter's author, a professor of literature—that de Man renounced journalism and chose to pursue a graduate study of literature, at Harvard no less. Whether de Man himself shared this contempt for public discourse, including journalism, is, to say the least, doubtful, and one may eventually be forced to defend de Man against his defenders, at least on this score.

The public voice of literature was, for Heine and Whitman, a key aspect in the demolition of tradition, the radical break with inherited forms in art and politics. In other words, the project of republican poetry and the democratization of culture is not thinkable without a revolutionary gesture, even when, as I have tried to show, the authors are well aware of the dangerous risks inherent in the project. Despite these risks, the project retains a plausibility because of the utopian hopes it awakens, and its failure is not treated as an inescapable fate; because political action is deemed urgent, it is also imaginably successful. How different then, how much more responsible and sober, is the argument which atones for de Man's political juvenilia by lauding the mature de Man's putative admonition against all politics. Whether this sort of reading of de Man's trajectory is adequate can remain open; more important is the intervention of another sublime critic, writing in the *New Republic*, in order to teach the lesson that politics slide into messianic revolutions which are always likely to end in fascism: "The political culture he championed in the *Le Soir* articles, a culture that claimed to be modern and revolutionary, was based on such a hope," i.e., a "messianic" hope in the possibility of "new beginnings."[27] Revolutions of the left, like those of the right, democratic or antidemocratic, are, by implication, always totalitarian. The dialectic of Enlightenment, inscribed in the ambiguity of republican poetry, turns out to be no dialectic at all but rather blind fate heading necessarily to catastrophe. For this good citizen, then, "the only activity that escapes the immediate ideological pressure is art itself," an analysis that clearly falls behind the level of "Doktrin" and "Drums." Art, already superior to journalism, is now declared superior to bad politics, or rather, to politics which are always bad.

But if politics are always bad, so is the public voice of a postauratic poetry, and so is any critique of modernity. Not in de Man's own texts but in the anxious prose of his defenders one finds the sophisticated version of the hegemonic cultural conservatism of the 1980s lodged in a solely ad hoc theory of fascism. It is a conservatism that has as little room for the terms of republican poetry and democratic culture as did Thomas Mann's formula of 1922. In the light of this double repression in the course of the century, Heine, Whitman, and the cultural alternative they represent might seem to fade into the recesses of an unretrievable past, thoroughly irrelevant to contemporary criticism. Yet it is exactly the shrillness of that repression that indicates the continued viability of the emancipation project, in politics and literature and in their potential congruence. Heine and Whitman investigate this potential and chart a terrain which is ours to rediscover or to repress. Their challenge stands in either case: to replace the hegemonic culture of conservative criticism with a culture that is critical of the conservative hegemony.

Chapter 3

Citizenship, Conversion, and Representation

Moritz Oppenheim's *Return of the Volunteer*

Emancipation did not come overnight: neither Enlightenment rationalism nor the tentative separation of Church and State in Fridician Prussia or Josephinist Austria immediately transformed the exclusionary structures that shaped the lives of the Jewish populations. No declaration of tolerance could instantaneously produce a civil society of secular citizens with equal rights regardless of creed. The confessional identity of states and cultures and the centrality of anti-Semitism to the Western tradition vitiated the reform efforts, even if one ascribes the best of intentions to their proponents. Yet the reformists' programs themselves were implicated in a dialectic of Enlightenment, so that Jews could just as well end up the victims of programs presented for their benefit or "improvement." Universalism was not only a fraternal invitation but a royal imperative as well, the authoritarian command to renounce the particularity of identity in order to gain the rights of modern citizenship; rationalist anticlericalism could be as antagonistic to the real forms of Jewish existence as traditionalist Christianity had been and, of course, continued to be.[1]

Beyond this philosophical ambiguity within the Enlightenment, the political and social history of the nineteenth century is anything but an unbroken narrative of emancipation. Even the most sanguine accounts of cumulative progress are, if at all honest, punctuated by a chain of reversals and retreats: the revocation of the Napoleonic Code after 1815, the riots of 1819, the conservative polemics against the liberal authors of the restoration era; the emergence of an intellectual anti-Semitism in figures like Paul de Lagarde and, later, the Wagner circle; the ramifications of Bismarck's antiliberal turn after 1878, especially the anti-Semitism debate incited by Heinrich von Treitschke; and, by the end of the century, the rise of a specifically anti-Semitic politics, in both

Germany and the Austria of Lueger and Schönerer.[2] We know moreover of the de facto, if not de jure, pressures to convert: the cases of Heine and Mahler are only the most prominent instances. That nineteenth century, an age of reaction and resistance, belies the optimistic accounts of universalism and amelioration. The bourgeoisie may have shared, by and large, an imagination of progress, but that is no reason for us, especially in the wake of the Holocaust, to imagine that progress, at least in the matter of Jewish emancipation, was predominant or untroubled.

These impediments to emancipation might be summarized as (1) the Enlightenment's philosophical denigration of any particularity, (2) an ideological opposition to Jewish integration, and (3) the social pressure to relinquish Jewish loyalties and to take up the majority religion of the German nation. Presumably this last factor was amplified by the waning significance of religious identity in a society undergoing rapid modernization; adherence to a faith that provoked the hostility of one's compatriots and peers must have seemed particularly inopportune in a context where the status of faith was increasingly dwarfed by a secular belief in the power of science and industry.

Without denying the explanatory validity of these factors, philosophical, ideological, and sociological, one does well to note that they remain extrinsic to the specifically religious matter which, if granted its own autonomy, is not primarily or purely a philosophical, political, or sociological datum. For the agent of religious experience—in this case, for the believer who is a Jew—the era of the emancipatory promise entails a crisis of religion (or, following Barth, it entails a new concretization of the crisis which religion always is).[3] Faith was no longer guaranteed by the ghetto walls, which were falling like the rabbinical "walls around the Torah." Nineteenth-century reform Judaism may have been an effort to adapt the religious tradition to a modernist sensibility, but the grand apologetics of Cohen, Buber, Scholem, and especially Rosenzweig were driven, at least in part, by an urgency to understand why one should not simply convert. (The same presumably applies as well later to Schoeps's interest in the problem of Jewish Christianity.)[4]

The temptation must have been great: not merely because of physical threats or careerist opportunism but because of an internally religious challenge as well, a challenge heightened by a development within at least parts of post-Enlightenment Protestantism. The argument was mounted that, since the apostolic era, the church had been tainted by an unchristian animosity to Jews, no longer tenable in an age of progress and brotherhood. Therefore the church was called upon to carry out the Pauline exhortation of directing its mission to Jews as well as to Gentiles; anything short of that would constitute a refusal of the Gospel; Jews should consequently not be stigmatized and reviled but embraced and converted.[5] Hence the increase in missionary activity, especially by the London Society for the Promotion of Christianity among the Jews, which undertook considerable activity in Germany.[6] Hence, most symbolically, the establishment of the joint Anglican-Prussian Bishopric in Jerusalem in 1841, charged specifically with a mission to the Jews. The first bishop there was Michael Solomon Alexander, a German Jew who arrived in England in 1820 and served as cantor in several congregations until converting in 1825. Active in the London Society, he rose through the Anglican ranks, until he took on the post in Jerusalem.

This is not the place to attempt to construct a phenomenology of religious conversion that would neither be vulgarly reductionist nor itself solely an appendage to a triumphalist *Missionswissenschaft*. Suffice it to say that the case of Alexander and others like him indicates what one might call a horizon of conversion for parts of German Jewry in the nineteenth century, i.e., the possibility of conversion out of a genuinely religious impetus.[7] No doubt such possibility could produce extreme anxiety, even if it were not realized in the form of a definitive choice to change one's confessional identity. No doubt, moreover, such possibility, no matter how genuinely religious it may have been, responded to nonreligious factors, such as the ambiguity of the Enlightenment, anti-Semitic agitation, and material need. (One can of course concede such a resonance between religious and nonreligious spheres without capitulating to accounts of religion as simply and solely a distorted reflection of social reality.)

One such factor requires cursory reference here, since it will become relevant for the further argument. Among the elements of anti-Semitic rhetoric in the first half of the nineteenth century (before the construction of a racial anti-Semitism in the second half), the trope of the "Wandering Jew" figures rather prominently. The key text was perhaps *Ahasverus oder die Judenfrage* by the conservative nationalist polemicist Constantin Frantz.[8] It should be remembered that in literary usage the "Wandering Jew" could vary considerably, from a fictional protagonist of travel literature to a maudlin object of sympathy.[9] Yet as Michael A. Meyer comments,

> it is the legend of Ahasuerus, the eternally wandering Jew, which Frantz conjures up for his readers. Condemned to roam about the earth for rejecting the messiah, the Jewish people can never find peace. It wants to mingle among the peoples and snuff out its peoplehood, but it cannot—not until the Second Coming of Christ. Thus efforts at Jewish religious reform and cultural integration—no matter how sincere—must always and necessarily be found wanting. They are futile attempts to escape a myth which the Jewish people must live out until the end of days.[10]

The point here is of course not to reconstruct Frantz's account in toto but to note a single component of the anti-Semitic imagination, the ascription of homelessness, a particularly interesting element since neither the text nor its context has anything to do with the Zionism of a later period. Reconstructing a possible sensibility of this period, one might conjecture a linkage that Frantz himself would probably have precluded: that individual apostasy might bring the wandering to an end or, in other words, that conversion might permit one to return home. The concatenation is clearly counterintuitive; one presumes that conversion entails, if anything, an entry into a new community of faith. Yet if the temptation of conversion responded on some level to the imputation of eternal wandering, conversion might have equally been experienced as a vehicle of return; and the desire to return home, to find a homeland, and to belong to a nation was certainly one of the most powerful elements in the nationalist nineteenth century. It is this constellation that I want to trace through various subtexts beneath the surface representation in the 1834 painting of Moritz Daniel Oppenheim, *Return of the Jewish Volunteer from the Wars of Liberation to His Family Still Living in Accordance with Old Customs*.

It is, so commentators have noted, "a signal work in the history of the artistic contribution of Jews. It is generally said to represent the first effort of a known Jewish artist to confront a specifically Jewish subject."[11] The characterization is worth pondering, without even exploring yet the apparent paradox that such a doubly innovative work takes as its *sujet* a return. Let me reserve that problem for later and note more simple matters first. The painting is clearly a product of legal emancipation, since heretofore Jews had been excluded from the arts by the confessional restrictions both on guild membership and on admission to the drawing schools and art academies which Oppenheim had been able to attend.[12] German Jews had been active as painters earlier only at the price of conversion: vide Ismael Mengs (1688–1764) who, as a Protestant, rose to court painter and director of the Dresden Academy, as well as his son, Anton Raphael Mengs (1728–79), who, a friend and collaborator of Winckelmann, converted to Catholicism in Rome in 1749.[13] Jewish topics, on the other hand, were not at all new in painting, if one is prepared to include under that rubric depictions of biblical scenes. Yet precisely the primacy of religious illustration, or rather, the institutional dependence of the arts on the religious project of the established Christian churches provided a further reason to regard as oxymoronic the notion of a Jewish painter. Oppenheim's *Return of the Volunteer* is therefore apparently modern in an additional sense; representing non-biblical Jewish material (indeed from the relatively recent past), it is indicative of the development of an autonomous institution of art, not primarily tied to ecclesiastical needs. The notion of Jewish painting—and of the *Return of the Volunteer* as a particularly prominent instantiation—is noteworthy, how-

Return of the Jewish Volunteer from the Wars of Liberation to His Family Still Living in Accordance with Old Customs. 1834 painting by Moritz Daniel Oppenheim, courtesy of the Jewish Museum, New York, and Art Resource.

Return of the Jewish Volunteer from the Wars of Liberation to His Family Still Living in Accordance with Old Customs. 1880 grisaille by Moritz Daniel Oppenheim, courtesy of the Jewish Museum, New York, and Art Resource.

ever, for a reason of greater cultural significance than the dismantling of exclusionary professional restrictions or the ongoing secularization of thematic
material. At stake is the problem of the *Bilderverbot*, the decalogic proscription of images of the deity: "Thou shalt not make unto thee a graven image,
nor any manner of likeness, of anything that is in heaven above, or that is in
the earth beneath, or that is in the water under the earth" (Exodus 20:5). The
most direct impact within Jewish cult was and remains the refusal to allow for
divine representations, a consistent and radical anti-idolatry in the name of
an invisible God, which was particularly provocative for anti-Jewish polemi-
cists of antiquity. Nevertheless, because considerable room remains for arti-
sans to produce extremely ornamental cultic objects, it is arguable that the
Mosaic injunction by no means precluded art but, on the contrary, provided
an ontology of art fundamentally antithetical to the mimetic paradigm that
would develop in classical Greece. Hence Adorno's comment: "The biblical
proscription of images has, in addition to its ideological side, an aesthetic one.
That one should not make a picture, that is, a picture of something, also means
that no such picture is possible."[14] A history of Western art that was prepared
to consider heterogeneous components and not, arbitrarily, privilege a Helle-
nistic origin would be obliged to pay attention to the dialectical interaction of
mimetic and antimimetic constructions of representation.

Without belaboring this matter which I have discussed at length in another
context, I want to underscore that the biblical text is itself by no means unam-
biguous on the question of the proscription.[15] The narrative of the revelation
at Sinai intertwines the *Bilderverbot* with the drama of its transgression in the
episode of the golden calf, entailing a sort of popular opposition to the severity of the new code (Exodus 32). In conflict, Moses and Aaron themselves represent competing modes of representation, script and image; Schoenberg's
opera draws attention to the continued relevance of the problematic in modernity. Yet the apparent victory of Moses is by no means unquestionably conclusive. The account is followed quickly by the construction of the Tabernacle which, as the sacred vehicle of the law, effectively enthrones the script,
but which is simultaneously adorned with the Cherubim, figures of the sort
that the script itself forbids (Exodus 32:7–9). The defeated mode of representation is reduced to a servile status as accompanying ornament; it is overthrown
but also preserved, *aufgehoben*. Therefore the assembly of the Tabernacle,
which in a sense brings to an end the events at Sinai, constitutes a compromise solution between the image and its refusal, between pictures and words,
between (in Lacanian terms) imaginary and symbolic dimensions, and between
a scopophilia and a scopophobia. The solution is moreover less a resolution
than the articulation of a tension between representational asceticism and cultic
populism that would certainly leave its marks on the religious history of ancient
Israel and, more germane here, that erupts as a subtext in Oppenheim's *Return*

of the Volunteer. Whatever may have been the painting's intentional message, which we have yet to consider, it is also about the conflict between verbal and visual representation, just as it is also about the problematics of conversion and return. Keeping these matters in mind, we do well now, before turning to the work itself, to turn briefly to Oppenheim, his concerns, and the character of his overall oeuvre.

Oppenheim was born in January 1800 in the ghetto of Hanau, and the events which transpired during his childhood make him a prime example of the first generation of German Jewry to grow up in a relatively emancipated context. The city was occupied by French troops on November 4, 1806, and it was incorporated into the Grand Duchy of Frankfurt on May 16, 1810, at which point French legal codes became applicable. On August 11, 1811, the new constitution of the grand duchy granted civil equality to all of its subjects; the ghetto thereby ceased to function as a legal institution.[16] For Oppenheim, this meant concretely that he was no longer restricted to attending the local Talmud-Torah school but could now enter the *Gymnasium* and the *Zeichenakademie*, where he apparently displayed enough talent to become a protegé of the local aristocracy. The countess von Benzel-Sternau was liberal enough to have kosher meals prepared for him in the castle, and his family was liberal enough not to resist his setting out on an innovative career.[17] He proceeded to study in the Munich Academy, where he became acquainted with the new technique of lithography recently developed there by Alois Sennefelder.[18] In Paris, he worked briefly with Regnault, a student of David's, and an element of the architectural geometry of classicism is evident in the *Return of the Volunteer.* Yet neither Munich nor Paris proved particularly conducive to his progress, and in 1821 he traveled to Rome where he worked at the S. Lucca Academy.[19] Short of a full biographical account, the following items are of particular interest. One of his paintings won a competition at the academy, but when it was discovered that he was both German and Jewish, he was denied the award. The sculptor Bertel Thorvaldsen took up his cause and prevailed on the commission at least to withhold the prize that year, if it was not prepared to grant it to the first choice. Thorvaldsen remained one of Oppenheim's two points of artistic reference, the other being Friedrich Overbeck, the Nazarene leader; Oppenheim had become close to German Nazarene circles during the Roman sojourn.[20] During a trip to Naples, he was introduced to Baron Carl Mayer von Rothschild, and a lengthy association with the family ensued which was crucial to Oppenheim's professional success; in his memoirs he describes himself with self-irony as the "painter of the Rothschilds and the Rothschild of painters."[21] In 1825 he returned to Germany to settle in Frankfurt, where he pursued an active and lucrative career, thanks especially to numerous portrait commissions (as well as the paintings of Otto IV and Joseph II in the Roemer), but that is only the part of the story that he tells. Research in the city archives has turned up evidence regarding the difficulties Jews encountered in gaining permanent residency in Frankfurt; it took Oppenheim more than twenty-five years. He had to submit at least ten requests for temporary extensions, and a request for citizenship, denied as late as 1847, was not finally granted until 1851.[22]

To be sure, his *Memoirs* were written late in life for his family members in the increasingly vitriolic atmosphere of 1880, which may explain the prominence of Jewish concerns in the narrative.[23] One is nevertheless struck by the degree to which Oppenheim refracts this Jewish material through references to the proximity of conversion. His report of his first encounter with the Jews of Rome, still confined to the ghetto, involves their suspicion of the stranger and their fear of forced conversion, and Oppenheim recounts one such incident he himself witnessed. In comparison, the efforts by his Nazarene colleagues to convert him appear relatively harmless, although the matter retains a surreptitiously existential urgency for Oppenheim.[24] In a passage on Philipp Veit, who had become head of the Städelsches Institut in Frankfurt in 1830, he notes: "His mother, Dorothea von Schlegel, lived with him; when her grandchildren wished her good night before going to bed, she blessed them and made the sign of the cross; to see the daughter of Moses Mendelssohn making a cross always saddened me." Or when he recounts to Veit how Mendelssohn resisted Lavater's efforts to convert him (Oppenheim painted the incident in *Mendelssohn, Lavater and Lessing*), he concludes: "Then Veit heaved a sigh and exclaimed, 'Who knows how much he is suffering for that now'—Veit was otherwise a very smart man."[25]

The remarks on Schlegel and Veit cast Oppenheim as melancholic and testy, simultaneously resigned and resentful. The politics of conversion can be worked out more interestingly, however, in a more complicated network of evidence involving two cases, Heine's and that of the Frankfurt physician and privy councillor Salomon Friedrich Stiebel. Heine arrived in Frankfurt on May 9, 1831, where, as Elisheva Cohen reports, he visited various acquaintances including Johann Baptist Rousseau, the doctor Aloys Clemens, and the book-dealer Löwenthal.[26] He had his portrait done by Oppenheim, at whose house he was invited for Sabbath dinner. Oppenheim recounts:

> I had invited some of his admirers and ordered, especially for him, authentic Jewish cuisine, "Kuchel und Schalet," which Heine enjoyed very much. I noted jokingly that he must feel homesick when he eats these dishes, like a Swiss hearing cowbells while traveling abroad. The discussion therefore turned to his baptism. When a guest asked about his motives, since he had never treated Christianity particularly nicely in his writings, Heine replied evasively that he found it harder to have a tooth pulled than to change his religion.[27]

Oppenheim refrains from commenting on the incident any further (in general, the *Memoirs* are not particularly reflective). Presumably he appreciates the wit of the exchange and therefore records the bon mots. Or does the record, for Oppenheim, serve to demonstrate the inadequacy of Heine's "evasive" response to his own challenge? That is, Heine's quip might be preserved here as evidence of an opportunist and cavalier treatment of a topic that Oppenheim—as we know from his thoughts on Schlegel and Veit—certainly took seriously. This reading of the sparse passage is supported by the anecdote which immediately follows, insofar as it entails a denigration of the convert, although not of Heine but rather via Heine. Here is Oppenheim's version:

> In one of his later writings [the Börne polemic], referring to his visit in Frankfurt, Heine speaks of the good Sabbath dinner at the home of the future privy councilor Stiebel. Yet he certainly remembers very well that he never had a Sabbath dinner at Stiebel's; doubtless he calculated with malice that the newly baptized Jew would be angered by the association with Old Testament cuisine. Speaking with Doctor Stiebel, I could ascertain that Heine's stab had not missed its mark.[28]

If Heine gets off easily in the first anecdote, Oppenheim evidently delights in the effectiveness of the poet's maliciousness in castigating the convert Stiebel. The tone has none of the melancholy which moved Oppenheim when watching Mendelssohn's daughter making the sign of the cross; on the contrary, he is forceful and aggressive, enjoying the embarrassment the apostate feels at the public recollection of his Jewish past. Presumably, for Oppenheim at least, the ostentatious exchange of confessions is neither as sincere as Stiebel would have one believe nor as unproblematic as Heine indicated in his ultimately weak dental analogy. That is, the temptation of conversion, the temptation of exchange, provokes a critical response that calls the viability of the exchange mechanism into question. Of relevance is a manuscript of a poem found in Oppenheim's papers and presented by Cohen, who surmises that it refers to Heine's dinner. "Despite appearances, it is not by Heine. It is however possible that Oppenheim, a clever amateur poet, was himself the author."[29] It is entitled "Memory," and the first two strophes dwell on the beauty of the Sabbath and the delicacies of the meal; the concluding two strophes address the problem of conversion:

Jedoch ich bekam bald die Nüss und die Sauc'
Durch deutsche "Krawalle" verleidet
Und deshalb vertauschte ich Abrahams Schoss
Mit einem der mehr ausgebreitet.—

Ich kenne nun beide und wahrlich ich seh',
Der Christoph ist gerad wie der Mausche.
Drum thut mir noch immer das Goldstück weh,
Das ich habe gespendet beim Tausche.—

[But soon I had my nuts and sauce / ruined by German riots / And that's
why I traded Abraham's lap / for another which was open wider. / Now I
know both and truly understand / That a Christoph is just like a Moses. /
So I still regret the piece of gold / That I donated at the exchange.]

For a strong argument, it would of course be desirable to be able to ascribe
the text definitively to Oppenheim. Yet lacking such philological certainty, we
can easily make do with the softer claim that the poem emerges in—or even
simply near—Jewish bourgeois circles in the 1830s (i.e., the era of Oppenheim's
Return of the Volunteer). The *Krawalle* refers to the anti-Jewish riots in Frankfurt in 1819 and, by extension, to an atmosphere of anti-Semitic agitation and
pressure.[30] The conversion described is a concession to the belligerence of the
surroundings. The convert finds, to his dismay, that the exchange was really
none at all, since nothing has changed—"Der Christoph ist gerad wie der
Mausche"—except that the name has changed, and the individual participates
in society through a character mask. Moreover the rhetoric of anti-Semitism
is appropriated in a manner reminiscent of Marx's usage in "On the Jewish
Question," insofar as the convert is parodied for remaining "Jewish," that is,
for regretting the loss of money, "das Goldstück . . . / das ich habe gespendet
beim Tausche." Indeed the same sort of connection is made directly through
the rhyme of *Mausche / Tausche*. However, the point of the poem is presumably not the assertion that Jews are differentially accumulative, since Chris-
tian/Jewish equality has been asserted only a few lines earlier. Rather, the
text—whether it is genuinely Oppenheim's or not is not crucial for the argument—demonstrates the implication of conversions in capitalist terms, i.e.,
conversion appears to provide a vehicle for upward mobility via entry into otherwise closed career tracks. Furthermore (and this is the radical twist) it suggests the fundamental fictionality and disfunction of the exchange structure:
the conversion feigns a transformation which is none at all—the logic of the
market fails to hold, at least in the realm of religious identity.

Imaginably Oppenheim might have been more concerned with the significance of conversion for painters. To be sure, his own career had been remarkable, despite his refusal to convert: born in a ghetto in 1800, he was granted
the honorary title of professor at the young age of twenty-seven by the grand
duke of Weimar on the recommendation of no one less than Goethe, and by
the mid-thirties he was clearly destined to become the portraitist of Frankfurt
high society.[31] Nevertheless he might have wondered about the case of Eduard

Bendemann, who converted in 1835 when he wed the daughter of his Nazarene teacher Wilhelm Schadow. Clearly a case of marrying the boss's daughter: in 1859 Bendemann succeeded Schadow as director of the Düsseldorf Academy.[32] Of greater interest, however, is the substantive difference in the works of Bendemann and Oppenheim during the thirties. Oppenheim's *Return of the Volunteer* dates from 1833/34; in 1832 Bendemann had completed *The Jews Mourning in Babylon*, and in 1836 would produce *Jeremiah at the Ruins of Jerusalem*. Ismar Schorsch comments trenchantly: "These celebrated paintings express more than the pathos of destruction and exile; they imbue the year 587 B.C.E. with a finality that is distinctly Christian . . . Oppenheim chose to read Jewish history differently and eventually became a spokesman for the religion he refused to abandon."[33] Yet to refuse to abandon, one must be acquainted with the real possibility of departure. Oppenheim's *Return* is certainly a manifesto for civil rights and an identity that can be simultaneously German and Jewish; as we will see, however, that optimism, that program of Enlightenment and emancipation rests on several subtexts that, at the very least, qualify the likelihood of progress. Oppenheim's considerable reputation in the second half of the nineteenth century, both internationally and especially in German Jewry, derived largely from a series of paintings commenced during the 1850s, the "Pictures of Traditional Jewish Family Life."[34] The full group includes the *Return of the Volunteer* (some twenty years earlier than the rest) and nineteen other images. The later works are arguably characterized by a realist aesthetic, with the specific connotation that term took on in Germany after 1848: depoliticized historical genre painting, depicting events from everyday life transfigured by a somewhat idealizing perspective.

Special attention is given to the accuracy of detail with regard to Jewish cult. The paintings appealed to a nostalgia for a disappearing ghetto culture, a reception made all the more likely by Oppenheim's clothing his figures in the outdated fashions of the rococo period: three-cornered hats, buckled shoes, etc.[35] Simultaneously the paintings could provide a non-Jewish public with a sort of ethnographic insight into the everyday practices of an observant Jewry; in 1867 and 1868, three of the paintings were reproduced in the *Gartenlaube*: *Beginning of Sabbath*, *Passover*, and *Sukkot*. Six of the images concern the life cycle, five the Sabbath, six other festivals, and three life outside the ghetto.[36] Schorsch provides the most sophisticated account of the agenda in the series: an effort to demonstrate the genuinely spiritual character of Judaism (against Kant's suggestion of its solely heteronomous character); to insist, in a covertly Hegelian manner, on its communal character; and to valorize the ghetto past for an upwardly mobile German Jewry otherwise potentially ashamed of its not-so-distant humble origins.[37]

The mass distribution of the images was instigated by the Frankfurt publisher Heinrich Keller. Since contemporary photographic techniques were inadequate to render the color paintings, Oppenheim redid them in gray gouache. The resultant "grisailles" were photographed and sold in portfolios, starting in 1866 for the first six images. The series of twenty was completed in 1881. In 1882, they appeared in book format, accompanied by explanatory notes by Rabbi Leopold Stein. The images were also mass-marketed on postcards, decorated pewter, and porcelain plates. "In sum, with a publication record of untold portfolio editions and at least four bound editions over a span of forty-eight years, Oppenheim's *Bilder aus dem altjüdischen Familienleben* may well have been the most popular Jewish book ever published in Germany."[38]

The final three images give expression to the "public credo of German Jewry," the viability of the double identity that eventually became the watchword of the *Centralverein*, "deutscher Staatsbürger jüdischen Glaubens," the harmonious balance of citizenship and faith.[39] The *Village Vendor* (*Dorfgeher*) depicts a peddlar setting out, kissing the mezuzah at the doorway, while his son, who presumably will accompany him, gives alms to an indigent Christian. *Jahrzeit*, the memorial service on the Day of Atonement, shows German-Jewish soldiers praying in a French farmhouse during the Franco-Prussian war. Both intend to demonstrate the possibility of Jews participating in German civil life while retaining a positive Jewish identity: citizenship without conversion. It is, however, in the *Return of the Volunteer* that Oppenheim's "uncompromising conception of citizenship" is given its most forceful expression.[40]

The members of a Jewish family are grouped around a table in a Biedermeier interior. On the left, the volunteer is seated, wearing a hussar's uniform; behind him stands an admiring young woman, probably his sister, while his aged father in front of him leans forward and stares at the medal on his chest: an Iron Cross. Behind the table, two younger siblings similarly direct their gaze at the volunteer, as does the mother too, standing in the foreground, holding a serving bowl. On the right, another young brother is turned away from the family but reaches out to the soldier's sword which is propped up against the wall. An equestrian image of Frederick II hangs on the left wall, an icon that combines both patriotism and Enlightenment aspirations.

While the father bends toward the cross, his left hand reaches out to touch an open book on the table; it is probably a prayer book, given the presence of other items of ceremonial significance: the kiddush cup, the pieces of challah, and the Sabbath lamp hanging over the table. However, the spice box, which would be used in the Havdalah service at the conclusion of Sabbath, still stands on the corner shelf. The point then is that the son has returned home on the Sabbath, in any case before the conclusion of Sabbath, and has therefore disregarded the injunction against traveling on the day of rest. The picture evidently both celebrates Jewish participation in the Wars of Liberation and works through the tension between duties to the military and the nation, on the one hand, and to family and religion on the other.

While I will want to comment primarily on the original version of 1834, the grisaille of 1880 displays some subtle though interesting changes.[41] Bracketing any contingent shifts in Oppenheim's style as well as specific consequences of the reproductive technique, one can account for such changes in two different ways, which are not necessarily mutually exclusive. Either the revision of the painting was driven by changed historical circumstances to which Oppenheim chose to respond with a different statement, or the reworking entailed an opportunity to correct unsatisfactory or ambiguous elements in the early version, i.e., the grisaille as a revisionist response to its own original. This latter line of argument therefore employs the reproduction heuristically, as an initial critical reading of the primary image.

The most prominent change involves the figure of the volunteer. In 1834 his right arm, in the blue sleeve of the uniform, is bent at the elbow, with the forearm reaching across his front toward the father. In the later version, the arm remains in the same position but is now in a sling, clearly an ostentatious display of the wound for which he received the decoration. Stein's comment in the 1882 book edition reads: "May the broken arm not symbolize the shattered expectations of the Jews nor the cross the return of the 'Christian State.' "[42] To treat the wound as a symbol of "shattered expectations" probably goes too far (and Stein does, after all, phrase the suggestion only as a negative wish), but it is not at all implausible to relate this shift in the illustration to the anti-Semitic challenges after the end of the liberal decade and at the beginning of the conservative Puttkamer era.[43] Yet it would be too limiting to address the matter solely with regard to a single moment in nineteenth-century German history. What is at stake, rather, is a response that highlights a constitutive element in the vocabulary of anti-Semitism. Oppenheim is forced to display the wound because the medal alone is apparently not adequate proof of genuine heroism at the front, and the medal is not sufficiently material evidence because, for the anti-Semitic imagination, the Jewish soldier is highly unlikely to be able to display military prowess. In this sense, *Return of the Volunteer* anticipates the Rubitsky case a century later in the United States, where of course doubts regarding the soldierly abilities of Jews even prohibit awarding a decoration.[44]

The association of Jews with military incompetence derives directly from the medieval iconography of the defeated Synagogue, counterposed to the triumphant Church, as well as from a sexual fantasy linking Jews and women, against the background of the assumption that the military is a necessarily masculine domain. The construction of gender will concern us more extensively below. For the moment, suffice it to note that Oppenheim is falling into a familiar trap: in order to argue for the patriotic loyalty of Jews, he is compelled to present them as ultrapatriotic. They not only fight, but they are heroes and have the wounds to show it; to claim that they can bear arms, they have to return home with an arm in a sling. And the younger brother on the right must eye the sword as an indication that he is already eager to enlist.

A second revisionist aspect involves some subtle changes in the composition of the image. In both versions, the seven figures are divided into three clusters: the sister, the soldier, and the father on the left; the children behind and the mother in front of the table; and the single brother with the sword at the right. In the grisaille, however, some details have been adjusted in order to underscore the overriding unity of the scene. Drapes now hang on both sides of the window in the background, embracing the family and muffling the severity of the bare walls in the original version which, borrowed perhaps from David's classicism via Regnault, seemed to underscore the separation of the three groups. The cohesion of the family is furthermore increased in the later version where the soldier is now turned toward the center, as he returns his mother's gaze; in the original, he faced forward and appeared to be straining to look at his sister behind him. The sister, who stands behind her brother in the original, crouches at his level in the reproduction. The result is to underscore the compositional symmetry of the revised arrangement: a line rises from the sister's head to the Sabbath lamp in the center (a line moreover identical with the direction of the rays of light), the mirror image of a line falling from the lamp, through the mother, and to the boy on the right. By lowering the sister, Oppenheim has diminished the prominence of the cluster on the left, which no longer competes with the definitive architectural center of the scene.

Elements of competition and separation are reduced in the grisaille in a further and telling manner. I have already pointed out the change of the soldier's line of sight from the sister to the mother. In addition, the sister, who originally looked over the soldier's head toward the mother, now admiringly stares at the soldier from behind. Thus, in the 1880 version, everyone, with the exception of the brother preoccupied with the sword and, of course, the soldier himself, is gazing at the wounded returnee. He is in effect the center of attention, and he directs his attention to his mother in the center of the painting. This arrangement successfully obliterates a decentering element in the original, a separate triangle of vision, in which the sister watches the mother watching the soldier who is stretching to see his sister and thereby, in effect, turning away from his father. This retraction from the father is all the more noteworthy since the soldier is set in a predominately female group (a fact that will bear centrally on the question of gender identity with regard to the sexual politics of anti-Semitism), which in turn accentuates the patriach's liminal setting stretched between the cross on his son's breast and the book on the table.

The compositional difference between the more fractured and dialectical original and the more transfigurative and cohesive reproduction can be explained in various ways. It might be subsumed under larger and familiar developments in aesthetics and philosophy in Germany between the 1830s and the 1880s, the displacement of the dialectic of negativity by a discourse of totality.[45] Alternatively, one might imagine Oppenheim underscoring family unity in the later version precisely as a response to the lability of traditional family structure, Jewish or not, as a result of the Industrial Revolution and the growing women's movement. Or the disappearance of the difficult contradictions in the reproduction might be blamed simply on the trivializing character of the developing culture industry.

Another approach is more timely here. If, as suggested above, one treats the reproduction as a critical reading of the original, one concludes that Oppenheim chooses to brush out contradictory moments that potentially subverted the intentional force of the initial statement. In other words, if the original is taken as an emphatic endorsement of the viability of a German-Jewish identity which does justice to both components of the hybrid, the very representation of that program may have contradicted itself, and the revisions in the grisaille therefore amount to an effort to redress, or better, repress those problems. To explore these contradictions and their ramifications, however, we can now leave the 1880 version behind us, having used it to focus on precisely those aspects of the original *Return of the Volunteer* which disappear in the revision because they threatened to destabilize the Enlightenment program.

There appears to be no external evidence from Oppenheim regarding his intentions in the painting. Nevertheless it is hard to imagine the foregrounded message to be less than the claims that German Jews can fight in a patriotic war and then return to traditional religious practices. The painting might also plausibly entail a protest against the rescinding of emancipatory legislation during the first post-Napoleonic years. This sort of interpretation pervades the critical literature, and it provides a convincing explanation as to why a group of Jews from Baden chose to present this painting (in fact it may have been commissioned by them) to the politician and civil rights activist Gabriel Riesser in 1835.[46] In his reply, Riesser, who remained a longtime friend of Oppenheim, also confirms the liberal reading of the *Return*. The key passage in his eloquent remarks is worth quoting at length:

> Praise to the wise artist, who has combined one of the holiest, if most transitory, moments of this century, with the ancient forms of Jewish life; who has overcome the superficial contrast between the two through artistic beauty and a great sense of humanity. As father and son unite, so do the past and the new age, inner faith and courageous patriotism, passive and active loyalty. Yes, like father and son, the ages should embrace in honor and love. Foolish the father who would dress his son in the clothes of the past and not draw pleasure from his youthful spirit, his joyous progress, his deepest participation in the strongest urges of the century! Foolish the declining direction of the past that would wrap the young, sprouting forces in its own shroud to have them wither in a cold embrace! But the son would be without honor who would be ashamed of his father and the past! We see in the

soldierly youth love for the fatherland coupled with a passionate attachment
to the religious life of the family, to which he has returned: in the melancholy expression of his features, we intimate his anxiety that the great struggle for freedom, which heaven has allowed him to join, the struggle for freedom of conscience and other freedoms, was fought in vain, and that new
battles and new sacrifices will be necessary. Oh! This is truly art! In its figures it combines only what is one in human arts, and which can be divided
only in deceptive appearance or in the delusion of prejudice.[47]

Riesser names the historical materials—patriotism, religion, and the disappointments of 1819—and, second, he locates them within a particular aesthetic philosophy of unity: father and son embrace, old and new join hands,
politics and faith, Germany and Judaism are reconciled. While the historical
reference points are indisputable, Riesser's explanation of them, the narrative
in which he places them, is not thoroughly convincing: the critical question
remains as to the plausibility of the reconciliation. In other words, since we
today no longer accept unquestionably the classicist aesthetics of totalization
which Riesser has clearly borrowed from the tradition of German idealism,
it is worth inquiring if the putative harmony is not belied by concurrent and
perhaps more substantive dissensions. On this score, it is noteworthy that
Riesser's rhetoric reaches its climax in a mode of admonition—"Thöricht der
Vater," etc.—as if the various reconciliations were not at all already achieved
but only declared to be desiderata. More to the point, however, are two curious concessions that Riesser makes in passages preceding the quote. With
reference to his own efforts in pursuit of civil equality—the activity for which
the presentation of the painting was designed to honor him—he asserts that
now, in the modern age, religion has become an increasingly personal, not a
collective matter, and that German Jews are bound together less by faith than
by their political struggle for emancipation:

> Common descent is today a dead, accidental, and meaningless fact; faith
> has very little to do with external life. . . . The common struggle for our with-
> held rights, for the recognition of our human value, for gaining the love of
> our fellow men—that is what unites us, that is what makes us an ethical
> community.[48]

His point may simply be that Jewry too is not immune to processes of secularization, but it is difficult to read these lines without being astonished by the
force with which they seem to undercut the terms of his effusive appreciation
of the painting. Descent, that is, filiation and family, are now cast aside as dead
matter—is that a reading of Oppenheim's wizened father? Religion, with which
the soldier could allegedly combine citizenship without a conflict of interest,

is declared to be of dwindling importance. Instead, a doubly political bat-tle—the political battle to enter the political sphere on equal terms—overshad-ows both the domestic sphere and confessional identity, both the father and the god of the fathers. If such tensions are read back into the painting, then the homecoming is a matter not only of reunion but also of separation: the patri-otic son cannot turn back to the old paternal ways, and the melancholy traits, which Riesser explains as a response to reactionary politics, are rather an expression of the discovery that he in fact cannot return home, or that the home has become an uncanny place of death.

Riesser's understanding and this alternative account are intimately linked with each other as two sides of the Enlightenment. The painting does indeed celebrate the Jewish volunteer's participation in the war of national liberation which was also his own war for civil equality within a democratic state: the Enlightenment project. If its goals are not realized however, it is due not sole-ly to the machinations of reactionary powers-that-be in the Europe of the Holy Alliance and Metternichian retrenchment but also to an internal dialectic. The emancipatory Enlightenment which frees the subject from heteronomous con-trol simultaneously rips apart the generations and renders the individual alien-ated and homeless: therefore the son turns away from the father, nearly recoil-ing in disgust. Enlightenment universalism, the discourse of tolerance, turns out to have no tolerance for concrete particularity.

While Riesser questions the contemporary significance of religion in order to privilege his own metier of politics, he also suggests that in the emancipa-tion struggle his own contributions are less significant than his admirers might imagine. Perhaps it is only rhetorical modesty, but in this context he formu-lates a contrast that is extremely important for the dissection of the painting:

> How infinitely little am I allowed to risk and sacrifice for the holy cause
> of freedom, as compared with the risks and sacrifices that freedom can ask
> of us and which are eagerly granted by those inspired by her pure flame!
> It has often saddened me to recognize how little our good cause asks for sac-
> rifice and danger, how it is only the echoing word that can reveal the burn-
> ing desire of the soul, and how the word is so undangerous because of its
> impotence, so unthreatened because unfeared.[49]

Riesser concatenates "revelation" and the "wish of the soul" with an asser-tion of the necessity of sacrifice. This all might be treated simply as an over-dramatic phrasing of the liberal cause in a religious idiom, certainly a con-ventional rhetorical ploy.

More however is at stake, for Riesser suggests a contrast between the "word" as insufficient and an unnamed but more effective mode of sacrifice. An obvious reading might be to imagine Riesser deferring to political prisoners, or exiles, or perhaps even the wounded soldier in the painting. We get further now by recognizing that the contrast is embedded in the painting itself: between the word, i.e., the open book, and the wounded body, the sign of whose sacrifice is nothing other than the cross. Significantly, the father is poised wavering between the sacred text, be it a prayerbook or Scripture itself, and the very symbol of the alternative religion, which is, moreover, the religion of the Son. What appeared to be a political manifesto for a German-Jewish hybridity—and it was certainly understood as such—turns out to entail a nearly antithetical subtextual component as well: the bearer of the Cross encountering the Jew, who, as the enfigurement of the Old Testament—Riesser's "alte Zeit"—is portrayed as old (a standard iconographic equation), and presents him with the invitation of conversion. Indeed, without the painting's title and without the soldier's uniform, a not so different painting might have turned into a Nazarene tract for a mission to the Jews.

Earlier we saw that for Oppenheim, with his emphatic Jewish identity, the existential temptation of conversion remained close to the struggle for equality and acceptance. Now we have been able to draw the same result out of the painting itself. To do so, it was necessary to bracket Riesser's (and presumably Oppenheim's) post-Schillerian aesthetics of harmony and to pay attention, perhaps even overread, the moments of contradiction. The payoff includes some counterintuitive insights that go far beyond the ostensible consciousness of the nineteenth-century German-Jewish bourgeoisie and begin to ferret out some of its repressed anxieties as well as more extensive difficulties within German-Jewish or Christian-Jewish relations. With reference to *Return of the Volunteer*, I want to survey some of these matters bearing on politics, history of religion, aesthetics, and gender constructions.

Understood as an expression of a strident liberalism, the painting depicts the possibility of the coexistence of a public loyalty to the state and private obligations to family within a modern construction of citizenship. On closer examination, however, it illustrates with equal force how the two spheres in fact collide; either they remain incompatible or the one suppresses the other. In Hegel's reading of *Antigone*, the legality of the state eventually overcomes family duty and traditionalist custom within the historico-philosophy of the dialectic.[50] In *Return of the Volunteer*, the son is the carrier of historical progress that is in the process of eradicating the ancien régime of the obsolete practices of the paternal world. For as the painting makes perfectly clear, he has traveled on the Sabbath and therefore set himself beyond the letter of the law to which the father's left hand is pointing. The law of the nation has superseded the law of the faith, just as for Riesser political struggle has come to overshadow the bonds of religion and consanguinity. Therefore the marginal location of the spice box, proof that the end of the Sabbath has not yet been celebrated, is more than an indication of temporality. It is also the refusal of the celebration of difference: the differences between the day of rest and the workweek, between the holy and the profane, between Israel and the Gentiles, i.e., a refusal of all particularity. The painting therefore does indeed give expression to a universalism, but it is not at all the universalism imagined by liberal optimism and pursued by activists like Riesser. Jews can enter the German nation as equals, so the *Return of the Volunteer* suggests, at the price of renouncing their differential identity, and the volunteer who has returned is not a son in the loving bosom of the family but a nemesis bearing the bad news of secularization.

Yet the son, the enfigurement of political progress, has had to pay a greater price than traveling on the Sabbath and, by extension, revoking the validity of religious law. In order to gain secular citizenship, he has had to shed his own blood (and even that may not have been enough, if his sad countenance is truly a comment on the political reaction). Furthermore we have seen how the magnitude of the requisite self-sacrifice increases between 1834 and the grisaille of 1880. If Jewish particularity was the object of a premodern traditionalist persecution, enlightened modernity promises to allow the Jew to escape persecution by surrendering particularity and by internalizing the violence in the form of mutilation and self-denial. Yet the archaic pattern is only sublimated, not abrogated, since the incremental sacrifice—overachievement—is nothing other than the recurrence of particularity and difference. Precisely the heroism of the returning volunteer marks him, with the Iron Cross or the wounded arm, as one of the chosen and therefore vulnerable to persecution. Because sacrifice identifies the victim, no sacrifice is great enough to escape victimization, as the following anecdote by Peter Altenberg underscores:

> A story was told of a wealthy Jew who lost four sons at the front, a fifth was blinded by the pressure of a shell, his wife lost her mind, and he was partially lamed by a stroke—to which a "Christian" [a member of the Christian Socialist movement] replied: "Partially! Even the stroke *naturally* gets these people only partially!"[51]

The *Return of the Volunteer* also stages a conflict bearing on the origins of anti-Semitism and the ideology of the Christian state, with regard less to politics than to the history of religion. Instead of casting the generational opposition as a historico-philosophical drama in which the new religion "returns" in an effort to redeem the old, one can focus instead on the father's choice between two modes of religiosity: faith in the word, to which he points, or the vision of the stigmata on the body of the son. This alternative is precisely not the conversion scene of the Jew encountering Christianity but rather a competition between Protestant and Catholic inflections of Christianity. That this competition played a particular role in German cultural history, especially during the nineteenth century, goes without saying. What is its status in Oppenheim's painting?

If the intrachristian conflict is staged in the presence of the Jewish patriarch, the point certainly cannot be that it is up to the Jew to choose between two options. The opposite is the case: the Jew is not subject but object, a function of the Christian division. He is the liminal position in the painting, between the book and the body, between the word and the image. (The antinomy is amplified by the right-hand margin depicting shelves of talmudic volumes, banished from the center of the scene.) Therefore the painting suggests that the source of anti-Semitism (or at least one source) is the Christian confessional conflict that generates a discourse on the figure of the "Jew," who serves as the accusation which each camp directs at its antagonist. For Catholicism, Protestantism can display dangerously hebraizing tendencies, with its privileging of the word and faith and an iconoclastic wing suspiciously close to the Judaic proscription of images. For Protestantism, Catholicism may represent a regression from the purity of apostolic faith, contaminated by Levantine admixtures and close to Judaism in its ritualism and in its external trappings inimical to a genuinely spiritual faith.[52] The point is clearly not that the one faith understands the other correctly or that either has any particular insight into the historical character of Judaism. Rather, denigrated religious characteristics are associated, rightly or wrongly, with an imagined Judaism in order to suggest that the adherents of the competing confession are ultimately fellow travelers of the murderers of Christ.

To read the painting this way, as a staging of the religious-historical origins of anti-Semitism (as opposed to, say, its sociological origins), means of course that whether the father chooses the "Catholic" decoration or the "Protestant" book, body or soul, the choice will be wrong, and he will remain the object of vilification. It follows then that no conversion—which is always a conversion to a particular confession—guarantees sanctuary, an insight very much in line with Oppenheim's comments on Stiebel. In addition, the painting perspicaciously identifies the antinomic character of anti-Semitism, which regularly denounces the Jew in oppositional terms: as peddler and as magnate, as communist and as capitalist, as Zionist and as cosmopolitan, as miserly and as pretentious, as prudish and as profligate. The series of binary opposites derives from the construction of the "Jew" as a function in the intrachristian conflict, which took on a special urgency in Germany during the process of national unification which effectively began with the wars from which Oppenheim's volunteer was returning. Their corollary with regard to specifically cultic matters can be discerned in anti-Semitic accounts of Judaism as simultaneously too abstract (its God is invisible) and too concrete (its panoply of peculiar rituals). In the *Return* these elements emerge as the tension between abstract verbality and the materiality of the cross.

The contemporary project for a Protestant mission to the Jews had, interestingly in this context, an emphatically anti-Catholic inflection, insofar as the argument was made that Jews had heretofore resisted conversion not simply because of a genuinely unchristian anti-Semitism but owing to the idolatry, the *Bilderdienst* of the Roman Church; the more sparse cult of Protestantism would presumably have greater appeal to a Jewish sensibility schooled on the proscription of images. As relevant as this material is to the confessional competition and the consequent generation of anti-Semitic tropes, it is central to the question of aesthetic representation posed by the *Return of the Volunteer*. Now it comes as no surprise that a Jewish painter—moreover a first-generation Jewish painter of Oppenheim's background—working on an emphatically Jewish theme inquires into the status of the *Bilderverbot*. Hence the prominent position accorded to the book, a painterly corollary to a literary ekphrasis, a description of a work of visual art in a verbal text.[53] Since we can reasonably surmise that the depicted book is of cultic importance, it is therefore implicated in the very decalogic injunction that might, in a radically iconoclastic reading, call the legitimacy of the painting itself into question. Yet such ascetic severity in aesthetic matters is countered by the fact that the law was broken long before the son traveled home on the Sabbath: on the wall hangs a picture of Frederick II who presumably fits somewhere in the list of creatures whose images were prohibited: "anything that is in heaven above, or that is in the earth beneath, or that is in the water under the earth." If one initially understands the painting in the painting as a testimony of a political credo, combining loyalty to the state with hopes for liberalization (not unlike photographs of John Kennedy and Martin Luther King in the black ghettoes of the United States), the *Return* can be taken in another light as well: as part of an investigation into the possible historical modes of art that proceeds from the image of the king through the inverted ekphrasis of the book to the evidently privileged representational locus, the decoration on the soldier's chest.

To understand the aesthetic value of the medal, it is useful to recall how it was transformed in the revisionist version of 1880, where the symbol of heroism was augmented by the material presence of the wound. Whether one attributes that change to political circumstances or to a slide from a realist into a naturalist aesthetics is of less import than the insight that it provides into the character of the symbol which, precisely as a symbol, operates by representing and therefore displacing a material event. The addition of the wound presumably indicates that the medal alone no longer adequately served its symbolic function of asserting a content not itself directly presented. That is, the symbol is a vehicle of abstraction and is consequently indebted to an aesthetic at odds with that which generated the iconic image of the Prussian king. Given the marginal situation of the icon and the location of the medal at the thematic center of attention (as opposed to the center of the construction near the book), the aesthetic statement of the *Return of the Volunteer* might be decoded as a historical passage from courtly representation to autonomous and abstract art, mediated via the *Bilderverbot*: from the political portrait through the book to the symbol.

This account obviously fits neatly into Peter Bürger's institutional history of art.[54] It also discovers within Oppenheim's painting a demonstration of the heterogeneous derivation of aesthetic autonomy, which sublates both mimetic and antimimetic, iconic and anti-iconic (which is not to say iconoclastic) positions. Indeed the incorporation of the book and the marginal volumes into the painting recalls the compromise solution of the Tabernacle, of course with a key reversal: the figurative Cherubim were reduced to the instruments of the script, while here script appears as subordinated paraphernalia in the construction of the image. The painting entails furthermore a graphic display of the connection between the artistic modernity of abstraction and the political modernity for which, one can assume, the volunteer had been fighting. Indeed, since the symbol, the Iron Cross, is itself a material presence (despite its function as a mechanism of deferral), one might come to the melancholy conclusion that it is only aesthetic modernity that the conquering hero has been able to bring home, while entry into a modernized civil society is still denied him by a resurgent ancien régime. The political defeat is compensated by an aesthetic victory; the institutionalization of affirmative culture becomes the alibi for political reaction.

That melancholy twist is not at all accidental, since the project of aesthetic autonomy, at least since Schiller's *Aesthetic Education of Man*, was frequently posed as an alternative to Jacobin politics: human progress should proceed through aesthetic education and not through political revolution. Does the *Return of the Volunteer* suggest that the same caution ought to hold for Jewish emancipation as well? At least we are admonished not to accept too quickly the forced reconciliations of a progressivist narrative culminating in the abstractness of the symbol as a historico-philosophically superior mode of representation. There is no reason to concatenate icon, book, and symbol in a sanguine teleology, since after all their organization in the painting is in no way linear. On the contrary, their constellation can as well be taken as anticipatory of highly problematic aspects of the culture of advanced capitalism. Abstract art is enfigured as the Iron Cross, a derivative religious symbol, pointing forward to the emergence of the *Kunstreligion* and the transformation of art into an object of conspicuous consumption. The liberal political strategy of arguing for civil equality on the grounds that the volunteer can sport the medal is frighteningly close to the pursuit of upward mobility via the accumulation of symbols of status, an all too familiar semiotic practice. In addition, the marginalization of Frederick should not only be taken as the assertion of the obsolescence of an aesthetics of political representation. It also declares the obsolescence of the classical Enlightenment, displaced by a more advanced, postromantic aestheticization of politics, concentrated again in the status of the symbol. Finally, and perhaps most saliently, the *Return of the Volunteer* stages the conflict between verbal text and visual symbol. Unresolved in this painting, which is itself so dependent on its own lengthy and awkward title, the tension foreshadows the central transformation of modern culture, i.e., the declining significance of print media eclipsed by the growth of visual representation.

A fourth and last zone of conflict has to do with family structure and the construction of gender. As already noted, the 1880 version erased evidence of tension in the original, notably a subtle repulsion between father and son. That opposition can be read in terms of the ancien régime and modernity (Riesser's two ages), religious tradition and national loyalty, or, in a conversion scenario, the old religion and the new. It can equally be read as an oedipal conflict, since the virile son, admired by mother and sister (and in 1880 staring into his mother's eyes), is juxtaposed with an unrealistically aged father, hunched over, perhaps ailing and close to death. The father is the adherent of God the father and therefore, once the son returns, part of an ancient world relegated to the past, as if the return of the son inherently implies the death of the father. The predilection for representing Jews as old apparently has both a religious and an oedipal derivation: to depict Jews as old means that the religion of the father and the "Old Testament" is obsolete. Conversely, given this subtext in representations of the Jewish patriarch, the question must at least remain open as to whether other discourses of antipatriarchy, including those which are apparently free of specific Jewish references, do not draw on subterranean currents of anti-Semitism in a Western culture which regularly defines itself in opposition to an Orient of mysticism and ritualism, wealth and poverty, and, above all, patriarchy. Both feminism and *Geschichtsphilosophie* (with its central paradigm of the New displacing the Old) might be investigated along such lines.

If the *Return of the Volunteer* represents the Jew as the father, it also presents the son as the Jew. Or perhaps not, since the religious identity of the son is at the very least ambiguous since he has transgressed against the law, he is the bearer of the cross, and he is set in opposition to the decidedly Jewish father. Yet the question of religious identity is compounded by a questionable gender identity: whether or not the son is genuinely Jewish, it is not at all clear that the son is genuinely male. He does after all participate in the predominately female triangle of vision with the mother and sister, and this trinity has an unmistakably erotic tone; the father scrutinizes the cross with curiosity, but the mother gazes at the soldier with love. Moreover the sister might well be taken to be a lover (perhaps, in the 1880 version, Oppenheim covers her head as a sign of modesty and turns the soldier's gaze away in order to preclude an erotic misreading).

Hence, within the family itself an opposition unfolds between the father loyal to the old law and a feminized group marked by the emblem of the religion of love. If we can treat the son—and to be sure, this is all very much in conflict with Oppenheim's presumed intentions—as the carrier of the cross, can we treat him, precisely in the role of Jesus, as a female figure? What is, after all, God's gender? My point is not to engage in feminist theological speculations but to locate the submerged conversion scene in the *Return of the Volunteer* in the context of undercurrents in European Christianity that bespoke an erotic interest in the body of Christ, whereby the wounds were covertly reinterpreted as female genitalia. E. P. Thompson comments:

> Christ, the personification of "Love" to whom the great bulk of Wesleyan hymns are addressed, is by turns maternal, Oedipal, sexual and sado-masochistic. The extraordinary assimilation of wounds and sexual imagery in the Moravian tradition has often been noted. Man as a sinful "worm" must find "Lodging, Bed and Board in the Lamb's wounds."[55]

As a particularly straightforward example of the eroticization of a female Christ, he cites the following hymn:

> O precious Side-hole's cavity
> I want to spend my life in thee
> . . .
> There in one Side-hole's joy divine,
> I'll spend all future Days of mine.
> Yes, yes, I will for ever sit
> There, where thy Side was split.

Given this alternative religious imagination, it is not at all wild to inquire into the gender identity of the soldier. If one can claim that he is a Christ figure—which at this point in the argument is a rather cautious claim given the iconography of the painting itself—then he may well have a female resonance too. The presence of such sectarian christological elements in the iconography strengthens the hypothesis that the *Return* is, despite its intentions, a complicated conversion scene: the antinomian son confronts the father pointing to the law, and the androgynous returnee confronts the patriarchal order. As strange as that result may be, it could provide a new explanation for the increased prominence of the wound in 1880, the eruption of a formerly hidden sexual undercurrent.

Moreover, this result returns the argument to the problem of anti-Semitism, which, as has been shown, has no difficulty in attacking Jews in mutually contradictory terms. The *Return of the Volunteer* stages the Jew as the father (indeed the potent father of a rather large family), but the painting may equally operate with the feminization of the Jew: either as Christ or, much more simply, as a mama's boy—the Jewish mother is rushing in with a bowl of soup. Indeed the emphatic insistence on his military heroism is probably a Freudian negation, masking its opposite, the image of Jews as weak, effete, and disarmed. The anti-Semitic association of Jews and women, a rhetorical castration, is familiar from Weininger's writings. Freud links it to fantasies provoked by ritual circumcision. It is in any case a powerful association that remains current, as in the recent lyrics in "Welcome to the Terrordome" by Public Enemy: "Told the rab, 'get off the rag'. . . . Crucifixion ain't no fiction . . . ," verses that dramatically link anti-Semitism and misogyny, while bringing into breathtaking proximity Christ's wounds and female anatomy.[56]

The equation of Jews and women might of course have made another kind of sense within the liberal politics of the nineteenth century. Both groups were excluded from participation in the public sphere on equal terms, and their vocabularies of emancipation could at times become close. From the standpoint of hegemonic privilege—Christian and male—both groups were outsiders, representing a threat. Given the deep-seated resistance to the emancipation project, even during the era of liberalism's greatest vitality, one therefore does well to pay attention to subtexts in liberal manifestos like the *Return of the Volunteer*. As a conclusion, the constellation of ambiguities within Oppenheim's painting—and, by extension, within the Enlightenment agenda in general—can be brought to the fore by confronting the painting with a noteworthy outburst by Wagner in his "Judaism in Music": "One's impression is as though the Savior had been cut out of a painting of the Crucifixion, and replaced by a Jewish demagogue . . . A race whose general appearance we cannot consider suitable for aesthetic purposes is by the same token incapable of any artistic presentation of its nature."[57] All the material which underlies Oppenheim's call for equal rights is packed into Wagner's single exclamation: the attack on the Jewish religion as inimical to iconic representation, the conflict between verbality and vision, a hostility to political liberalization, and an erotic component as well, since the polemic was directed against the Jewish actor Josef Kainz who competed with Wagner for the favors of the homoerotic King Ludwig II of Bavaria.

Given Wagner's central importance in the ideological history of the radical German right, this is by no means cultural-historical marginalia. To the contrary: it is articulate evidence of the depth and multiple inflections of the opposition encountered by the proponents of Jewish emancipation in nineteenth-century Germany. Hence tentative answers to the question postponed at the outset of this essay: why is the illustration of progress and innovation staged in a narrative of return? A conservative response might suggest that the progressive program is only a veneer, an ideological layer weakly imposed on top of ultimately irrepressible contents of permanence and stability, eternally returning. The ambiguity of the painting would, in this reading, demonstrate the inability of the Enlightenment—represented by Oppenheim and Riesser—to resist the return of religion, the return of Oedipus, and the return of myth. By dismissing ambiguity as weakness and failure, however, such conservative pessimism would only reveal its own authoritarianism and ignore the success of the painting in indicating what a successful Enlightenment might be. The *Return of the Volunteer* is the return of the *Freiwillige* and the return of freedom. Freedom returns not because it is defeated—the soldier has triumphed—but because it has unfinished business to take care of, as it discovers overlooked zones into which emancipation has yet to be extended: custom, religion, family, sexuality, and, not least of all, aesthetics. For the diachronic narrative of progress, which is initially, as narrative, a literary undertaking, comes to encounter synchronic structures, visual representation and the world of sight, and it renders them historical. It is in that historical space that the community engages in its self-construction.

Chapter 4

Piedmont as Prussia

The Italian Model and German Unification

If contemporary cultural theory has a keen eye for the artificiality of national identities, treated as little more than rhetorical inventions, the underlying fact—the construction of the national state as a political unit—remains much more impervious to criticism, at least of the academic sort. A strange omission indeed, as states all around crumble, reunify, and redraw their borders. Is only identity up for grabs or is a scrutinization of the large territorial state itself also overdue? Far from being a natural or necessary frame for politics, the national state was a by-product of nineteenth-century economy and culture; its persistence today represents the reification of the political imagination, impeding the emergence of more supple, communitarian, and democratic forms of social life. Only the fixation on the naturalness of nationhood—in a phenomenological sense, a "naturalistic" reduction—eclipses other political options. To strip the national state of its appearance of organicity, reexaminations of the historical origins are called for, and no example is more instructive than one which links the production of the two new nation-states of the European nineteenth century: Germany and Italy. Standard accounts present the establishment of these two nations as the obvious and long-expected outcomes of organic teleologies. Nothing could be further from the truth, and the contradictory impulses within nationalization become particularly evident when one discourse is refracted through another: the German account of Italian nationhood.

No staple of German culture is more stereotypical and more persistent than the image of Italy as the treasure trove of art and ruins. A landscape strewn with remnants of erstwhile grandeur, monuments and museums of exquisite form, a people understood as devotees of sensuous appearance, and therefore irreversibly superficial—this is what the German traveler has found, at least since the eighteenth century, again and again during the obligatory *Bildungs-reise* through Italy. Of course, this is precisely what the German traveler expected to find, as the underlying structure of Kantian philosophy was projected across the map of Western Europe: pure reason in France, practical reason in England, and Italy as the place of aesthetic judgment, indeed of a purely aesthetic judgment which is therefore devoid of political substance. Italy as the locus of art has meant, within canonic German culture, the plausibility of a place without politics, and the apparent privileging of Italy—and the trip to Italy—is a particularly compelling instance of the "unpolitical German," to use Thomas Mann's phrase, and the *Sonderweg*, the peculiarity of German modernization, with its relatively underdeveloped political public sphere.

The German aestheticization of Italy is itself an extremely complex phenomenon, combining both a conservative escapism and a utopian search for an alternative to domestic disappointments: conservative as a vehicle to deny the political challenges of the moment, utopian as a vision of a qualitatively better mode of existence. Hence the ambivalence of Jakob Burkhardt in a letter to his friend Hermann Schauenburg of February 28, 1846, announcing his impending trip to the south; unlike others who vocally oppose the age, Burckhardt boasts:

> I, in contrast, oppose it silently but totally, and therefore flee into the beautiful, languid South, which is dead to history and, like a miraculous tombstone, will rejuvenate me, so tired of modernity, with its ancient mysteries. Yes, I want to escape them all: the radicals, communists, industrialists, academics, chic, the reflecters, the abstract, the absolutes, the philosophers, the sophists, the statists, the idealists. . . . On the other side of the mountains, I must find new ties to life and poesy, if I am to survive.[1]

Deeply disappointed with contemporary society and politics, Burckhardt chooses to flee, to run away from communists, industrialists, and all the other species he imagines are absent in Italy. For it is in Italy that he expects to regain a deeper tie to the vital currents of poetry and art: an unmistakably modern and romantic gesture, precisely when it is presented as an alternative to modernity. Modern political life is the precondition for the desire for a place where no politics exist, and which the Germans try to find south of the Alps.

The internal complexity of this image of Italy was subject to a critical exploration in the third of Heinrich Heine's travelogues, the "Journey from Munich to Genoa," of 1828. Participating parodically in the genre of the voyage to Italy, the text reserves some especially poignant references to Goethe's paradigmatically aesthetic account. Yet much more is at stake than Heine's competition with the gray eminence of Weimar. The left Hegelian critique of classical autonomy aesthetics, itself personified by Goethe, led to a growing interest in genres marginal to the emerging bourgeois canon of high art, including the travelogue. For the travelogue (and other potentially "operative" modes of writing) could allow for a degree of politicization, no matter how mitigated by censorship, that the classic-romantic work of art tended to prevent. Among the descriptive and informational elements expected in a travelogue, the "Journey from Munich to Genoa" intersperses a barely submerged reflection on politics, from the derogatory references to the Prussian state, through the ubiquity of Austrian military presence, to the decoding of signs of Italian resistance to foreign occupation. Yet very much in line with the established conventions of the genre, this resistance is located precisely within the aesthetic dimension itself.

In other words, Heine's alternative to Goethe's Italy of art is not a politicized Italy, i.e., Italy as a sovereign political subject, but an Italy of politicized art, and this politicization of art, projected onto Italy, is at least in part a function of *querelles allemandes*. Heine's praise of "a genuine piece of Italian music, from some popular opera buffa," fully in the manner of Rossini, leads into a denunciation of established German music criticism's hostility to this popular form and popular art in general;[2] the same high culture/low culture tension that grounds the formal parody of Heine's literary text is now made thematic in the commentary on musical taste: "The opponents of Italian music, who approach this style as judgmentally as they do others, will someday face their well-deserved punishment in hell and may be damned to hear nothing in all of eternity except for fugues by Sebastian Bach."[3] German high culture's inability to comprehend Italian popular form is a consequence, according to Heine, of its ignorance of the Italian people and its history, which find expression in the music. The work of art is the displaced voice of the oppressed nation:

Poor, enslaved Italy is prohibited from speaking, and it can express the feelings of its heart only through music. All of its hatred for foreign rule, its enthusiasm for freedom, its rage over the feeling of powerlessness, its melancholic recollection of former glory, its attentiveness and thirsting for help: all of this is hidden in those melodies that slide from a grotesque intoxication with life to elegiac whispers, and in those pantomimes that leap from flattering caresses to threatening anger.[4]

If popular form is, on the one hand, an expression of popular desire, it is, on the other, also a consequence of repression: Heine plays out the "esoteric meaning of the opera buffa" against the presence of the "exoteric gendarme" who is always on guard against any "revolutionary coloraturas."[5] This is certainly a far cry from the safe haven for poetry and life which Burckhardt would envision less than twenty years later. Yet while Heine constructs Italy as a place of politics (or rather, of politics displaced into aesthetic form), the politics are not in any way specifically Italian, i.e., the question of foreign occupation does not lead directly to a thematization of Italian nationalism. To be sure, Heine has a keen eye for indications of patriotism, but the patrimony of the patriots offended by the Austrian presence is not self-evidently the unified nation. Heine can identify hostility to foreign domination and the Metternichian order in general, but he presents no evidence of a counterprogram involving the pursuit of a specifically Italian national liberation. On the contrary, the same philosophical idealism that leads the left Hegelian Heine to his politicization of art, pushes his thinking away from such national particularisms and toward a universalist vision: "there are no nations any more in Europe, but only parties," indeed only two parties—the party of oppression and the party of emancipation—and this opposition takes on a global character. "What is the duty of our age? Emancipation. Not only the emancipation of the Irish, the Greeks, the Frankfurt Jews, the West Indian blacks and other such oppressed people, but rather the emancipation of the whole world. . . . "[6] Heine is staking out a position that draws dialectically on both Napoleonic heroism and the emancipatory rhetoric of the anti-Napoleonic wars, and it is a position which would be inherited by left liberalism and socialist internationalism. Yet in its internationalism, it bypasses the question of nationhood, the Italian question. At this level, then, left-wing Heine shares with conservative Burckhardt and Goethe a reluctance to understand "Italy" as itself a term of political contestation. Metternich's quip that "Italy" is only a geographical concept has as its corollary for Heine as well as most other German travelers the suggestion that Italy is only a cultural term. The circulation of "Italy" as a designation of potential political valency—and not only of aestheticized politics—does not commence until much later, in the historical unraveling of the treaties of 1815 and the emergence of new political structures in Italy and Germany nearly simultaneously.

The early-nineteenth-century German blindness to a political Italy is evidenced, perhaps most dramatically, in the position of the 1848 revolutionaries: whether moderate or radical in their political agendas north of the Alps, they tended to side with the Austrians against the Italian revolutionaries (just as they tended to oppose the national aspirations of other groups in Central Europe).[7] It was therefore not at all the European revolution that undermined the borders of 1815, but the tectonic shift initiated a decade later by the Crimean War, including the reemergence of France as a continental power, and as a power that began to challenge Austrian hegemony in northern Italy. The site of this shift is Piedmont, and the metamorphosis of the German perception of Italian politics between 1859 and 1871 testifies to several reinventions of the concept of Italy—as functions of both the political process being played out on the peninsula and the simultaneous process of German national unification. In addition, the several versions of the articulation of "Italy" simultaneously entail widely disparate cultural-theoretical implications with regard to the substance of national identity.

During the War of 1859, Austrian forces engaged Piedmont, which received massive support from France; at the Peace of Villafranca, Austria was compelled to cede control of Lombardy, and Piedmont emerged as the strong force around which a unified Italy would soon crystallize. German perception of the war depended on several complexities. As a member of the German Confederation, Austria could expect support from the other German states, and in particular from Prussia, the key military force in Central Europe. Nevertheless, the legitimacy of such a claim was mitigated by arguments to the effect that the Austrian Lombard campaign derived from imperial Hapsburg concerns and not from the specific needs of Austria as a German (rather than an imperial) power. If these formal legal waters were muddied, it was of course a result of the ongoing political conflict between Austria and Prussia and the competition between *grossdeutsch* and *kleindeutsch* models of German unification. Hence considerable maneuvering: to force Prussia into the role of subsidiary ally or to highlight Austria as a dynastic power not at all congruent with German national interests. Finally, the debate on the "Italian War" had a cultural dimension, pertaining to the ability to articulate and mobilize "national" interests: within the public sphere, there was a subtle shift in the vicissitudes of German national identity. Yet this shift takes place, interestingly enough, with barely any perception of Italy at all. Instead, Lombardy becomes a field which reflects conflicting loyalties to Austria or to Prussia, and secondarily, conflicting evaluations of France and, especially, Bonaparte.

At the outbreak of the war, German public opinion was largely pro-Austrian, which is to say, hostile to France, to Piedmont, and to any claims for a unified Italy. This was especially true in southern Germany (where the ties to Austria were historically stronger), but it was true as well in Prussia. The associated rhetoric, which included exhortations to greater German military assistance to Austria, was particularly successful "because it continuously appealed to elementary popular sentiments, a vague notion of 'Germanness,' and to the need to unite Germanic forces against the Gallic enemy. In a period of growing national consciousness, it could employ key slogans and vigorously invoked the memory of 1806 and 1813, superficially overcoming profound differences."[8] As may often be the case, a current war can provide the opportunity to fight a previous one; in this case, the belligerent rhetoric of 1859 mobilized the patriotic backdrop of the anti-Napoleonic wars of a half-century earlier, including the images of 1806 (Prussia's defeat) and 1813 (the Wars of Liberation and Austrian primacy). Lombardy therefore gave the German public an opportunity to imagine a unified German nation, in which the tensions between Berlin and Vienna were subsumed in a national cause. The fight for the Austrian possessions in Italy therefore represented a fight for German interests, a fight moreover against the same enemy and against a leader of the same name as in 1813.

The imagery was powerful and seductive, leading at first to considerable public sympathy for Austria and hostility toward the Prussian government for its reluctance to enter the war. What was the nature of the reluctance? We know that Bismarck, for one, recommended a diametrically opposite course of action: to seize on the hostilities between France and Austria—Piedmont is still regarded only as the incidental issue, not as a full political subject—in order to resolve finally and conclusively the intra-German competition by annexing the southern states, unifying Germany, and excluding Austria. Bismarck, however, was in Petersburg and did not prevail on the Prussian leadership. Yet his emphatically anti-Austrian calculation represents what, in a more moderate form, came to circulate in Berlin: apprehension regarding ceding leadership to Austria and legalistic doubts pertaining to obligations outside of the strictly German sphere of the confederation. The result was a policy that wavered between neutrality and only minimal support for Austria: a moderation which Bismarck regarded as a lost opportunity for a *kleindeutsch* resolution and which the southern German advocates of a *grossdeutsch* program denounced as a betrayal of a German confederate.

Surveying the alternative positions in the German debates on the War of 1859 (and these positions of course existed in a full range of nuances), one ought to take note of important similarities and differences. None of the significant participants on either side of the issue seems to have regarded Piedmont or Italy as the crux of the matter. For the *grossdeutsch* camp, it was a war in Italy between France and German interests; hence the appeals to Prussia to expand the war by attacking France on the Rhine. Since a Bonaparte was attempting to revise the order of 1815 and the subaltern status of France, the German press could hoist the nationalist flag of anti-Napoleonic heroism. For the *kleindeutsch* camp, the war in Italy was not between France and German interests, but between France and Austria, and Austria's defeat was hardly unwelcome. Certainly, the outcome of the war had, among its political implications, a weakening of the pro-Austrian camp within Germany.

Yet while the supporters of Austria and of Prussia shared, despite their otherwise divergent evaluations, a blind spot for Italy, their constructions of "Germany" differed sharply, and not only with regard to the obvious difference as to the geographical scope of the imagined nation. In addition, the two positions presented rather different constellations of state, nation, and people. While the *grossdeutsch* camp mobilized patriotic images of national history and appealed to pan-German sentiment, the Prussian discussion in 1859 remained much less popular and much more conservative, in the sense that it focussed solely on the issues of state power and political interest. In other words, despite a disregard for any putative Italian national aspirations, the *grossdeutsch* publicists appealed directly to German nationalism as a vessel of cultural and historical identity, while the *kleindeutsch* accounts were more "realistic" in their politics and therefore more cautious and less popular in their claims. Thus for the commentator of the *Preussische Jahrbücher*, Theodor von Bernhardi, the whole notion of an "Italian Question" is discounted as a fabrication of Napoleon, despite Bernhardi's own otherwise primarily anti-Austrian stance.[9] Indeed, the fiction of Italian nationality is treated as an invention of the emperor in Paris as well as a consequence of the Viennese Kaiser's manipulation of nationalist policies in order to undermine Magyar ascendancy. Bernhardi therefore provides what might today be termed a discourse-theoretical account of national identity: an invention designed to consolidate established power and therefore in no way an expression of the experience of the members of the putative grouping and certainly not a consequence of some prior "essence."

Neither side recognizes a legitimate Italian national interest (although one might argue that Prussia's implicit reluctance vis-à-vis Austria was, de facto, supportive of Piedmont and, hence, of Italy). Yet the Austrian side, with a romantic and popular account of national interest—German national interest, that is—clearly occupied a stronger symbolic and rhetorical position within the German debate, while the Prussian realists could understand power only as vested in the state rather than in the nation. Therefore the efforts to define a difference between Austrian and German national interest, which would have greatly benefited the *kleindeutsch* progress, lacked the same sort of cultural symbolism that the other camp wielded so well. Consider Bernhardi's analysis of the conclusion of the war:

> However, the real reason behind the conclusion of the peace agreement was, as the Austrian government press admitted with admirable naiveté, that Prussia was arming to attack France: not however as a blindly obedient vassal of Austria, but independently, to counteract French supremacy in defense of all truly German interests. That is what Vienna wanted to prevent: the point was not the defense of Germany but of Austria's system! If Prussia had entered the war at this point, it would have naturally taken over the leadership which Austria had either lost in battle or could not claim, lacking an army to send to the Rhine. Austria sued for peace not because of a threat to Germany but of a threat to Austria's position within Germany, which was, as the Austrian press put it, "worth more than Lombardy"—at least from the standpoint of Austria's special interests.[10]

Obviously, Bernhardi is repeating the Prussian defense that the conflict in northern Italy was an Austrian matter, outside of the area of responsibility of the German confederation; this allows him to treat Austrian policy as outside of and, indeed, inimical to a genuine German interest. Furthermore, he is suggesting that Austria accepted the Peace of Villafranca so suddenly as a result less of French military force across the Alps than of the imminence of Prussian entry into the war. Whatever the accuracy of the claim, Bernhardi's calculation remains solely on the level of interstate diplomacy and lacks any reflection on national, as opposed to state, interests. This is indicative of the relative weakness of his discourse-theoretical articulation of national identity; he seems nearly as blind to a German nation as he is to an Italian one: the key players are always only the states and their diplomatic representatives, and public opinion is only the product of a manipulative press. There is no exploration of the popular pro-war sentiment as possibly the expression of a collective national identity, as if the nation had no identity except as an expression of the state. His efforts to relocate Austria outside of German national interest therefore seem painfully shallow and ineffective, just as his announcement of a Prussian attack on France rings hollow, since his substantive hostility is aimed at Vienna. If, as Bismarck suggested, 1859 was a missed opportunity, it may have been so owing not only to the vacillation of the Prussian court, i.e., the inadequacy of leadership, but also to an underdeveloped notion of nationhood and the requisite symbolism. The point is that the rhetorical capacity of the *kleindeutsch* advocates of a Prussian-led unified German nation appears to have been considerably weaker than that of their opponents, particularly in terms of the ability to manipulate cultural symbols.

During the stages of German and Italian national unification in the following decade, however, richer and more powerful accounts of nationhood would develop, and the revisions of "Germany" would draw repeatedly on the model of Piedmont and Italy. In effect, during this period of rapid transition, two separate stories intertwine: on the one hand, the new nation-states, Italy and Germany, take shape, while, on the other, a significant adjustment takes place in the relationship between politics and culture. Challenging the legitimate, dynastic authority, and doing so in a historical context where the mobilization of public opinion has taken on new importance, the new political order derives its legitimacy from cultural claims; culture in turn finds its erstwhile apolitical status—the aestheticized Italy of the unpolitical Germans—growing increasingly untenable.

Seven years later, in 1866, the conflict between Prussia and Austria came to a head; Prussia's rapid victory in the hostilities led to its undisputed ascendancy within Germany and the final exclusion of Austria from German matters. It led furthermore, indirectly, to Austria's loss of Venice and the emergence of a unified Italy. The literary and cultural significance of this turn is marked in Hermann Baumgarten's classical essay "German Liberalism: A Self-Criticism," the key text which redefined the relationship of the liberal public to Bismarck's leadership and his specific formula for national unification. Liberal reticence vis-à-vis Bismarck is treated as an expression of a political inability that has long hampered Germany's role in Europe, and in order to convince his readership of the viability of a reinvention of the terms of German nation-hood, Baumgarten has recourse on several occasions to the lessons of the Italian model. If, in 1859, the Italian War was the site for intra-German conflicts, by 1866 it becomes an example to emulate and an enabling metaphor for German unification.

This profound shift entailed a revision of the evaluation of Bonapartist France. Previously viewed either as the anti-German (qua anti-Austrian) aggressor or (by Bernhardi) as the conspiratorial manipulator of an "Italian Question," Napoleon suddenly becomes a heroic figure, avenging the French nation on the Holy Alliance, shattering "the grand solidarity of conservative interests" that had prevailed since 1815, and enabling Cavour to promote Italian independence.[11] Before examining the treatment of Cavour more closely, one should note that for a moment at least Baumgarten even invokes Napoleon's own Italian background, i.e., he is depicted not as the imperial aggressor but as the admirable patriot who promotes Piedmont against Vienna, encoded as freedom against reaction. The competition among states, which had structured the German discourse of 1859, is now filled with resonant values: Napoleon's battle against conservative legitimism, Napoleon against the ancien régime, Napoleon and Cavour against the "hierarchical-Catholic" powers supported by Austria.

It is against this background that Baumgarten censures the German, especially southern German liberals, so severely. Fearing Prussia, they supported Austria in 1859, but at what costs? "How could it have been possible that liberalism felt obliged to defend Austrian despotism in Italy, to side with the Papal State against free Sardinia, and to ally with the clerical and feudal parties against liberal Europe?"[12] One more expression of German backwardness, one more failure to play a historical role—the misjudgment of 1859 is the point at which the "self-criticism" of liberalism sets in, and Italy provides the counterexample: "The single, grand, glowing victory of liberalism in this century was won in Italy. In Italy, however, I believe that the many aided the one leader in obedient subordination, and the one who was truly victorious was an aristocrat."[13] From a merely incidental backdrop in 1859, Italy has become the grand model for liberal politics and the blueprint for German unification. More precisely, however, Baumgarten indicates that the liberal fear of Bismarck is misplaced, insofar as Piedmont too had its towering aristocratic leader. Cavour is implicitly the corollary to Bismarck, in Baumgarten's account, which is to say, at this crucial juncture in the history of German liberalism, the point at which the alliance with Bismarck is forged—and more radical, left liberal directions are abandoned—it is the Italian model of Cavour's leadership that facilitates the transition: Prussianized Germany as an imitation of Piedmontese Italy.

The terms of the metaphor are complex. Baumgarten proceeds from an assumption of a history of German failure—disunity, political ineffectiveness, cultural escapism—and he has a very particular reading of Italy. Italy's distinction is its political class: "Next door to us, Italy awoke, but Italy did not bend as we did. Italy had a man, who combined great courage with greater wisdom, and it had a king with a truly royal sensibility."[14] Presumably Germany had lacked both: a political leader and a responsible monarch. Moreover, while German culture was trapped in a philosophical idealism that militated against political action, Italian sentiment was revolutionary and prepared for substantive deeds.

> Italy was not rotten with eccentric dogmatisms, and Italy did not benefit from that equanimity—or should we say spiritual breadth?—which can tolerate the most miserable condition of the fatherland, drawing compensation from a well-kept house and profound immersions in ideas and fantasies. Italy had the healthy resentment of a people mistreated for three centuries, and directed it toward its tormentors, and it gave this resentment over to a wise mind, more interested in political success than in mere opinions.[15]

Here Baumgarten articulates a sort of political corollary to literary realism, the privileging of the fact over the ideal. Indeed the opposition of "success" and "opinion" is obviously reminiscent of Bismarck's own notorious contrast of blood and iron to parliamentary speeches and decrees. This realism, however, is a far cry from the discourse-theoretical power analysis of 1859 in Bernhardi's essay. For all of Baumgarten's evident interest in state formation and the establishment of power, it is clear that his account is structurally dependent on extensive cultural claims and references to historical experience. State power and national experience have become two independent variables, both of which are indispensable for a comprehensive analysis.

The passage is furthermore a breathtaking inversion of the traditional coding of aesthetic Italy. In 1846 Burckhardt fled the politicized north for the rejuvenating return to the poetic sources in Italy. Here, twenty years later, Baumgarten looks to Italy as the site of the model revolution, where a politicized people found a politically effective leadership. In retrospect the flight from politics to Italy turns out to have had little at all to do with Italy; it was, on the contrary, a specifically German fantasy, as Baumgarten complains. Germany, and German liberals in particular, have fled responsibility and feared the consequential deed. Their culture of profundity has been only a cozy escape from political exigency, the expression of the comforts of provincialism. Instead of intellectual escapism, insensitive to the real needs of the *Vaterland*, it is action that Germany requires.

So while measured against Bernhardi, Baumgarten certainly expands the analysis to include national identity, historical experience, and cultural substance, the crux of the matter is not at all autonomous aesthetic culture. It is, rather, the capacity for political leadership, the leadership of the aristocracy, and Cavour as the aristocratic individual par excellence.

> These sentiments and aspirations of the Italian people were shared with equal passion by the aristocracy, both in diplomacy and in the army; everywhere the aristocracy played a leading role in the national battle. While the continent groaned under a reaction that stretched from Prussia to Spain, small Sardinia dared to be constitutional, and with its modern economy, prepared a thrust which would fundamentally change the situation of Europe.[16]

Bernhardi was concerned with the interests of the Prussian state; Baumgarten's considerations are directed at transforming the continent, economic modernization, and a revolution of the established order. His politics are, however, counterintuitively aristocratic, insofar as he suggests that it is precisely the aristocrat who can best carry out the revolution.

> The genuinely decisive impulses did not come from the Italian people, nor did they come from an Italian party; they came from Cavour. He arranged for Italy to participate in the Crimean War, he forged the alliance with France, and he incited the war which brought salvation. These sorts of changes can only be prepared and executed by an individual, and it is only an individual who, in politics, can provide the instinct of a people with the strength to reach its goal.[17]

The ultimate source of the national identity, the genuine inventor, is therefore the great individual: not the state, not the people, not history. Just as Cavour made Italy, so Baumgarten suggests, liberals should give up their pointless opposition, and allow Bismarck to make Germany.

This is also the defining moment of Baumgarten's liberalism. The larger political vision includes a fundamentally Enlightenment promotion of cultural modernization, as expressed in his critique of the liberals' siding with Austria in 1859. Instead of choosing, as Germans, to support Austria against Piedmont, they should have chosen, as moderns, to support liberal Piedmont against the Austria of cultural reaction. If this orientation toward individual rights stakes out Baumgarten's difference with conservatives to his right, its culmination in the heroization of the great individual also distinguishes him from a democratic left: "Of course our age is ruled in important aspects by democratic tendencies, but precisely this democratic character makes outstanding individuals all the more indispensable. For a democracy needs a leader. Only aristocracies can provide the masses with an opportunity to act collectively."[18]

The ostensible point of Baumgarten's argument is to urge liberals toward the center—or toward the right—so as to become capable of governing in an alliance with Bismarck. The theoretical import is the articulation of a model of nationhood that combines the competing rhetorical modalities of 1859—the popular nationalism of the *grossdeutsch* camp and the conservative realism of the *kleindeutsch* essayists—thereby, of course, modifying both. It is the nation, and not the state, which is at stake; but without the political leadership of the elite, the nation remains mute and inactive. At this point, however, Baumgarten blurs the difference between the political class, for him coincidental with the aristocracy, and the single political leader: Cavour or Bismarck. Hence the mixed ramifications of the argument. On the one hand, Baumgarten appropriates Italy as a model for emulation by German liberalism in an alliance with the Prussian minister, the constellation which indeed prevailed during the liberal *Gründerjahre* of the 1870s. On the other, to the extent that Baumgarten "misreads" Cavour and overemphasizes his individual role, he appears to be setting the stage for the authoritarianism—or Bonapartism?—that would come to characterize the political culture of Bismarckian Germany, gravely mitigating any liberal potential.

By 1871, a third reading of Italy emerged, one that again reversed the relationship between Italy and Germany and which had deep-seated consequences for German political and literary culture. Between 1859 and 1866, Italy had moved from invisibility within the German political discussion to an exemplary status. In 1871, in the heat of German nationalism, it was demoted; still related to unified Germany, unified Italy increasingly took on the hallmarks of the inferior state, while simultaneously the interconnection of the two states became a source for the articulation a new identity for the German Empire.

The nuances of this redefinition are particularly evident in Wilhelm Lang's essay "Deutsche und italienische Einheit," which commences with an admiring reference to "the miraculous parallelism in the history of unification in the two nations." [19] Yet as much as Lang applauds the two unifications and as much as he is prepared to discuss their similarities, he refers repeatedly to the secondary status of Italian unification, judged a mere by-product of German history: "Once again the Italians are profiting from the battles that the Germans won. Just as Königgrätz brought them Venice, so has Sedan won them the Capitol." [20] Baumgarten's admiration for the political prowess of the Italians, contrasted with German enervation, has given way to a patronizing reduction of Italy to a sideshow: "And is not the Italian uprising, no matter how independent it may be in its motivation and development, and no matter how deep its roots in the history of the people may be, in its decisive crises actually only an episode in the history of the German uprising?" [21]

Italy is secondary in a further sense, however. As much as the two unified states resemble each other, their modes of unification, the internal substance of the nation-state, are fundamentally different: the centralized Italian *Einheitsstaat* and the federal complexity of the German *Reich*. Lang compounds the difference with the aesthetic metaphors of classical lines as contrasted with "Gothic" ponderousness, and with suggestions of different velocities: the Italians moved much more quickly toward a more modern form, but the German solution, for all of its intricacy, may be more respectful of history and therefore ultimately more stable.[22] Indeed while both processes are characterized by the term *Erhebung*, or uprising—the uprising of the nation to achieve independence and unification, presumably against a foreign power—Lang associates the Italian path with more emphatically revolutionary imagery, as opposed to Germany's more conservative trajectory. Even more important, however, is that the revolutionary surplus in Italy is linked now, for the first time, to an ethnic characteristic: "radical uniformity, that flows in the blood of the Romanic peoples."[23] Note the connections: the centralized state is likely to produce greater homogenization and leveling than the gothic *Reich*, while propensities to both radicalism and conformism are treated as congenital features of Romance cultures. Leaving aside the interesting connection of radicalism and conformism—the barely hidden suggestion is that democracy equalizes—one has to take note of the sudden invention of Italy as one of the "Romanic peoples," which in effect reduces Italy to a subsidiary of France, in 1871, in the context of the Franco-Prussian War and the Paris Commune, hardly a neutral linkage. Thus Lang proceeds from the assertion of a mirroring relationship between Germany and Italy, to a blurring of the difference between Italy and France, and, finally, to an emphatic contrast between the conservatism of German nationhood and the mercurial adventurism of the French.

> Even given the strong motivation provided by the unification idea in the gloriously led war of national defense [the Franco-Prussian War], the German people never succumbed to the temptation, which the French periodically cannot resist: to trust in the risk of improvised inventions. Equal to the will for unity was the strength of preserving, and the equilibrium of these two forces became incarnate in the compromise of the new order, the best feature of which is certainly that no aspect of it appears to have been forced. For it thoroughly lacks force or enthusiasm, that most pleasurable form of terrorism.[24]

Baumgarten had limited the status of democratic tendencies within his account of political theory by insisting on the need for an aristocracy and for the leadership only great individuals could provide. Lang faces a similar quandary: the establishment of the nation-state represents a revolutionary reconstruction of the political order, in particular owing to its dependence on forms of mass mobilization. Where Baumgarten put a brake on the revolutionary potential through the invocation of the leader—Cavour or Bismarck—Lang introduces the role of national character and appeals to French and Italian developments as counterexamples to the healthy historicism of the German path. The *Reich* is a compromise, and therefore not radical; it is organic and therefore not forced or artificial; and it is not violent, since it took shape without "enthusiasm"—a negatively coded term—and, therefore without terrorism, present presumably in the Commune of Paris and, so Lang implies, potential in Italy as well.

Evidently Lang places Italy in a liminal position. As a relative of France, it shows signs of succumbing to excessive democracy and conformism, while as a mirror of Germany, its national unification is a key step in the modernization of Europe. If, as we have already seen, Lang treats the finalization of Italian territorial integrity as an "episode" in German history, the culmination of nationhood, the occupation of Rome, is integrated even more emphatically in the German national narrative. The establishment of a secular Italian state is represented as the completion of the Reformation and even of a longer German history with roots in the Middle Ages:

> The fall of the worldly papacy completes the world-historical atonement, which has been carried out by the German people, just as three hundred years ago the German spirit challenged the omnipotence of Rome. From the height of the conquered Capitol, we can oversee the deep connections of German and Italian history, which have interacted for centuries, and which continue to do so today. It is as if ancient guilt were being avenged. During the September days, who could not think of the collapse of the German emperors, the end of Conrad, and how papal and French treachery brought about his downfall. Through the victory over France, a new empire emerges, while the national Kingdom of Italy establishes its control over the city of Peter.[25]

The Italian national state and the German Empire—the latter self-evidently superior to the former—are nevertheless on the same side in their victory over the papist and Frankish alliance. On the same side, where they have belonged since 1859, the unified Germany and Italy have transformed the conservative order, but at this point, the rhetoric of German unification and its incorporation of Italian identity hardly sound progressive. On the contrary, "Italy" now becomes evidence within the German *Kulturkampf*—the state's attack on the Catholic church—a cornerstone of the illiberal culture of the empire and certainly proof that centralization and homogenization could operate within the "gothic" form of the nation-state as well as elsewhere.[26]

The two processes, the political formation of the nation-states and the aestheticization of political discourse, have interacted to produce a curious result. In order to legitimate the revolutionarily new political subjects and,

at the same time, to put a limit on democratizing tendencies within the potentially revolutionary situation, cultural identity is invented and invoked. Which
identity, which invention? In 1859, the memory of 1813, the anti-Napoleonic
liberation, was invoked; in 1866, Baumgarten appealed to Napoleonic revolu-
tionism as the facilitator of Cavour and, mutatis mutandis, Bismarck as well;
in 1871, however, it is the distant history of the-Reformation and the medieval
conflict of Kaiser and Pope. The success of the secular Italian state in occu-
pying Rome is integrated into the anti-Catholic rhetoric of a Protestant Germany in a way that will lend itself to justifying the state's claims against the
Church: Prussia as Piedmont against Rome. At this point, the conservative
criticism Lang directed toward the excessive uniformity of the Italian model
could be redirected against Lang himself and the German model as well, i.e.,
that any national unification tends toward authoritarian solutions. It is, furthermore, a line of thought that can flush out a further implication of the metaphoric connection. If, as Baumgarten and other liberals would soon have to
concede, Bismarck's solution and the "Prussianization" of Germany entailed
a degree of illiberalism and central control inimical to their own ideals; and
if Piedmont and Prussia, Cavour and Bismarck, stand in some mirroring relationship to one another, that is to say, if we face a general problem of unified
nation-states rather than a solely German question; then one might begin to
explore the possibility of a critique of the nation-state and the historical process of national unification, which, however, would not be a conservative critique in the sense of a defense of the political order established at the Congress
of Vienna. There ought to be an imaginable alternative to the centralizing
aspects of the political culture of the nation-states without appealing to Metternich; whatever may have been wrong with the politics of Bismarck, Cavour,
and Napoleon III, it is certainly not that they dismantled the Holy Alliance.

Socialist internationalism may have attempted to transcend the principle
of the nation-state, but it never opposed national unification, which it inherited from the politics of enlightened liberalism. It is rather in the anarchist tradition that one finds the most emphatic rejections of the national models, coupled with a preference for decentralized, local power. Thus Proudhon: "On
fait appel aux nationalités, et le premier usage qu'on fasse de l'indépendance
est de les engloutir: Napolitains, Romagnols, Toscans, Lombards sont moins
en Italie que les Hongrois, les Bohémiens, les Croates en Autriche!"[27] Power,
so he suggests, is most appropriately vested in the regional and historical unit,
rather than in the centralizing invention of the nation-state. Proudhon does
indeed end up defending the legitimacy of the 1815 treaties, not because of any
loyalty to Metternich or legitimate dynasties, but because he views the
Bonapartist—and Bismarckian—revisionism as part of authoritarian agendas
for the establishment of strong states hostile to democracy. An investigation
of Proudhon's extended polemics around the unification of Italy would go far

beyond the scope of this essay; the point, however, is that the process of national unification—in the context of the internal resonances between unified Germany and Italy—was neither natural nor somehow self-evidently desirable.[28] The centralized state bureaucracy of the Kingdom of Italy was perhaps not the only possible alternative to the Austrian occupation of the north, nor was the authoritarianism of Wilhelmine Germany an unavoidable political-cultural destiny. As far away as the details of nineteenth-century European history may seem today, the issues have, if anything, become overriding again, in the context of German unification, the regionalism of the Lombard League, and the disintegration of Yugoslavia. As Europe unifies, the future of the nation-state is ambiguous to say the least; dismantling the fictions of the nineteenth century may be the first step toward participatory democracy on a local level.

Chapter 5

Literary History and the Politics of Deconstruction

Rousseau in Weimar

A self-reflective project of "literary history" has to proceed by inquiring into the consequences of introducing historical material into discussions of aesthetic objects. For very quickly one encounters objections from formalists of various sorts, be they New Critics or deconstructionists, who insist that historical paradigms ultimately deflect attention from the authentically literary character of the text at hand. To reply that formalism may not provide a fully satisfying account of literature as definitively nonhistorical is, of course, not itself an adequate counterargument but only a defensive move in a still unresolved debate. Without at all capitulating to the formalists, one can certainly concede that some literary-historical undertakings might well be insufficient, insofar as they reduce literature to a function, reflection, or epiphenomenon of a presumably prior history. A successful literary history would have to be able to explain why literature, precisely when it is most literary (and not with regard to some secondary feature of literary texts), is also involved in historical processes.

Without such an account, literary history runs a risk (and this has often been its fate) of becoming a peripheral ornament to a larger and allegedly more serious history: English or French or German literary history transformed into a series of illustrations of the long march of the respective state through the centuries. This nationalist potential, based on a nineteenth-century disciplinary paradigm still very much in force in the organization of literary studies in the universities, is compounded by a conservative aesthetic bias in favor of the literary past. To be sure, an alternative history is imaginable, one that incorporates reflections on change, progress, and the future, rather than focusing solely on the weight of tradition. Yet without an adequate theoretical foundation for literary history, such an alternative imagination is highly unlikely, and literary history runs the risk of slipping into a cultural conservatism hostile to aesthetic innovation.

Literary history: if the first problem is to avoid burying literature under history, the second is to determine to what extent history is always itself a partially literary construction. We encounter history by reading historiographical texts written by authors who, sometimes, possess significant literary skills, and these historians build their stories on the basis of other texts, the allegedly genuine "historical documents." Does this mean that history is only a set of narratives related by professional (and probably also nonprofessional) storytellers? Is the past only an effect of language, and is progress, a particular version of the story of the past, nothing more than a figure of speech? To answer in the affirmative would dissolve not only history but all real objects into fiction and subvert the possibility of even an only tentatively objective science.

To reduce literature to history might be labeled an antifictional position, insofar as it diminishes aesthetic autonomy as soon as the literary text is treated as a mere reflection of an objective world. To reduce history to literature might similarly be labeled an antirealist position, transforming the material of social existence into literary constructions. The possibility of a genuinely critical literary history requires a dialectical balancing act, refusing to collapse either term into the other, maintaining the separation of the fictional and the real, while simultaneously insisting on their interaction: the impact of real history on imagined worlds, the intervention of imagination into real processes. This sort of political literary history stands at odds, however, with some influential neoformalist literary theory, especially the deconstructive criticism influenced by the work of Paul de Man. Yet much more is at stake than "only" the interpretation of literary texts or the possibility of literary history. The neoformalist attack on literary history is simultaneously an attack on history, in particular an attack on history as an account of progress and the possibility of egalitarian social transformation. It is therefore not at all accidental that seminal deconstructive texts by de Man and Jacques Derrida focus on Rousseau as the primary theoretician of political modernity and critic of social inequality. A political history of deconstruction that would explore the relationship between its critique of Rousseau and its rise to prominence in American universities in the Reagan era is still to be written. In this chapter, I want to explore some of the central theoretical issues in three stages: (1) the dispute as to whether Rousseau's account of history is fictional or realistic; (2) Heinrich Mann's appropriation of Rousseau as both a literary-historical term and a powerful program for the politicization of literature; (3) conservative resistance to the politicization of literature, with reference to Carl Schmitt and de Man, especially with attention to the connection between the young de Man's fascist journalism in occupied Belgium and the exclusion of history in his mature literary theory.

History and Equality in Rousseau

"O man, whatever country you may come from, whatever your opinions may be, listen: here is your history [voici ton histoire] as I believed it to read, not in the books of your fellow men, which are liars, but in nature, which never lies."[1] Rousseau's promise, at the outset of the *Discourse on the Origin and Foundations of Inequality among Men*, moves in two directions at once, deriding as mendacious the authoritative texts, "les livres de tes semblables," while laying claim to the even greater authority of an incontrovertible nature. Despite the intention to provide a powerful incentive for the subsequent narrative, the duplicity of the commencement threatens the very credibility of the text, since the argument might quickly encounter the objection "Who's the real liar here?" or "One man's nature is another man's text," in which case Rousseau's own book would become indistinguishable from the degraded books of his fellow men, and his apparent claim to have literally entered an extratextual objectivity designated as "nature" would dissolve as just so much false consciousness.

A fine objection indeed, except that Rousseau himself is aware of it and has integrated it into the construction of the *Discourse*: in the cautious and tentative progress of the prefatory sections, in the problematization of both the anthropological topic and the archaeological method, and in the self-ironization in the sentence following immediately on the one already quoted: "Everything that comes from nature will be true; there will be nothing false except what I have involuntarily put in of my own."[2] Evidently Rousseau's text too knows that it may well have been corrupted, involuntarily or not, and it conceivably may stand at as great a distance from a truthful nature as do the competing texts; its touted authenticity turns out to be a strategic pretense. Is authenticity ever otherwise; can a text escape from the domain of fiction and deception; or, more pointedly, how tenable is this spatial metaphor of separation that suggests the very possibility of escape and the presence of an exterior to texts, an exterior that might be named, as Rousseau did, nature or truth, history or politics? Can one imagine books that don't lie?

No one, presumably, will argue for the empirical veracity of the state of nature described in the first part of the *Second Discourse*. Following Jean Starobinski in the introduction to the Pléiade edition, one can nevertheless posit two arguments militating against the purely fictional and ahistorical character of the material: first, that the rupture with contemporary facticity is a prerequisite for the imagining of a radical intervention into history ("He stands outside of established society, severing all immediate ties, but only in order to think through the conditions of existence of a community of greater justice and happiness");[3] and second, that Rousseau's concern is not historical events themselves but the process by which an initially extrahistorical humanity enters into history, or, better, produces history itself, i.e., a metahistorical narrative in which the state of nature functions at most as a "regulative concept" or a "theoretical postulate."[4] Not hard facts, to be sure, but neither is the construct of a state of nature then appropriately denigrated as an arbitrary fiction.

All of this is important because Starobinski, rejecting readings of Rousseau that underscore the theatrical and performative character of his texts, presents him as a critic of inequality and a theoretician of history as a crucial component in the process of both identity formation and transformative practice. It is important furthermore because de Man, begrudgingly conceding that "this existential notion of freedom is impressive enough in itself," returns to the problem of fiction in the *Second Discourse*, in particular, to the putative incompatibility of the fiction of the first part and the "concrete realities of political life" in the second part.[5] And the matter is now very important, for if the fiction of the state of nature turns out, as de Man would have it, to be fundamentally incompatible with the practical critique of inequality, then the constellation of history, subjectivity, and an egalitarian freedom, i.e., Starobinski's Rousseau, will itself turn out to be, at best, an arbitrary fiction, at worst a gripping hallucination, and it is precisely in order to demonstrate as much that de Man mounts his attack. In other words: against Starobinski's Rousseau, the advocate of equality and historical progress, de Man undertakes a deconstruction by playing out fictional and realistic, metaphoric and referential elements in the *Discourse* against each other. If de Man is right, then one of the founding documents of the modern political narrative of progress is only a narrative and is, moreover, internally flawed.

The confrontation between the two critics takes the form of a dispute over a brief passage in the section on language. Rousseau has argued that the mind grasps ideas only in their verbal form, which is why animals, lacking language, can never acquire ideas or ever—the text continues—"acquérir la perfectibilité qui en dépend."[6] In fact, for Starobinski, Rousseau claims that the larger version of perfectibility "is not the result of language but much rather its cause."[7] Since "perfectibility" is the term used to name history, in particular, a history of progressive teleology, the point of Starobinski's insistence is to describe language as an element within historical change. De Man's goal is the reversal of this relationship and the demonstration that perfectibility is an intralinguistic function—language generates history, which is foremost a narrative operating in terms of rhetoric, not social transformation—a claim which would obviously have far-reaching consequences for the understanding of the relationship between literature and history. Put simply: Starobinski locates literature (somehow) within history, while de Man treats history (definitively) as an outgrowth of literature.

That the stakes are very high here is betrayed by some of de Man's formulations: with a remark on the grammatical construction and an objection to Starobinski's paraphrase, de Man seems to imply that Starobinski has a faulty command of the language; although Starobinski has commented on the passage in a footnote, de Man speaks of its "repression" and claims that it is "overlooked" and "avoided"; and, before proceeding to his own explication of the text, de Man heightens the argumentative suspense by commenting that "there must be an unsuspected threat hidden in a sentence that one is so anxious to defuse." What then is the "unsuspected threat" that leads "a critic of Starobinski's intelligence and subtlety" to misread the passage on language?[8]

The threat involves de Man's claim that the text demonstrates how perfectibility, i.e., the possibility of history, is always already within language and therefore not at all primarily a process of social change, let alone egalitarian modernization. For the very process of mental conceptualization is not a referential one but thoroughly intralinguistic, including the construction of a metalanguage with a figural character that serves to guide the apparently literal language of denomination. "All language is language about denomination, that is, a conceptual, figural, metaphorical metalanguage."[9] Yet when the metaphor poses as authentic denomination, when it forgets that naming is an arbitrary act of language, and when it falls into the literalism presumably necessary for the political life of civil society, it becomes blind to its own figurality and is, as de Man puts it, "the deceitful misrepresentation of an original blindness."[10] De Man's case in point: the treatment of human equality in the second part of the *Discourse* is not the product of some egalitarian anthropology grounded in a state of nature that never lies but is rather an effect of language, in particular, the construction of a metaphor of numerical equality; when this misrepresentation is taken literally it becomes, as de Man puts it, "a lie superimposed upon an error."[11] The "error," for de Man, is to equate individuals who are always different and therefore never equal; the "lie" is the suggestion that the equation, itself inadequate, has an objective validity rather than a solely rhetorical force. For de Man, in other words, the discourse of equality, for which Rousseau's text is both a prime example and a highly influential source, may have considerable persuasive power; it is, however, not therefore true.

In order to achieve this subversion of Rousseau's egalitarianism, de Man has to shuttle back and forth between the *First* and *Second Discourses* in remarkable ways and manipulate the text, about which I will have more to say later. At this point, however, I want to step away from this politically charged material in order to ask the more modest question as to what all this might have to do with the possibility of literary history. On a methodological level the answer is, of course, everything, since the controversy between Starobinski and de Man, the relationship between language and history, bears directly on the very legitimacy of a historicizing approach to cultural material. Presumably any periodic rubric—my example will be "the Weimar Republic"—is intended to designate more than an accidental collection of texts; perhaps it suggests that chronological proximity implies some further, logical association. Whether such an association could take the form, say, of a "grounding" of literary texts in a historical context is, to say the least, called into question by de Man's reading of Rousseau, for if history is just another fiction, then a historicizing commentary on a literary text only replaces one fiction with another one and therefore produces no cognitive gain. Is "the Weimar Republic" a tenable literary-critical category or is it only another story? If we accept de Man's reading of Rousseau, we would likely resist any ascription of priority to a temporal context over the textual entities somehow associated with the period. Indeed it would be consistent to reverse the intuitive historicizing hierarchy and treat the period, the "Weimar Republic" or whatever, as itself a figment of a linguistic imagination. In that case, it might make sense to investigate the rhetorical strategies of historians writing about interwar Germany, but there would be little reason to relate a novel written in Berlin in 1930 to the context of its production, for one would only be slipping from one fiction into another. Is literary history possible at all? Probably not, if we accept the terms of de Man's arguments. Nor is it adequate to reply with a naive invocation of the conventions of national literary historiography, an answer implicated equally in conventionalism and nationalism. However, one might begin to provide a more effective answer by addressing the problematic relationship of literature and history, language and perfectibility, and, furthermore, by responding to the questioning with a question: what drives a theoretical school like deconstruction toward the repression of extralinguistic material? What pushes de Man toward a refusal of history? Instead of reducing history to a function of language, it may be more useful to ask how literature participates in historical processes and how history may impinge on the language of literary criticism.

Literature Intervenes in History: The Weimar Republic

There is, however, a more precise connection between the dispute over Rousseau and the problem of the Weimar Republic, understood now not as a gray and abstract paradigm of literary history but as the particular historical material. For while there may always be some general relationship between literature and history which a theoretical metadiscourse could have as its object, the Weimar Republic was characterized specifically by a widespread and self-aware politicization of literary life. On this point, some considerable critical consensus exists, although the explanations of the phenomenon are multifold: the experience of the trenches eroding the plausibility of aesthetic autonomy, the involvement of writers in the revolution of 1918–19, the impoverishment of intellectual strata in the course of the inflation, the "age of mechanical reproduction," the transformed public sphere of the republic, etc., etc. Whatever the explanation, it remains the case that across the literary spectrum of the twenties, from Ernst Jünger on the right, through Thomas Mann in the center, to Bertolt Brecht on the left, the involvement of literature in politics and history appeared to be the order of the day. At least in the self-understanding of Weimar authors, the character of literary language was considerably less metaphoric and much more denominative than de Man would later have it for Rousseau.

In fact—this is now the lexemic connection in the argument—it was Rousseau who provided the model for a politicized literature and the intervention of literature into history. The text itself, Heinrich Mann's "Geist und Tat" (Spirit and Deed) of 1910, antedates the republic by eight years, but it greatly influenced a younger generation, notably the political expressionists, and can be treated as perhaps a blueprint for the politicization of the literati in the republic. Mann's Rousseau provides the paradigm of the "ratio militans," the intellectual as the engaged writer of the so-called activist movement, and opens, more generally, onto the question of operative literature during the twenties.

"Of all who ever wrote," writes Mann, "Rousseau had the greatest, most tangible success."[12] The quick elision of the difference between the adjectives, implying that the greatest success would be the most tangible, suggests that, for Mann, Rousseau's success involved the transition from abstract writing to a dimension of incremental reality, in other words, from theory to practice. (For de Man, the similar gap between fiction and the real was grounds to deconstruct Rousseau's egalitarianism.) This reading is confirmed in the subsequent text, as Rousseau appears as the source of ideals which eventually inspire the people to engage in revolutionary activity.

It would be a misreading, however, to assume that the transition involves a reductive correspondence or a repression of fiction in the interest of some more relevant facts, a return to nature, as it were. For Mann reading Rousseau, writing intervenes in history not when it corresponds to the factual but, on the contrary, precisely to the extent that it can articulate negation. Therefore Mann immediately glosses the assertion of Rousseau's success with a characterization that amounts to a chain of contradictions: "A sorry figaro who loves nothing but his passion and wants to be taken seriously. A vagabond, looking for a people and dreaming of a state. A sick man yearning for a good and healthy nature. A misanthrope counting on a distant . . . good humanity. An enemy of the privileged who desires countesses. . . . " Note the oxymoronic foundations of the activist writer—the serious figaro, the patriotic vagabond, the humanitarian misanthrope—a figure repeated often enough to suggest that it is precisely the contradiction that is at stake and not the particular substances. Yet the materiality of the images remains interesting, since, in each case, it is an initial factual identity that is modified or retracted by a subjective moment of resistance—desire, dream, illusion—as if the fictional negation were precisely the prerequisite to activist intervention. (This was of course Starobinski's suggestion: that Rousseau had to break with his milieu in order to imagine a better community.) This accumulation of reversals is eventually itself reversed in a peripatetic moment when the movement is suddenly inverted: no longer from reality to fiction but from literary fiction to revolutionary politics: "who is so just and true in his novel of the state that a whole people henceforth wants to be just and true . . . and takes up his struggle [seinen Kampf weiterkämpft]."

Thus the political possibility of literature depends not on an extrapolation of some literalist mirroring of reality but on the negative distance—autonomy, if you like—which permits for an interventionist moment. Without the counterfactual ideals of fiction, politics, for Mann, cease to be possible, immobilized by the lethargic weight of the given order. Hence his refusal of any deterministic politics:

> The necessity of things? The "development"? It never means anything more than a minimal possibility of life. Not freedom: just living. Not justice: just living. Not human dignity: just living. To count on the development means to surrender to nature, and no one ever saw her waste anything.[13]

In Mann's account, therefore, Rousseau has suddenly become an antinaturalist, the critic of the world of natural facts, and only therefore the model for an activist political writing. The power of the egalitarian agenda derives not from the questionable truth value of the fiction of the state of nature but from the capacity of the fiction to call the really existing inequality into question. With this in mind, de Man's reading, as a commentary on the inaccessibility of an adequately referential language for a political writing, turns out to be less than satisfying; his argument depends on the straw man of a naive literalism which he can easily debunk but to which, of course, nearly no one subscribes. If language always involves a figural component, it does not follow that a hierarchy must be constructed that denounces denotative language as degraded or that the language of civil society, i.e., political language, is always "a lie superimposed upon an error." In contrast, Mann's Rousseau displays the dialectic between the return to nature and a critical antinaturalism, that is, between referential and figurative moments; and it demonstrates how the figurative moment, as a refusal of the referential, is itself a political act, the grand refusal of a fallen nature. For de Man, a literalism ignorant of an intralinguistic priority is trapped in a self-deception; for Mann, a self-referential language ignorant of politics ignores its own construction and abuses its own nature (or better: its own antinatural nature). Instead of asking, with de Man, why Starobinski represses the question of language, one should inquire why de Man represses the question of politics. "An intellectual," writes Mann, "who collaborates with the master caste commits treason against the spirit"— which brings us to Mann's Nietzsche.[14]

Mann presents here one of his clearest and most radical accounts of literary geography: in France, generations of authors from Rousseau to Zola wage a constant struggle against entrenched power and are applauded by a "people with literary instincts," while in Germany an indolent people coexist with a conservative and self-enclosed intelligentsia: "They think further than anyone else, they think to the end of pure reason, they think into nothingness: and the country is ruled by divine right and an iron fist. But why change anything: Whatever has been achieved elsewhere, the Germans have surpassed it in theory."[15] A hypertrophic intellectual culture side by side with underdeveloped political institutions: Mann points out the refusal of German intellectuals to take up the political fight—for fear of change, for love of comfort, and out of an adulation of power. He names Nietzsche as the paradigm of this quietism, just as Rousseau served as the model of the activist writer.

Yet the treatment of Nietzsche is in fact more complex; just as Mann turns Rousseau into a critic of nature, he hints at the possibility of a democratic inversion of Nietzsche. Describing the preference of German intellectuals for individual protection and subservience, he indicates that they could not "believe in democracy," a term he glosses as "ein Volk von Herren," a people of masters, an evidently Nietzschean turn of phrase: as if Nietzsche's contempt for democracy was itself implicated in the slave mentality that Nietzsche otherwise attacked; or phrased positively, as if a genuine democracy offered the only chance to universalize a Nietzschean aristocracy. Such a transformation would depend, however, on the politicization of the literary intelligentsia, a shift from Nietzsche to Rousseau, from the German to the French model of literary life.

The name of that shift might be "the Weimar Republic." I have already suggested that the culture of the republic was characterized by a heightened awareness of literary politics. Interesting evidence is provided by Mann himself in his 1944 autobiography, *Ein Zeitalter wird besichtigt*. Writing in exile, he looks back at the republic and comments on the important status literature achieved in it, especially in some crucial institutions like the Prussian Academy of the Arts and in certain policies of the Ministry of Education. Perhaps most interesting, however, is his account of a reading he gave in the Karstadt department store on the Hermannsplatz in Berlin:

> A department store has lots of displays; here it gave its customers a chance to take a look at literature. The women came and went. They hardly knew my name; maybe half a sentence stuck with one or another of them. My anonymous appearance in the flowing masses who gave me no special treatment—this is one of my purest memories of public life in the republic.[16]

This 1944 statement about the writer intervening in public is obviously much less heroic than the model of intellectual leadership he had associated with

Rousseau thirty-four years earlier. Gone is the enthusiasm of intellectual avant-gardism, replaced by nostalgia and the melancholy of defeat. Yet considering the republic from the standpoint of both framing texts, it appears to have been a period in which a certain literarization of public life took place, and in the autobiography Mann goes on to comment on the historical status of that cultural moment:

> Twenty-five years earlier [that is, during the empire] a department store presented the "miraculous mandrake root" as a special attraction in a glass case. You weren't supposed to buy it; you were just supposed to stare. In the decade before the second war, the department stores (I can't say if in Germany too [Mann was in exile]) were constantly pumped through with the noise of a radio jazz music. A saleswoman who was not deaf to it must have suffered a nervous collapse. During the German Republic, it was deemed proper and useful to have authors read aloud to everyone who passed by and listened. That means that the German Republic was better than its reputation and its spirit better than the events [ihr Geist besser als die Tatsachen] that brought about its end.

The account invokes a larger cultural history: between the immobilizing superstition of the premodern empire and the expansion of the culture industry in an era of mass mobilization and war, the republic is the placeholder of literature, where political democracy and cultural democracy began to coincide. A certain cultural conservatism is of course unmistakable when the writer privileges the moment of literary performance—his public reading—over and against the iconic spectacle of the mandrake root ("nur staunen sollte man") and the mechanical reproduction of popular music. The literary intellectual, not surprisingly, values the written text more than visual or acoustic experience. Yet this is precisely the staging of the intervention of the literary that Mann had called for in 1910, the literarization of public life, or—what amounts to the same thing—the Weimar Republic as a literacy campaign: bringing the author to the public represents the integration of literature into politics and the democratic culture of the republic, while the competing models, the mandrake and the music, are deemed symptomatic of authoritarian cultures that operate through the manipulation of the pacified masses.

Initially Mann attempted to validate the democratization of culture, the literacy campaign, by appealing to the authority of Rousseau. One need not overstate the case by insisting that Mann gets Rousseau absolutely right or that, for whatever inexplicable reason, Rousseau could turn out to be the hidden prime mover of the literary and cultural revolutions of Weimar Germany. It is, however, important to recall that, as Robert Darnton has shown, Rousseau did help to initiate a radically new mode of reading, marked in particular by

a rejection of a certain elitist literary world and by the insistence that literature could have an instructional and perhaps more widely operative value in
everyday life. [17] As great as the difference may be between the Rousseauistic
readings prevalent during the ancien régime and Mann's Rousseauism on the
eve of the Weimar Republic, as multifold as the possibilities of reading may be,
it is important to pay attention to some continuities within the permanent cultural structure of the *longue durée* of European modernity, the tension between
an elite culture of conservative self-referentiality and a vernacular liberalism
of a politicizing literature. Arguing for intervention, political change, and anti-
elitism, Mann invokes Rousseau, and the choice is by no means arbitrary (just
as de Man's effort to dismantle the possibility of Rousseauistic politics is
equally overdetermined). "Rousseau in Weimar"—what is at stake is the very
possibility of a literature, and a literary criticism, adequate to a republic.

Opposing Progress: From Schmitt to de Man

What the democratic culture of the republic would come to regard as intervention—"eingreifende Literatur"—appears from the standpoint of conservative authority to be an interference in the exercise of power. While Mann
appeals to Rousseau in order to articulate an egalitarian literary-politics, the
premier legal philosopher of Weimar, Carl Schmitt, undertakes a dismantling
of Rousseau in order to demonstrate the logical untenability of an egalitarian
politics and the obsolescence of liberalism. Thus, in the introduction to the
1926 edition of his *Crisis of Parliamentary Democracy*, we read that

> the equality of all men as men is not democracy but a specific form of
> liberalism, not a state form but an individualistic-humanitarian morality
> and a Weltanschauung. The murky connection of the two is the basis of
> modern mass democracy. Despite all the attention devoted to Rousseau and
> despite the correct insight that Rousseau stands at the outset of modern
> democracy, no one appears to have noticed that even the political construct
> in *The Social Contract* combines these two different elements in an in-
> coherent fashion. The facade is liberal: the grounding of state legitimacy
> on the free contract. But later, as the crucial concept develops, the *volonté
> générale*, it turns out that for Rousseau, a true state exists only where the
> people is so homogeneous that a one-mindedness prevails. [18]

In such a situation, however, a heterogeneous element, which might well be
integrated by means of the liberal contract mechanisms, would necessarily be
excluded from the body of the homogeneous people, i.e., Schmitt reads
Rousseau (as he does the Weimar Constitution) to argue for the incompatibility
of liberalism and democracy or, what amounts to the same thing, the incom-

patibility of universal equality and popular sovereignty. In fact, genuine popular sovereignty, the rule of the people, is impossible when universal civil rights accord political influence, via free speech, to everyone, including minorities; consequently, in Schmitt's account, democracy is more likely a matter of a dictatorial regime in which the leader serves as the vessel of popular will than a possible outcome of parliamentary liberalism and its atomized special interests. Rousseauistic egalitarianism is a bad metaphor: according to Schmitt because it blurs political authority, according to de Man because it blurs the linguistic process of conceptualization.

This is not the place to enter into an extended discussion of Schmitt's work; suffice it to say that he recurs to a Hobbesian defense of the state, *autoritas non veritas facit legem*, and his project in the twenties, at least, appears to be the defense of political authority against the threat posed by the articulation of norms and truth claims in a public sphere. To put a fine point on the conflict: where the Rousseauist Mann argues for political intervention by the literati, as a group with a privileged access to language, the Hobbesian Schmitt attempts to protect the authority of the state (whatever state has authority) from the interference of the authors and the vagaries of public speech. Hence his admiration for the antiliberalism of a conservative like Donoso Cortes:

> He straightforwardly defined the bourgeoisie as a "discussing class," *una classa discutidora*. It has thus been sentenced. This definition contains the class characteristic of wanting to evade the decision. A class that shifts all political activity onto the plane of conversation in the press and in parliament is no match for social conflict.[19]

"No match for social conflict" means that for Schmitt reading Donoso Cortes a Rousseauistic public can never be the plausible carrier of state authority. Some more effective agent of sovereignty is necessary, and Schmitt will locate it in the myth of the dictator; he concludes *The Crisis of Parliamentary Democracy* with a paean to Mussolini and Sorel. Adequate politics depend, apparently, not on the ethics of a state of nature, not on universalistic norms, not on egalitarian principles, but on the aesthetics of a fiction—like Sorel's myth—beyond rational scrutiny or parliamentary accountability. Politics belongs to the realm of figural, not literal, language, since its concern is *autoritas* and not *veritas*. In fact, one can read Schmitt's ostensible project—the defense of the autonomy of political sovereignty against the threats of literarization or, for that matter, social and economic claims—as coincident with a defense of a version of aesthetic autonomy: except that the aesthetic object has ceased to be the traditional work of art and is the dictatorship itself, the aestheticization of politics, to cite Walter Benjamin's familiar designation of fascism.[20]

One could pursue the connection to Benjamin here, both because of the not uninteresting overlap with an aspect of Schmitt's work and because he presents, in the 1934 essay "The Author as Producer," a left-wing critique of Mann's activism. To oversimplify: where Schmitt resists the political intervention of literary figures, Benjamin complains that left liberals like Mann do not go far enough, only allying themselves, in a patronizing manner, with the proletariat rather than recognizing the proletarianization of the status of the author within the means of production. That is of course well-trodden ground and should be familiar; a more fruitful line of inquiry would involve an issue that Benjamin labels the "literarization of living conditions," which resonates apparently with the interventionist model I have associated with Mann's Rousseauism.[21]

That "literarization," the introduction of literature into the public sphere, or, to repeat my own formula, the Weimar Republic as a literacy campaign— that shift in the organization of literary life can be treated against the background of a *longue durée* of a hierarchical opposition of elite and popular culture, and it can be located at a specific moment, a surge of democratization in the early twentieth century. The language game of vernacular liberalism challenges the language game of cultural elitism and evokes several responses including the Schmittian defense of autonomous political sovereignty and an equally anti-egalitarian defense of aesthetic autonomy, for example the conservative project of the American New Criticism or, more germane to the topic at hand, the aestheticism of the young Paul de Man.

Reviewing de Man's contributions to the collaborationist Belgian press of the early 1940s, one finds a variety of competing models and claims, ranging from the innocuous to the egregious; this is not the time for a complete survey. I do want to comment on an issue raised in the most notorious article, "Les Juifs dans la littérature actuelle," which includes of course the strong anti-Semitic remark that has been widely reported.[22] My concern is, however, something else, the relationship de Man posits between literature and history, or what it is he could mean precisely by a "littérature actuelle."

Disputing a radically anti-Semitic position that claims that postwar literature has succumbed to an excessive Jewish influence, he asserts that, no, Jews are only second-rate authors and therefore uninfluential and, somewhat contradicting himself, they have used their influence to spread the claim of their literary importance. His central point, however, is not to worry: no matter what role Jews may play in postwar Europe, the literary sphere has been impervious to their influence, indeed it has hardly been affected by the cataclysms of war and revolution:

> It appears that aesthetic evolutions obey very powerful laws that continue their action even when humanity is shaken by considerable events. The world war provoked a profound upheaval in the political and economic world. But

artistic life has been stirred relatively little, and the forms which we currently recognize are the logical and normal consequences of what previously existed.

That is to say that historical events do indeed transpire in some objective realm in the exterior, but they have no impact on the self-enclosed world of art. Therefore it is not surprising that Jews, whom de Man locates by definition in that exterior, have no access to the genuine dimension of European aesthetic culture:

> That [Western intellectuals] have been able to protect from Jewish influence a domain as representative of culture as literature proves their vitality. One couldn't have expressed much hope for the future of our civilization if it had let itself be invaded by a foreign force without offering any resistance. Preserving an originality and an intact character, despite the Semitic meddling [l'ingérance sémite] in all its aspects, European life has shown that its profound nature is healthy.

Clearly the issue of anti-Semitism overlaps here with the relationship between aesthetic culture and history. The Jews are not only ciphers of an alterity, a foreign force; they also are the pressure of the historical moment, the challenge to the permanence of tradition. Bourgeois liberalism's interference in the affairs of Schmitt's sovereign has become the "ingérance sémite," Semitic meddling in de Man's European affairs. Indeed one can note an interesting point of convergence, since Schmitt's effort to defend the sovereign from political literati mirrors de Man's protection of literature from the threat of politics. In the one case, state authority, and in the other literary authorship, is separated from the vagaries of history. De Man's key point, however, is that genuine literature, including a postwar literature—such as the literature of the Weimar Republic— is not a function of historical change, i.e., either all literature is always *actuelle* or the term has simply a descriptive sense that does not address the truly literary aspect of the texts at hand. For this aspect is hardly touched by external events, even those as large as the world war.

Does literature ever encounter a temporality outside of itself? Is literary history possible? The question has already been posed once and with regard to the same author. Rereading de Man after the discovery of his earlier pieces, one will want to reexamine the question of history and politics and their relationship to literature; it is on this score, if any, that some continuity might exist. It is, however, most likely a continuity with some considerable shift: in the early writing, history is a present that occurs outside of a hermetically sealed literary realm, i.e., literature is never touched by external events. In contrast, in the late essay on the *Second Discourse*, it appears that perfectibility is only a consequence of language, i.e., history is the result of an intralinguistic process.

The two accounts share an effort to protect language from putatively objectivist claims of history—in the early version by asserting a rigid autonomy, in the latter by dissolving history into language, and thereby erasing the space in which politics might take place. In the Rousseau essay, he can do so only by forcing the text of the *Discourse* in ways that border on distortion. Although his concern is the linkage between the two parts, he essentially represses the first few paragraphs of the second part, including the pre-Proudhonian attack on private property ("The first person who, having fenced off a plot of ground, took it into his head to say *this is mine* and found people simple enough to believe him, was the true founder of civil society.")[23] What de Man does here is much more of a "repression" than is Starobinski's treating the passage on perfectibility in a footnote. When de Man does quote, from paragraphs 5 through 7, he omits with a three-point ellipsis passages having to do with the role of technical progress in history. Finally, he glosses Rousseau's term "cette importante Vérité," which in the original refers to the recognition of a common humanity, as "the suspicion that human specificity may be rooted in linguistic deceit."[24]

I have already posed the question as to why de Man might push toward a refusal of history. The sort of discussion that has to take place is obvious: a scrutinization of his late work to determine whether it is constructed to provide an alibi for the repressed collaborationism. The chapter "Excuses" in *Allegories of Reading* is presumably the crucial text here, insofar as it argues, with reference to Rousseau's *Confessions*, that all confessions are always inadequate because they are implicated in a logic of exculpation.

More interesting, however, than a hypothetical biographical continuity in de Man's work is the response of some of his defenders to the recent discussion. Consider, for example, Geoffrey Hartman's suggestion that, as unfortunate as the essays in *Le Soir* may be, it is crucial to hold onto the lesson of the mature de Man regarding the potential danger of any politics (as if one could avoid political catastrophes just by steering clear of politics).[25] Or consider Werner Hamacher arguing that, because no confessional language could ever be adequate to the Holocaust, the appropriate response is not to speak of it; ergo, de Man's silence was the laudable *Trauerarbeit*, while his critics are to blame, probably for their *ingérance*.[26] Or consider, finally, the argument that de Man's collaborationist prose was not as bad as it might have been in the early forties and that the difference indicates that de Man was, in effect, a resistance hero.

What strikes one in arguments like these is a considerable loss of reality, a repression of history that erases both de Man's personal history and the legitimacy of a discussion of history altogether: as if literary-critical methodology were being bent to accommodate the construction of the alibi which de Man's doubting defenders imagine he needs. So the question much bigger than de Man's past is the future of historical inquiry in literary studies and the very legitimacy of categories such as "literature and the Weimar Republic." War, revolution, the republic—the current debate involves whether these will be treated as historical events, processes, structures, or, to borrow de Man's own image, only as written documents masquerading as history. That a historical account of literary development might have a conservative implication, especially perhaps a nationalist one, is self-evident. It is by no means evident, however, that the language game of vernacular liberalism, the project of emancipation, could ever do without history. It is in the historical dimension that victims imagine something better, just as much as it is also to the perpetual future that they are forced to postpone gratification. The dialectic of history provides no guarantees, except that without history there are no dialectics, no change, and no progress. Yet while deconstruction may attempt to repress history, one can certainly ask questions about the vicissitudes of deconstruction within history.

Deconstruction as History: Troping to Pretoria

Deconstruction combined a theoretical skepticism toward language—no meaning is fully fixed or exhaustively definable—with a practical realism in pursuit of institutional power. The radical doubt, on the one hand, permitted the deconstructive critic to claim an oppositional stance, an ostentatious hostility to authoritarian structures, reason and universalism, logocentrism and Western metaphysics. The conservative Realpolitik of the deconstructive academy, on the other, permitted it to occupy positions of considerable authority in many of the most prestigious American universities during the deconstructive decade: from the publication of the English translation of *Grammatology* in 1976 to the public debate in 1988 over Paul de Man's collaborationist activities in Nazi-occupied Belgium. Is it fair to label the apparent tension between radical claims and institutional conformism unprincipled or hypocritical? Presumably the deconstructive critic's reply would point out the question's own reliance on two contradictory terms, theory and practice, a splendid example of just that sort of binary opposition endemic in post-Socratic philosophy which it is the proclaimed program of deconstruction to dismantle, along with subject and object, male and female, etc. It is as if an appreciation of an egalitarian agenda in some fields, such as gender or race relations, necessarily required the obliteration of differences in all fields: a strangely totalitarian consequence of a credo that otherwise flaunts an anarchic, libertarian posture. Refusing to provide an account of its own institutional practice, deconstruction appears frighteningly naive when it occasionally makes political claims, despite or rather because of its neo-Heideggerian extremism, which thrives on an unlimited irresponsibility. For it is, after all, "always already" only verbal radicalism; hence the rallying cry that there is nothing beyond the text. Far from trying to change the world, deconstruction does not even want to interpret it but smugly abolishes it instead, writing it off as a figment of the imagination of language. Wars and revolutions are, if noticed at all, regarded as just so many texts and documents: fine enough, unless you get in the way of a bullet.

If one turns a deconstructive eye on deconstruction itself, it is not too hard to find traces of its history within its own texts. Jeffrey Mehlman has documented the deferential, indeed obsequious language Jacques Derrida opted to use in essays and addresses at major universities: the enfant terrible turns out to be a regular guy. In "Living On," included in a volume edited by Harold Bloom, Derrida sports "a key in the *récit*, a 'Yale' key." In "The University in the Eyes of Its Pupils," a 1983 lecture at Cornell, "reason perched precariously above its abyss is the Cornell campus atop its suicidal gorges," or, "the topolitics of the Cornellian point of view." And at the University of Virginia, Derrida appealed to Thomas Jefferson and wrapped himself in the Declaration of Independence, read as a protodeconstructive investigation into the duplicity of signification. For Mehlman, this amounts to "literary adulation" to ensure "academic respectability," a strategy that has effectively ensconced a new literary-critical orthodoxy that dwells on the pretense that it is anti-establishment.[27] Yet one can experience this antinomy as painful only if one expects deconstruction, as does Mehlman, to live up to its subversive self-advertising. On closer examination, however, there is no reason to expect the literary-critical establishment of the 1980s to be anything but conformist, despite its plethora of adversarial gestures. To be sure, Mehlman exposes the degree to which deconstruction is ready to curry favor, and—true to the deconstructive project—he traces the self-subversion of the deconstructive text. But a deconstruction of deconstruction, like all deconstruction, turns out to be ultimately inadequate, providing at best a precious but always unilluminating reading, prudishly fearful of going beyond the text. Deconstruction wants to handle texts without getting its fingers dirty; before it picks up a book, it puts on gloves to avoid contamination with reality. A full account of the political history of deconstruction's rise and fall would have to go further than the text and ask about the context, the academy, contemporary culture, and wider social changes.

That full account would entail a cultural history of the United States from the sixties through the Reagan presidency. The political struggles and social transformations of the civil rights era and the student movement accelerated developments already inherent in the multiversity of the postwar period. Traditionalist readings of cultural material grew obsolete in the age of Sputnik, just as Eurocentric cultural hegemony became dysfunctional after decolonization. The curricula of literary studies were in desperate need of reform and expansion, and the inherited methods of reading were equally ripe for change.

the trace of the Reagan era, the subterranean complicity of populist fundamentalism and deconstructive antifundamentalism.

So the "academic respectability" of deconstruction is not at all just a product of politic deference or opportunist metaphors, no matter how many tenured positions that rhetoric may have extorted from deans. It is not the case that the pursuit of institutional integration meant a betrayal of a radical project, proudly disrespectful of tradition. There was never anything to betray: deconstruction has operated as an ideological transformer, stifling discussion, buttressing conservatism, and halting the secularization of cultural studies. This operation moreover is not a consequence of context—let us lend no credence to an "encirclement" hypothesis, whereby an original and pure (and presumably "French") deconstruction was somehow distorted by the putatively hostile environment of traditionalist English departments or an American antipathy to theory; it is, rather, the consequence of key deconstructive tenets, especially (1) the privileging of language, (2) the opposition of writing and speech, and (3) the critique of Western metaphysics. Each point, as will be shown in turn, has had a debilitating effect on the critical imagination.

To privilege language means to marginalize other dimensions of existence, both the physical cosmos and alternative aspects of human experience. Deconstruction is not the sole contemporary account that focuses on language; one thinks immediately of Habermas' theory of communicative action and Foucault's discourse theory. Yet for both Habermas and Foucault, despite the immense distance that separates them, language operates at least upon or within other material. Deconstruction alone refuses to go beyond the linguistic text or, what amounts to nearly the same, casts everything as a function of language. Deconstruction is the restaurant where one can order only the menu; to inquire, crudely, as to the whereabouts of the beef elicits the anemic response that it is in the text, à la carte. Let them eat tropes!

It is, however, not language in general that deconstruction takes as its object of study but the written text, as opposed to the spoken word. What is at stake in this polemical opposition (a false opposition, since writing and speech are obviously not mutually exclusive)? A theory of spoken language might plausibly depend on the presence of speakers, i.e., human subjects engaged in dramatic exchanges of meaning. Language would consequently be regarded as a vehicle for potential, if flawed, communication and understanding. This argumentative route—Habermas pursues a version of it—tends to tie the sense of the utterance to the intention of the speaking subject. From the standpoint of deconstruction, this model of spoken language, labeled "phonologocentrism," is rejected because of its reliance on a philosophy of "subjects," which, in good Heideggerian fashion, is denounced as part of a Western metaphysics of subject and object. Furthermore, the equation of the meaning of an utterance with the intention of a speaker deflects attention from language itself and onto the specific historical, perhaps even objective, consciousness of the speaker. The indeterminacy of language would thereby be surrendered to a psychology of the interlocutors; the freedom of the signifier, a moment ago separated from history through the privileging of language, would suddenly be bound up again in extralinguistic material.

Deconstruction privileges language as writing and therefore labels itself grammatology. If the spoken word might be confused too quickly with a speaking subject whose physical presence is necessary for speech to occur, the written word can circulate independently of an author, who quickly disappears from the scene. Deconstruction gains considerable latitude by its scrutinization of the word but tends to lose interest in the historical vicissitudes of its writer: intentions, context, politics. The result can be traced in a 1985 exchange on the topic of South African apartheid in *Critical Inquiry*, which casts important light on the political substance of deconstruction.

"Racism's Last Word" is a translation of Derrida's contribution to a catalogue of an exhibition entitled "Art contre/against Apartheid." To be sure, Derrida passionately opposes the South African regime, its segregationist policies, and its brutal violence, as well as the complicity of other states engaged in supportive and lucrative trading relationships. Yet it is not so much a political account that Derrida provides, familiar as he is with the details of South African history. His central concern is instead a meditation on—or deconstruction of—the word. This grammatological blindness to the variegations of material history and fixation on the single term produce a text which may be ethically inspiring but lacks analytic focus; one learns very little from it. Thus his respondents, Anne McClintock and Rob Nixon, comment:

> For most of the essay, Derrida allows the solitary word *apartheid* to absorb so much of his attention that the changing discourses of South African racism appear more static and monolithic than they really are. Paradoxically, what is most absent from Derrida's essay is an attentiveness to racial and class difference: his insights are premised on too uniform a conception of South Africa's discourses of racial difference, while his historical comments are too generalized to carry strategic force.[29]

Indeed, Derrida's fetishization of the word seems particularly narrow in the light of the political and social developments that have recently begun to unfold in South Africa.

What one can learn a great deal about from Derrida's text, however, are the philosophical and perhaps political allegiances of grammatology. The original problem in South Africa is, for Derrida, not apartheid but *apartheid*, the word. More than its etymology, it is its grammatical status, an abstract substantive, that is implicated, so Derrida suggests, in a logocentrism of hierarchy, domination, and separation.

> the glaring harshness of abstract essence (*heid*) seems to speculate in another regime of abstraction, that of confined separation. The word concentrates separation, raises it to another power and sets separation itself *apart*: "apartitionality," something like that. By isolating being apart in some sort of essence of hypostasis, the word corrupts it into a quasi-ontological segregation.[30]

The real practices of apartheid are then, apparently, not the result of interest or ideology but the consequence of a linguistic form, in particular the capacity for abstraction in—here another nod to Heidegger—Western language. In other words, it is not the case that "apartheid" is a name given to a set of social practices that ensure social hierarchy, exploitation, and racial separation. Instead, Derrida gets it backwards: the linguistic practice of forming terms that indicate abstract essences, exemplified by "apartheid" (but presumably also by "emancipation," "freedom," or "equality"), generates the social practice. Derrida is of course not thoroughly wrong when he continues, "there's no racism without a language," but the point is platitudinous and irrelevant; without a language, there would be no Freedom Charter. Or rather the point is relevant only for Derrida in his attempt to exploit the example of South Africa to pursue his own sectarian philosophical agenda. The suggestion that the apartheid state can end only when the whole edifice of Western thought is overcome could hardly provide much comfort to the victims of South African racism.

An alternative to the linguistic problem of "apartheid" is—no surprise—for Derrida imaginable only as language: "a language at once very old, older than Europe, but for that reason to be invented once more." Apartheid is the result, perhaps even the ultimate goal, of Western metaphysics; it "would have had no chance outside a European 'discourse' on the concept of race"; at stake is the "occidental essence of the historical process." South African specificity disappears beneath the broad-brush account of a monolithic western tradition. Against the background of Derrida's account, it is nearly incomprehensible to read that Nelson Mandela could invoke the American Declaration of Independence (in a manner very different from Derrida's in Virginia) and the authority of Washington, Jefferson, Lincoln, John Brown, W. E. B. DuBois, and Martin Luther King—American heirs to a, if Derrida insists, "European" discourse of Enlightenment and emancipation.[31]

Antiphonologocentrism, the priority of the written text over the spoken word, means that deconstruction prefers to ponder the mysteries of authorless inscriptions, silent and permanent, rather than listen to what living subjects say or watch what they do. If change or history takes place for deconstruction, it is because of the instability of language, and not because of the social practice of human beings. This erasure of the subject derives from the critique of Western metaphysics and is related to Heidegger's antihumanism and Foucault's neo-Nietzschean "end of man."[32] Neither historical practices nor economic imperatives drive imperialism, in this account, but a metaphysics of the Occident that has been operative for at least two and a half millennia: apartheid as a *Seinsvergessenheit*, whose real crime is the "presentation of some present."

But for that very reason, because all the dialectical nuances disappear into a monolithic metaphysics of presence, this description ends up blind to effectively critical categories, especially those in the Western lexicon. Emancipation, Enlightenment, modernity, liberalism, democracy—all this is jettisoned: "the customary discourse on man, humanism and human rights, has encountered its effective and as yet unthought limit. . . . " Hence, presumably, a human rights critique of South Africa, one based perhaps on the Freedom Charter, is disallowed, since it would rely on an anachronistic anthropology. In the heat of the polemic with his critics, Derrida becomes more consistent and even suggests that the opponents of apartheid are not simply ineffective but in fact complicitous with apartheid become of shared philosophical assumptions and discursive arrangements; for deconstruction the dialectic of victim and culprit is a binary opposition hopelessly lodged in Western metaphysics—the goal becomes a blurring of the borders. Both the South African state and its opponents valorize the term "democracy," and that common humanist episteme is, for Derrida, precisely the problem. Freedom, thus teaches one of the premier philosophers of the late twentieth century, is slavery. By this point, however, it is clear that Derrida is merely projecting the terms of Parisian antitotalitarianism, the fashion of former radicals on their short trek into the towers of learning, onto South Africa about which he has nothing to say.

The critique of the metaphysics of presence sovereignly ignores the key issue for the anti-apartheid movement: representation—one person, one vote. One need not invest the prospect of a representative government with exaggerated hopes in order to recognize the material urgency of this single point in the real political situation, where language is one capacity of society, but hardly the sole substance. If literary criticism chooses to ignore history, it is criticism that is impoverished. History is not brought to an end, nor are its challenges diminished.

Chapter 6

German Primitivism/Primitive Germany
The Case of Emil Nolde

Early in the summer of 1937, the most prominent Nazi painter, Adolf Ziegler, led the operation that removed all representatives of so-called degenerate art from the public museums of Germany. Many of the works were soon shown again in the "Exhibition of Degenerate Art" that opened in Munich and were later destroyed, sold (both domestically and abroad), or, most cynically, confiscated by Nazi leaders for their private collections. As was typical of the bureaucratic confusion that characterized the National Socialist dictatorship, there appears to have been no precise administrative guideline as to which works or which artists were to be judged contraband (one result of which was to augment the insecurity of the public which, never sure of the legal limits, was pressured into a posture of vigilant self-censorship). Yet, according to one count,

> sixteen thousand works of art—paintings, sculptures, drawings, and prints—by nearly 1,400 different artists were gathered up [including] more than a hundred works by the sculptor Lehmbruck; between two and three hundred examples each of Dix, Grosz, and Corinth; between three and four hundred by Hofer, Pechstein, Barlach, Feininger, and Otto Mueller; more than four hundred Kokoschkas, five hundred Beckmanns, six hundred Schmidt-Rottluffs and Kirchners, seven hundred Heckels, and more than a thousand Noldes.[1]

Theda Shapiro numbers the confiscated works by Nolde at 1,052, making him presumably the artist most strongly persecuted, at least in this numerical sense, by the cultural policies of the fascist state.[2]

This sort of introduction to the case of Emil Nolde appears to set the stage for a heroic narrative of the modern artist martyred by the political dictatorship that denounced his work as degenerate as early as 1933 and, in 1941, issued an official prohibition on his engaging in any further painting. It is perhaps interesting to note that an East German encyclopedia, eager to highlight the antifascist pedigree of any major cultural figures, underscores this aspect of Nolde's biography, without however mentioning the other side of the story: his membership since the twenties, long before it had become opportune, in the Nazi party (or rather, its corollary in Denmark to which northern Schleswig where he resided had been ceded under the terms of the Versailles Treaty).[3] So the plot thickens, and the anticipated story of the beleaguered modernist, glowing with the glory of aesthetic autonomy but hounded by the stooges of totalitarian evil, just will not do, since there are villains of sorts on both sides of this barricade. The same Nolde whom the Nazis lumped together with other artists allegedly representing a putative "cultural bolshevism," corrupting liberalism, and Jewish art market had himself long espoused a virulent cultural nationalism, was "exceptional in his racism," and articulated notions of regional authenticity arguably homologous to the "blood and soil" tenets of German fascist aesthetics. Protesting the inclusion of his works in the Exhibition of Degenerate Art, Nolde wrote to the Minister of Propaganda, Joseph Goebbels, with the patriotic plea that "my art is German, strong, austere and sincere."[4]

None of this historical information, of course, amounts to conclusive evidence for a judgment on Nolde's oeuvre or for a determination of the substance of a fascist aesthetic. One would certainly not want to proceed by accepting the Nazi position and then simply reversing it, i.e., by arguing that because the Nazis opposed Nolde, his work ergo displays an anti-Nazi substance. One would thereby not only surrender any autonomous critical capacity but also end up with unacceptable results in the cases of figures appropriated by the fascist regime; Nazi celebration of Dürer, Goethe, or Shakespeare tells us nothing about the aesthetic character of the works. Consider also the case of the author Oskar Maria Graf, whose writings, presumably owing to their peasant coloration, were not consigned to the flames of the book burnings in May of 1933 but who, on the basis of his own leftist sympathies, issued a public protest of his exclusion. Similarly, Nolde's protest that his works were included in the Munich exhibit has the status of any artist's self-judgment: it may have historical or biographical interest, but it is by no means binding for a serious aesthetic-theoretical consideration. In short, the Nazi condemnations exculpate Nolde as little as do his entreaties condemn him.

Similar caution is called for in the face of claims found in the highly politicized larger aesthetic discussion of the thirties. One could point to Georg Lukács, during his most socialist realist period, arguing that expressionism represented an artistic corollary to fascism, a judgment which the Communist obviously meant to be a denunciation.[5] On the other hand, a minority position within the German fascist camp briefly tried to claim expressionism positively as the genuine artform of the Nazi revolution.[6] Yet these claims and counterclaims by no means cancel each other out. It would be very wrong to conclude that the plethora of incompatible political judgments on the same set of aesthetic objects, and on Nolde's work in particular, indicates that the relationship of politics to art is ultimately arbitrary and that art, therefore, basically stands outside of politics. For one is still faced with the magnetic attraction this art exercised on the political imagination, as well as the frequently volatile political character of the self-understanding of early-twentieth-century artists and writers. To understand this connection, the attraction, repulsion, and resonance between Nolde's expressionism and German fascism, one must first renounce any simple solution, forego the security of tendentious judgments, and presume that the political substance of a serious work of art is likely to be ambiguous and multivalent. With this methodological caveat in mind—particularly crucial given the sensationalism of the topic—one can turn to the specific construction of the artistic practice.

For the sake of this argument, I want to focus on Nolde's primitivism, rather than on some other, perhaps equally constitutive element, such as his personal reclusiveness, his predilection for religious topics, or his use of color. For both the distance from and proximity to the fascist discourse on art are particularly prominent with regard to the issue of primitivism, a term which refers simultaneously to his exoticist interest in artifacts displayed in ethnographic museums, his cultural critique of modern civilization, and the ramifications of his journey to the South Seas in 1913–14 on a mission sponsored by the imperial German colonial ministry. Most obviously, it was the integration of stylistic features apparently borrowed from encounters with non-European culture that set him at odds with a fascist aesthetic compulsively concerned with European supremacy and racial purity. Writing in the *Völkische Beobachter* on July 7, 1933, the chief ideologue Alfred Rosenberg insisted that a

> definitive ideal of beauty has ruled the artists of Nordic origin. This powerful and natural ideal is nowhere more beautiful than in Hellas, but it prevails as well in Palma Vecchio, Giorgione and Botticelli, who painted decidedly Gretchen-like figures. This ideal appears in Holbein as it does in the image of Gudrun and Goethe's Dorothea. It rules the face of Pericles and the Rider of Bamberg.

Against the background of this Western tradition, Rosenberg turns to Nolde (and to Karl Barlach); he at first concedes that "both artists undoubtedly display an explicit talent, a seascape by Nolde in the Kronprinzenpalais, for example, is strong and weighty. Yet," he continues, "next to it are a few attempts at portraits: negroid, impious, raw, and lacking any genuine inner power."[7]

That Rosenberg was willing to put forward a minimally nuanced judgment is indicative of the fact that the internal fascist debate on expressionism had not yet been resolved. Therefore Nolde, the regionalist painter of the maritime German north was treated as acceptable, but the modernist Nolde who, like other expressionists as well as the cubists—think of Picasso's *Demoiselles d'Avignon*—integrated a non-European iconography into his portraiture was condemned. For he stood beyond the pale of a racial aesthetic uniting Greek antiquity, the German Middle Ages, and the Italian Renaissance. His primitivism evidently amounted to a proscribed aesthetic miscegenation. It is paradoxical, but not wholly unexpected, that one can find Nolde himself elsewhere effectively concurring with a similar cultural racism, although tempered by more relativism than Rosenberg might have allowed:

In the long run, no race may be better or worse than another—all are equal before God—but they are different, very different, in their stage of development, their life, their customs, form, smell, and color, in all their internal characteristics, and it is not at all the intent of nature that they should mix. . . . Some people, and especially those who are already mixed, have a burning wish that everything—people, art, cultures—be mixed, whereby the human community of the earth would end up consisting of mixtures, bastards, and mulattoes. Of people with impure faces and negative characteristics. Some places in the tropics are frightening examples of complete race mixing. The sweetness of sin is unconscientious. There is a striving for self-corruption.[8]

If this first version of primitivism entails direct appropriations of iconographic elements from non-European settings, a practice which both Rosenberg and Nolde programmatically condemn (even though Rosenberg accuses Nolde of engaging in it), a second, more sophisticated version evaluates the primitive positively as a more powerful and authentic vehicle of expressive representation. Now it is Nolde himself who is cast as the primitive, the prototype of a young, German art, counterposed to an increasingly established and tame impressionism of French, which is to say excessively civilized, provenance. Commenting on his break with the Berlin Secession in 1910 when his *Pfingsten* was rejected, one of his strongest proponents, Max Sauerlandt, contrasted Nolde's style with that of Max Slevogt: "While Slevogt's color plays the role of a means for an individualizing characterization and has become a vehicle for an illusionist depiction of reality in the idealizing sense of an impressionistic naturalism, Nolde's color has grown into a pure form of expression for emotional values, a 'hieroglyphics of sentiment.'"[9] The terms of Sauerlandt's prose set Slevogt as the paradigm of a post-Renaissance—and in this sense "modern"—artist, exemplifying the metaphysics of a means/ends rationality, the subjectivity of bourgeois individuality, illusionist aesthetics, and the determinist materialism of an external, sensory perception. In contrast, Nolde is posed as both postmodern and more original; he goes beyond the logic of bourgeois culture by retrieving the archaic expressivity of a nonsubjective language of hieroglyphs.

This substantive primitivism transcends the obsolete representational aesthetics of the nineteenth century by returning to an origin of emotion, instinct, and power. Moreover it is this constitutive primitivism that both precedes and explains Nolde's interest in Oceanic art:

> The by no means ironic modern artist took these exotic grotesques, the artful masks of the South Seas, so seriously and was so profoundly moved by them because of the mystical power of sentiment that led to a stylistic heightening of expression far beyond any banal depiction of reality. He found here an essential stylistic element of his own art in a most naive and penetrating version. Like the anonymous carvers of the South Seas, he recognized that the mimic expression of the gesture or the facial features, when most intense, has something purely grotesque and is internally related to the rigor of a mask.[10]

Consequently Nolde's relation to the non-European material is by no means a matter of borrowing or "mixing," which—Sauerlandt was writing in 1933—might be denounced within the terms of fascist racism. On the contrary, Nolde, presented as the radical alternative to French cultural hegemony and the terms of liberal-bourgeois culture, discovers or rediscovers the terms of his own aesthetic in the antimimetic art of the islanders. Perhaps Sauerlandt was tilting his argument in order to make Nolde palatable to the new rulers; in any case, primitivism here ceases to be a geographical import inimical to European identity and instead turns out to be congruent with the German nationalist rejection of the impressionist canon, the fascist critique of civilization, and the Nietzschean call for a new barbarism.

An additional, third dimension of Nolde's primitivism might be considered a combination of the other two, the encounter with the non-European world as a central component in the demolition of the terms of nineteenth-century liberalism. Yet where the Nazis denounced a putative influence of Oceanic or African art in racial terms, what is at stake now is the legacy of colonialism. European expansionism was always an internally contradictory project; while it drew its legitimation from an ideology of a civilizing mission, narratives of progress, and a "white man's burden" imagined to be a vehicle of benign improvement, the real experience of the colonizers faced with the overt or covert resistance of the colonized populations entailed practices of violence, domination, and inhumanity antithetical to the sometimes sanguine intentions and illusions with which they had set out. Whatever colonialism's impact may have been on its victims, the process of victimizing also transformed the colonists, rendering increasingly implausible the terms of bourgeois liberalism. In other words, in the wake of colonial violence, the ideals inherited from the Enlightenment and the French Revolution grew more and more intangible; thus Hannah Arendt could argue that the brutality of the colonial administrations served as a proving ground for the inhumanity of the totalitarian regimes—fascism as colonialism come home.

The nexus of colonial politics and primitivist aesthetics is further complicated by a two-stage process of mediation. Modern artists, cubists and expressionists alike, first discovered works of non-European art in the metropolitan centers, especially, if not exclusively, in the various ethnographic museums that had been founded during the final third of the nineteenth century. Colonial artifacts were displayed as specimens of anthropological interest, and one can trace how painters like Nolde struggled to transform them from objects of a scientific scrutinization into sources of artistic innovation. When Nolde asks, "why are Indian, Chinese, and Javanese art still classified under science and anthropology?" a certain solidarity with the colonized cultures is evident, insofar as he ascribes to them an otherwise denied capacity for genuine aesthetic representation. Yet this anticolonial gesture turns out to be part of a dubious political agenda, a revaluation of the primitive as an alternative to a European civilization allegedly too rational, egalitarian, and feminized: "In the original, primitive state, it is not women and children who have a playful, ornamental desire but rather strong, manly men. . . . "[11] Here and elsewhere, Nolde defends the primitive art of the colonies as a vehicle with which to carry out an agenda of antiliberalism in order to rediscover the primitive in Europe, where "manly men," rather than women or, presumably, effeminate impressionists, ought to be celebrated as the genuine creators of art.

Yet the anthropological collections themselves were not only displays, scientific or artistic; they were also institutions firmly rooted in the larger process of colonial expansionism, with all the violence that entailed. Therefore the artistic appropriation of primitive art, even if framed by an anticolonial and antiprogressivist gesture, was presumably implicated in some way in the colonial practices of domination. In Nolde's case, that complicity can be traced through a second stage in the reception of non-European artistic forms. After the initial encounter with ethnographic material around the beginning of the second decade of the century (when he completed his paintings with the most explicitly exotic topics), he subsequently undertook a journey through Russia and the Far East to the German Pacific colonies. That the journey was sponsored by the colonial ministry as part of an effort to research the cause of the declining birthrate in the colonies—understood as an economic threat to the viability of the colonies—only makes more emphatic the connection between the politics of expansionism and primitivist aesthetics.

Facing colonialism, Nolde is horrified by its brutality (even though he patriotically reserves the strongest criticism for Germany's colonial competitors). Yet he also accepts colonialism and its destruction of the indigenous cultures as an inevitable fate, thereby subverting the possibility of an effective anticolonial critique: " 'The law of the strong' is a natural law, just like for animals and plants—this is the only comfort, if it is comfort at all, for us humans with our societies to protect animals, our humanist doctrines, and our Christian faith of love."[12] The reality of colonialism is proof enough that humanism—and all the other illusions of the European nineteenth century—are pointless. Thus armed with an oppositional stance that declares itself helpless, the melancholy colonist easily slips into his preordained role: "Each of us was given a 'boy.' Young brown natives, Tulie and Matam, were ours."[13]

For all of Nolde's counterposing primitive authenticity to civilizational veneer, for all of his explicit attacks on colonial practices, he participates in them with no apparent discomfort: not only in his prose or his behavior as a traveler, but in the construction of the scene of painting itself. "When painting the natives became difficult, we showed the picture of the Kaiser of Germany and said, 'This big fellow Kaiser wants to see what you look like and that's why you are being painted.' "[14] Other strategies were available too:

> I had my watercolors and painted; some of them soon noticed; others, frankly, did not. Near me lay my revolver with the safety off, and behind me stood my wife, covering my back with hers, also cocked. I have never worked in such a tense situation, but everything before my eyes was so beautiful, so splendid. As [we reembarked and] the ship once more started across the flat sea, the pages went from hand to hand and gave us so much joy.[15]

As Nolde grows into the role of the colonist, his primitivist expressionism reveals itself to be an aestheticization of colonialism, transfiguring domination into a source of pleasure and an aesthetic justification of exploitation. Painting is implicated in what Renato Rosaldo has called imperialist nostalgia; Nolde prides himself on his contributions to the expedition while simultaneously regretting its results.[16] In the end, his solidarity with the victims of colonialism is displaced by a stronger solidarity with the agents of colonialism, even at the price of moving close to the sort of scientific rationality he condemned in the ethnographic museums:

> During my childhood years I had heard and read about Stanley and Livingstone, and I was later very interested in the adventurous polar journey of

Fridtjof Nansen and the expeditions of his friend Knud Rasmussen too. I believed to have also contributed to genuine research with my many works, perhaps just a little when compared with the great scientific travelers, but something special and almost opposite. My vision had been "artistic" and alive, not "scientific" and photographic, like so much before. And such primitive types [*Urtypen*], as in my drawings of the natives of New Guinea, probably no longer exist. In our economically active, but modern civilizing age, everything original and essential disappears, never to return. Where are enclaves of primitive soil being preserved, with their people, their animals, their plants in an untouched primitive state, for the benefit of anthropology in the coming centuries or millennia? Few have the foresight to think of the human community [*Gemeinschaft*], nearly everyone thinks only about one's little, proper "me."[17]

Evidence like this pushes us toward a rather hypotactic argument: Nolde's painting derives centrally from a complex discourse of primitivism, which is a function of colonialism, which in turn is a crucial stage in the prehistory of fascism. Indeed one might reorder the linkage more polemically by suggesting that the cultural ramifications of colonialism are transformed through the aesthetic practices of some wings of European modernism and thereby made available to the fascist hegemonies in the wake of the First World War. Yet even if one were able to prove conclusively the individual claims within the larger concatenation, and despite the seductively compelling character of the full argument, it remains more suggestive than convincing: because of its generalizing abstraction and because of the many counterexamples, where primitivism is located on trajectories toward nonfascist or antifascist positions, e.g., Carl Einstein's interest in African art or, for that matter, Picasso as the painter of *Guernica*. If colonialism was the necessary precondition or, better, context of primitivism, primitivism contained too many multivalent potentials to be regarded as a self-evident term in a fascist aesthetic. If Nolde's primitivism fades into his fascism, it evidently has to do with the specific character of his primitivism, and a closer look is in order. For unless that specificity is clarified, the whole inquiry could be disqualified by the objection that Nolde's political affiliation remained thoroughly external to his artistic achievements.

Reexamining the last quoted statement, where Nolde puts himself in a line with Stanley and Livingstone, one cannot help but be struck by the tension between Nolde's insistence on the difference between his own "artistic" and other "scientific" undertakings and, paradoxically, his inability to name that artistic difference. On the contrary, art, like science, is engaged in a project of preservation and collection, driven perhaps by a heroic resistance to the march of progress (which Nolde accepts as inevitable). But it remains a collection of objects that appear to have no validity except that they are otherwise disappearing; and that imminence of disappearing is probably the definition of the primitive. Because of a catastrophic historical vision—modernization will soon eradicate all authenticity—Nolde imagines himself at the penultimate moment, and the ensuing urgency forces him to rescue the material through depiction of the *Urtypen*. Thus, for all of Nolde's expressed contempt for the illusionist fictions of impressionism and naturalism, his painting always remains figurative. His reception of primitive art never leads to the formal abstraction of the cubists, nor does his expressionism take the decidedly allegorical turn characteristic of Beckmann. The primitive material remains primarily a matter of topicality: figurative representation of primitive objects.

Yet the objects are after all always primitive archetypes, never individuated subjects. Note how his professed admiration for the scientific and artistic project of collection finally flips over into a mysticism of community, counterposed to the egoism of individuality. Nolde's project seems stretched between the objects of collection and transcendent values, between reification and religion, with no intermediate dimension of formal rationality, secular sociability, or subjective practice. The islanders of his portraits are trapped in an ethnographic present where no change is possible. They are profoundly expressive but never active or nuanced, and, one is tempted to argue, the same erasure of history, the same proscription on innovation—formal or thematic—characterizes his paintings of noncolonial topics as well. This structure explains the power and the ambiguous politics of his oeuvre. The simultaneity of radical objectification, compulsive preservation of the figure, and overarching religiosity reproduces the amplification of commodity fetishism into the aesthetics of fascism: the meaningless world of sensory data forced, as it were, into meaning by a charismatic prophecy. Yet even if that prophecy remains unmediated and therefore becomes terroristic, the promise of redemption can still draw on utopian values; hence the expressive beauty of the renditions.

The point then is not at all to suggest that Nolde's paintings ought to be treated as tendentious vehicles of a fascist message; Nolde may have believed that was the case in his letter to Goebbels, but he was evidently wrong. The whole question of fascist aesthetics has to be posed in a more interesting way. To be sure, there were cases of crude propaganda, and the border between propaganda and serious aesthetic works may at times be blurred, but for Nolde's work what is at stake is not the intentional meaning but a structural homology between his expressionist paradigm and the cultural ideological character of German fascism.

In *La peinture française (1905–1914) et "l'art negre,"* Jean Laude cogently presents the by now standard account of a basic difference between the French and German reception of primitive art. For the Parisian cubists, so the argument goes, African masks suggested new solutions to aesthetic problems and contributed to a rationalization of form within the emergence of modern art; for the German expressionists, on the other hand, non-European material was of interest as a topic marked as authentic, religious, and redemptive, documentation of a cultural alternative to a desiccated modernity. Overstated in this fashion, the dichotomy ignores a good deal: expressive values in cubism, formal innovation within expressionism, and counter examples within each camp. The account depends moreover on familiar clichés regarding French rationality and German irrationalism.[18]

Nevertheless, for some of the German expressionists, and perhaps most emphatically for Nolde, the association of primitivism and irrationalism did hold, as described by Carl Einstein:

> Geographical exoticism may have depended a bit on the expansive imperialism of the prewar era, but it also entailed a protest against excessive sophistication, derisively pointing out its opponent's alexandrianism. The more the biological basis, the breadth of human existence, expanded, the more important did the primitive become, who had preserved forgotten links and stages of human behavior. For the European yearning for past times and distant places, the primitive cultures became the frequently abused means to expand history backwards. This tendency also grew out of the struggle against the rational enlightenment; reason was regarded as only a final tip, resting on the predominant forces of dream, instinct, and emotion; among the primitives one could still find mythical cultures, the hierarchy of the instincts oppressed in Europe, the tyranny of dream and ecstatic ritual.[19]

Einstein himself tended toward an account much closer to that of the cubists, i.e., a rational appropriation of the innovative aesthetic models evident in African and Oceanic art. Still his characterization of the expressionist stance is not only a critical caricature. On the contrary, it foregrounds the internally contradictory character of Noldean primitivism: simultaneously an emancipatory search for a greater range of experience and a regressive flight from the Enlightenment, leading to a desire for "hierarchy" and "tyranny."

These two components in expressionistic primitivism—the dynamic expansion of expressivity and a search for a static order—indicate how, in Nolde's particular case, modern aesthetics could take a right turn and end up with considerable fascist sympathy. For National Socialism could be misunderstood as a path out of a stultifying modernity and back to an authentic culture of genuine experience, i.e., the search for a primitive alternative to modern culture which had led Nolde to New Guinea might have appeared to come to a conclusion when Germany was redefined as the locus of the better primitives, and Nolde was clearly eager to participate in this illusion. It was moreover an illusion that had a long history and considerable currency; one finds it in the young

Paul de Man's readings of Ernst Jünger (representing mythical Germany versus a rational and psychological France), just as it remains the structuring aspect in Laude's differentiation between expressionism and cubism.[20] In the latter case, ironically, the attack on expressionist irrationalism, clearly made with the best of political intentions, falls into the trap of adopting the cardinal point of the right-wing agenda: Germany as the bulwark of the anti-Enlightenment and the counterrevolution.

To make this simple equation on the political level (Germany as the locus of irrationalism) or on the aesthetic level (German expressionism as mystical, regressive, or irrational) is a grave error that obscures the complexities of the real situations. For early-twentieth-century Germany was a modern society, just as German expressionism was part and parcel of modern European art. The point is not German irrationality, political or aesthetic, but rather that the ideological assertion of this German specificity was (and apparently remains) a crucial component of the German and European cultural and political discourse. Irrationality as a refusal of knowledge or an intentional restriction of cognitive capacity is necessarily regressive and a retreat from the best of the Enlightenment legacy, the admonition to use one's mind: *aude sapere*. In this sense, fascism was indeed irrational, for example in its restrictive policy on aesthetic experience which is itself a form of knowledge. Yet the critique of reason that is driven by a genuine discontent with characteristics of modern society—alienated labor, the loss of community, the domination of nature—can hardly be denounced as fascist. On the contrary, that agenda is central to an Enlightenment that can scrutinize itself critically, a self-reflective Enlightenment. The internal contradictions of fascism included the ideological mobilization of these discontents and their simultaneous repression, insofar as fascist policy entailed both a flaunted irrational antimodernism and an aggressively forced modernization. Nolde found himself trapped in this dialectic: the German primitivist enamored with the illusion of a primitive Germany. That fascist Germany was not a return to primitive origins indicates the false consciousness inherent in his political solution. If his artistic solution, historically, was not untouched by that political context, it has a more important ramification as well. For the authenticity of his works depends on an expressive value and experiential authenticity, categories which shed a critical light on the modern world and goals that remain a sine qua non of an emancipated society.

Chapter 7

A Solidarity of Repression
Pabst and the Proletariat

The lesson of Nolde's vicissitudes in Nazi Germany involves the limits of intentionality: the painter's desire to identify with the fascist state was unable to influence the state's rejection of the painter. A similar disjunction operates in the case of Pabst's *Kameradschaft* (1931), one of the most explicitly political films of the late Weimar Republic. For the ostensibly leftist celebration of proletarian solidarity betrays, under scrutiny, a much more ambivalent agenda. True, the final sequence of the film seems to demonstrate unambiguously the establishment of the solidarity promised by the title. The last of the German mine workers, who volunteered to rescue their French comrades trapped in an underground disaster, return to the border after the successful conclusion of the operation. The thronging mass that greets them is in a festive mood, explained by a French worker who leaps onto a platform and, framed by the French and German flags, delivers a rousing speech proclaiming proletarian unity, pacifism, and internationalism. With appropriate symmetry, the German worker who initiated the rescue movement, Wittkopp (Ernst Busch), responds with a parallel address in German: workers are the same everywhere—"Kumpel ist Kumpel"—and will refuse to be pushed into war; even if "the people on top" are caught in disputes, the miners have learned the importance of solidarity and *Kameradschaft*.

Yet despite the uplifting assertions of an international working-class community of interest, what appears to be unambiguously conclusive at the end of the film is in fact open to some considerable doubt. An epilogue (which is missing in the versions generally available in the United States) shows German and French guards in the mine shaft reconstructing the border barrier that had been broken through during the rescue efforts. Several explanations for the omission of this sequence have been offered, ranging from the "derisive howls and hisses from audiences" when it was first screened in Berlin, to objections from German censors. According to Siegfried Kracauer, Pabst intended the coda as a critique of nationalism, but it was misunderstood as an attack on the Treaty of Versailles (as the document which established the postwar boundaries) and therefore very much part of the nationalist agenda.[1]

Whatever the significance of this sequence and its excision, the ideals announced in the double speeches are in fact undermined by more than the epilogue's fiction of a reerected fence. As the epigraph proudly asserts, *Kameradschaft* is "founded on fact," in particular on the factual past of the mine disaster at Courrières in 1906, when German workers did indeed rush to the aid of the trapped French miners. While maintaining a camera style designed to evoke the realist authenticity of a documentary, Pabst shifts the event to the postwar era and to Lorraine—the border runs right through the mine—in order better to stage the issue of national divisions and working-class internationalism. The film is consequently able to produce the message of the final speeches and their optimistic ring. Yet that message rings hollow, as soon as the source of the ostensibly documentary material is taken into account: if the solidarity of 1906 could not prevent 1914, why should the viewer in 1931 trust an unreflected repetition of that solidarity to prevent a new war?[2] Therefore the ambiguity of *Kameradschaft* is by no means dependent on a subversive epilogue, missing or not, but is rather a consequence of the historical construction of the foregrounded message of solidarity. The concluding ideals turn out to have little plausibility on their own merit, which is to say that *Kameradschaft* has less value as a vehicle of internationalism than as evidence with which to study the failure of internationalisms and the weakness of working-class solidarity on the eve of National Socialism.

In fact, the very manner with which the film attempts to assert its message of solidarity turns out to demonstrate its instability. The lengthy encounter in the mines, so profoundly intense, intimate, and, as will be discussed in a moment, full of sexual and mythic undertones, is seemingly summed up in two sloganeering speeches, as if the public language of political leaders were adequate to articulate a collective identity or a socialist hegemony.[3] The concluding sequence enacts, one might say, a linguistic turn in the much richer analysis carried out by the text, privileging the speech of the cadre over both the preceding material experience, the substance of the extended narrative, and the concrete multiplicity of the assembled workers. Yet speech, to which the film ascribes the power to assert the identity of comradeship, turns out to be inadequate, as Wittkopp is forced to announce at the commencement of his address: "What the French comrade said, I could not understand; what he meant, we could all understand." Thus even in the context of this political speech, which announces the self-evident socialist message of the film, speech itself is presented as insufficient and relegated to a secondary status vis-à-vis a more effective mode of expression—*meinen* rather than *sagen*—and the construction of the collective is thereby shifted from rational communication into an irrational domain of opinion and a nonverbal semiosis.

This contradiction—Wittkopp's speech insisting on the limits of speech—obviously undermines the plausibility of the solidarity which is the central message of his own speech, i.e., Pabst's proletarian community is stillborn. To the extent that this failure has to do with the structure of language and, in particular, the hierarchical relationship between cadre and collective, the final sequence of *Kameradschaft* could well be contrasted with another document of Franco-German peacemaking, the Strassburg Oath of 842; in the latter case, both the Carolingian leaders and their military followers participate in speech, producing presumably a more complex network of loyalties and collective identities. In contrast, the modern film silences the collectives and permits only the leaders to speak. By presenting two separate speeches, one in French and one in German, it effectively reproduces the national division that the speakers themselves want to deny.

However, the ambiguity of politics in *Kameradschaft* and the failure of Pabst's ideals are not solely a result of this distorted communicative structure at the end of the film. From its very outset, the film presents a critique of nationalism that never thoroughly measures up to the values of pacifism and socialism that are so urgently underscored. *Kameradschaft* begins with a game between two boys, one German and one French; the opening shot shows a marble rolling across the ground. Through a montage of editing, the boys, who quickly begin to quarrel, are set in relation to tensions between France and Germany along the border in the context of the growing German unemployment. The point of the gaming commencement is, however, not simply that adults are behaving like children but, more important, the suggestion that the wrong game is being played since the aleatory moment of free play, the rolling marble, has been displaced by an inappropriate game of agonistic embattlement.

The gaming that follows in the film is exclusively agonistic: the muted class struggle between workers and management; the heroic struggle with nature; and, especially, the reminiscence of the wartime struggle in the single flashback of the movie. Even aspects of the celebrated solidarity are tied closely to images of combat: the procession of the German rescuers leaving their town recalls soldiers leaving for war, they have to smash through the border and survive a volley of shots, and when they arrive at the gates of the French mine they are initially mistaken for troops. The images of comity depend ultimately on an iconography of enmity, since the body of the film presents no alternative to a confrontational agonistics, i.e., the struggle with the national enemy—which is ostensibly rejected—is preserved in the militarization of the vocabulary of solidarity and is displaced into another terrain of struggle: interestingly, less the struggle with another class than the struggle to master a threatening nature.

None of these permutations returns to the utopian moment of aleatory play with which the film opened, the rolling marble; nothing has retracted the fall into agonistics, and the film's initial problem, the need to return to a nonrepressive *homo ludens*, is never solved.[4] Clearly the solidarity envisioned by the film is not a solution, since it is very much implicated in processes of struggle and mastery, despite the rosy rhetoric of the concluding speeches. Given this discrepancy between the end of the cinematic text with its message of socialist harmony and the opening assertion of an ontology of struggle and repression, it is crucial to pay close attention to the nature of the social bonds represented in the course of the film and not only to the terms of the social contract announced at its conclusion. Is the comradeship of *Kameradschaft* a matter less of a pacifist internationalism than a comradeship-in-arms of men conquering nature? What are the grounds for the collective identity of the workers? If it is true that the proletariat has no fatherland and, as Wittkopp puts it, all the workers are the same—"Kumpel ist Kumpel"—then one has to ask what force holds the community of comrades together.

A likely answer is some considerable homosocial attraction: the decision to launch the rescue expedition is made as part of a spectacular shower room sequence replete with glistening nude male bodies, and a fight with a delirious French miner (who has succumbed to the haunting memories of the war) concludes when the victorious German affectionately strokes the cheek of his now unconscious and prostrate opponent. Yet more important than these examples of an ostensible male eroticism, extensive evidence points to the exclusion of women as a crucial aspect of the construction of the male collective.[5]

The point is not that there are no women working in the mines (that, presumably, is a moment of verisimilitude in the film) but that both the German and French miners, all men, are constructed as groups from whom women have been emphatically separated. Phrased another way, the separation which has been caused by women can be healed only when the women are separated away and the men come together in the dark, deep inside the earth. The origin of this problematic is the dance-hall scene which follows immediately on the initial exposition. Three German miners enter the music-filled *Kursaal* on the French side of the border. The film cuts to an attractive young couple, Emile and Françoise, dancing with obvious affection for each other. When one of the Germans asks her for a dance, she refuses, which is taken for a nationalist affront, and a melee is only narrowly avoided when the German withdraws from the woman.

This separation of a male collective from a female sphere is repeated on the French side as well. On their way home, the couple overhears an engineer commenting on the fire in the mine; Françoise insists that Emile give up his job, and when he refuses, she decides to leave. The following morning, we see Emile enter the mine, and Françoise departs on a train just as the disaster strikes. By now, however, a network of sexual imagery has become apparent: Emile chooses the fire in the phallic mine shaft over Françoise's female sexuality, just as the three Germans retreat from Françoise into the conviviality of an infantile eroticism (one of his companions pleads with the rejected suitor to "leave the women alone and come back to the rabbit," a reference to the pet they have inexplicably brought with them: an indication of both childishness and genital renunciation, since the alternative to the woman is the genderless neuter of the *Kaninchen*). Furthermore Françoise's path back to the mining town is marked first by her abandonment of her suitcase—a sign perhaps of her renunciation of an independent life but certainly for Freud a standard symbol of female genitalia.[6] This latter association is confirmed by the fact that Françoise proceeds back to the mine by taking a ride with a nun, an incontrovertible indication of the denial of female sexuality.

The underlying sexual economy turns out to be one in which male solidarity is produced in response to a threat by women (the encounter in the dance hall) and is preserved through the negation and subordination of women (Emile prefers the mine to Françoise). Precisely this logic is played out outside the gates of the mine. In the belief that the mine management has prematurely given up the search for the buried workers, the crowd, composed mainly of women and led by Françoise, tries to storm the gates. Françoise is in the front of the surging mass and is shot in a slightly elevated position, calling to those behind her, not unlike the famous iconography of the figure of the revolutionary *Liberté*. Yet just at this moment of radical confrontation, the German rescue company arrives with all its military demeanor. This unexpected turn of events quiets the crowd and bewilders Françoise, who can only mutter, "Les Allemands, c'est pas possible."

Even the moment of rescue, therefore, is constructed through the ostentatious displacement of women: instead of the radical crowd led by the female allegory of liberty, the heroic role is reserved for the uniformed German volunteers, fresh from the showers. The price of the male bonding turns out to be a simultaneous displacement of a radical alternative—the impassioned crowd led by Françoise—by a more disciplined and hierarchical group. Excluded from the male discipline of the socialist organization, the anarchic energy of the unruly mass presumably could eventually be occupied by antisocialist, especially fascist movements that more effectively articulated values of spontaneity and a populist antipatriarchy.[7] It follows then that the apparent shallowness of the ideals of *Kameradschaft* and the weakness of working-class solidarity had to do with the implicit misogyny in the symbolism and political practice of the working-class movement. To the extent that the collective of proletarian solidarity was de facto a matter of male bonding, it could not be a radical one. On the contrary, this reading of the film should show how, despite the rhetoric of socialist revolution, such male bonding was implicated in an establishmentarian defense of the status quo from a putative female threat—the threat at the borders, the imminence of separation and castration—and the need to sublate the wound in the healing collective of a male whole.

These sexual politics of the community are explored in the overriding iconographic concern: the construction of identity through the establishment of division and the anxiety over an impending disruption of the border. At the outset, the borders are of course treated as evidence of unnecessary enmity and belligerence: the border drawn between the two children or blocking the passage of the unemployed workers. These images are obviously fully compatible with the message of internationalism illustrated by the German miners' breaking through the underground wall marking the 1919 border. Yet the miners are not the only force to break through walls: the catastrophe first appears as the eruption of a flaming explosion tearing through the brick containment wall and setting off the collapse of the sides of a mine shaft. Masses of stones, flooding water, and impenetrable smoke pour into various frames, obscuring the images of the figures and threatening their lives. So despite the different evaluations of a positive socialist internationalism and a murderously brute force of nature, both appear on the screen as the activity of masses challenging borders. *Kameradschaft*'s judgment of the mass is therefore intriguingly ambivalent. Proletarian solidarity is applauded as an alternative to the divisiveness of national borders, but the homologous power of the elements, breaking down the divisions erected by technology, is portrayed as the ultimate danger.

The radical crowd storming the gates of the mine can arguably be associated with a position of class struggle: the enemy is the owner or, at least, the manager. The genuine lesson of the film, however, is a different one: workers of the world unite, not in a struggle with the bourgeoisie but in a struggle to control nature. The ambivalent portrayals of the sublime mass—never-ending solidarity and the infinite elements—are resolved to the extent that the film sets the two against each other: proletarian solidarity of the masses overcoming the threat of the masses of the elements. The pacifist theme provides an excuse to redirect an initial aggression pointed at a foreign enemy (across the national border) toward nature in the form of technological mastery.

Yet this redirection of aggression is also an introversion; the mass (of workers) is turned against the mass (of nature), and one is forced to ask to what extent it is in effect turned against itself. Is the conquest of nature, which the film portrays as a struggle with external nature, in fact a displacement of a repression of an internal nature? *Kameradschaft* explores the viability of mechanisms to control the masses, who appear in their full spontaneity at the moment of catastrophe. As the train carrying Françoise pulls out of the station, the alarm whistle sounds at the mine, and suddenly, in a series of shots, the otherwise placid pedestrians of the city break into a frantic run. This sudden transformation is the genuine crisis of the film: the crowd is born, perhaps the only convincing echo of the aleatory chaos of the game of marbles, and the film suggests several competing analyses of this origin—the moment of terror that disrupts the petit bourgeois routine of everyday life as well as the undeniable concern and compassion for the endangered workers.

However, one shot in particular is crucial, showing the panicked crowd rushing off but reflected in a store window displaying a series of indistinguishable caps. If there is a radical moment in *Kameradschaft*, this is it, although it is not the moral intended by Pabst. The shot sets up a relationship between, on the one hand, a commodified culture—the exhibition of wares—whose ultimate product, however, is the spectacle, the reflection in the window, and, on the other, the emergence of the crowd. Yet this crowd of consumers, *flaneurs*, and dislocated individuals has the propensity to explode in the spontaneous combustion of a Luxemburgian anarchy, culminating in the riot at the mine gate.[8] This radical threat to the society of commodities is averted by the discipline of a male socialism that arrives in the nick of time to save the capitalist organization. Proletarian solidarity appears to be a version of crowd control. The mass is turned against the mass, and this self-negation unfolds in two different ways: the sequences within the mine, representing an effort to master nature, are both a metaphor for the repression of the masses outside the gates and a displacement of the control of an internal nature necessary for the establishment of the promised comradeship.

While the displacement of the radical crowd is an important indication of the political underbelly of socialist solidarity, the film ultimately places greater emphasis on the second trajectory of self-negation, the instinctual archeology of the male bond. The workers conquer nature and thereby conquer themselves. This dialectic of technological progress is staged in a primitive setting, with man pitted against elementary forces of fire and water gushing through elongated shafts. *Kameradschaft* therefore seems to display some remarkable similarity with Freud's reading of the myth of Prometheus. Both explore the libidinal economy of technology, and both pose the problem in terms of male collectives mastering fire (both, by the way, are works of 1931). Most important, however, is the shared recognition of a homoerotic or homosocial foundation for the technological community of men.

Freud begins his comments on the myth with a consideration of the hollow stick in which Prometheus transports the fire; he interprets it as a penis symbol with reference to the oneiric rhetoric of inversion: "What a man harbours in his penis-tube is not fire. On the contrary, it is the means of *quenching* fire; it is the water of his stream of urine." By associating fire furthermore with the heat of erotic desire, Freud can suggest "that to primal man the attempt to quench fire with his own water had the meaning of a pleasurable struggle with another phallus."[9] The elementary ambivalence of fire and water is clearly present in the iconography of the catastrophe in *Kameradschaft*: both push through the shaft, presumably a threatening resurgence of libidinal energy which it is the labor of the film to master in the interest of civilization and technological progress.

As for Freud, the film too suggests that this progress requires a reorganization of homoeroticism, i.e., a renunciation of the pleasurable play with another phallus and the consequent establishment of a homosocial community: the handclasp of the German and French rescuers in the darkness of the mine. Simultaneously this male community of self-repression can itself function as a mechanism of repression vis-à-vis the threat of the female crowd. Yet in Freud's reading the myth also preserves a knowledge of the costs of progress and the suffering caused by repression: Prometheus' deed is a crime for which he is punished, that is, the crime against nature inherent in any denial of libido. On this point, the film diverges markedly: the conquest of nature, internal and external, is presented as unambiguously positive, and suffering is relegated to a past characterized as lacking adequate control. This refusal to identify and critique the experience of repression means that, for all its progressive self-presentation, *Kameradschaft* boils down to a lesson in discipline and self-control. This conservative apology for civilizational repression belies the socialist aspirations of the film's conclusion and is an important symptom of the sort of weakness that prevented the working-class movement from mounting a plausible response to the challenge of an antirationalist fascism.

The negativity that adheres to the Promethean myth, which insists on the criminal and even blasphemous character of progress, is preserved in classical psychoanalysis as the notion of a necessary discontent in civilization. Historical development has been paid for with an enormously painful repression and instinctual denial: in particular, Freud discusses the sublimation of homoeroticism in the taming of fire as the initiation of technology.[10] That same process of libidinal repression is staged in *Kameradschaft* which, however, refuses to treat repression as an object of criticism. Instead repression, denial, discipline, and technological progress are celebrated and presented as unambiguously positive. One consequence of this affirmative stance is the extraordinarily timid character of the political message, a strangely meek socialism without class struggle, as if the excessive repression of nature robbed the movement of any real spunk.

A second consequence is the importance of technology, which overshadows any vestigial romanticism of the worker as producer, and the crucial technology for *Kameradschaft* is ultimately the film itself. The anxiety about borders which the film thematizes is no doubt a consequence of the relatively new use of the moving camera, which was so central to Pabst's exploration of a realist cinema. Despite the considerable editing and montage in the film, innovative camera movement contributed to a redefinition of the frame of the shot, and, as Noel Carroll has commented, "The feeling engendered is that the cameraman is pursuing an unstaged action, shifting his point of view as the event develops. . . . Throughout the film, camera movement has the look of following the action rather than delimiting it." [11] This spontaneity and movement, however, like the obliteration of the borders within the film, set off a crisis: the organization of space has gone out of control, and in both cases, the formal construction of the film and the content of its narrative, the answer to the crisis is technological progress, in particular the technology of the sound film.

Sound, and not proletarian solidarity, is arguably the real hero of *Kameradschaft*. The sound of the factory whistle calls the workers, and the alarm siren announces the disaster. Pabst uses sound to indicate explosions taking place elsewhere than in a particular shot, and Françoise and Emile can overhear, without seeing, a conversation regarding the underground fire. More important, certainly, is the role of sound in the rescue operation, when a stranded French miner attracts the attention of a German volunteer by banging on a metal pipe with his wrench. Finally the intended message of the film is presented in the concluding oratorical performances of the double speeches.

The central role of sound—in 1931 still very much a new technology—is in fact announced in the film itself in a way that indicates its complicity in the network of sexual politics and repression. Renouncing her plans for independence, Françoise rushes back to the site of the mine disaster by hitching a ride with a nun; the imagery of sexual denial has already been mentioned. When asked if she has a relative in the mine, Françoise replies, "my brother," then pauses, and adds, "son ami," his friend, i.e., not her own friend or lover, but her brother's colleague. This reply is compatible with the analysis of the construction of the homoerotic collective. Yet the pause in the middle of the phrase draws attention to another ambiguity: the ambiguity not of the relationship but of the phoneme itself, which can be taken either as a possessive adjective or as an independent noun, in which case "son, ami" turns into "sound, friend." In this version, then, Françoise's cryptic answer identifies the mine less as the locus of male solidarity than as the site of an innovation having to do with the technological reproduction of acoustic phenomena.

This account might well appear plausible if one keeps in mind the uses of sound already enumerated. It turns out to be irresistible if one reexamines the final rescue episode, which can be treated as the climax of the film. The three Germans from the dance-hall sequence did not join the rescue crew, but instead set off on their own to dig their way through from the German side of the mine to the French side, where they eventually end up trapped together with two French men, a young miner and his grandfather. Finding their escape route blocked, they give up all hope, and one of the Germans comments, "Well, we'll take the electric tram to heaven," at which point a telephone rings; earlier shots have indicated that a telephone operator in the mine office has been trying to determine if and where anyone was still caught below, i.e., the five remaining victims have literally been saved by the bell or, in other words, by friend sound, the electric tram to heaven.

Friend sound, "son, ami," is electrically reproduced sound, itself the technological innovation of *Kameradschaft* as well as the result of the technological progress which *Kameradschaft* records: the control of fire. Although the film refuses to explore the dialectic inherent in the mastery of nature, it does in fact draw attention to alternative appropriations of technology. The telephone, which is the actual agent of rescue, has already made a number of appearances in the film: forced to allow his employees to set off on their rescue expedition, the manager of the German mine rings up his French opposite number and suggests that he deserves credit for what was in fact an act of spontaneous solidarity; and when the German workers crash across the French border, the border guards call ahead. That is, in the two earlier cases, the telephone, as a cipher of the new technology of acoustic reproduction, is deeply involved in the structures of control and domination, while in the final sequence it works as a tool of emancipation.

This investigation of the technologically most advanced means of communication is located within a historical theory of the media. Like many texts of the Weimar period, *Kameradschaft* suggests that a culture of verbal literacy—individual reading in a bourgeois private sphere—belongs to an increasingly distant past. The metaphor for such anachronistic reading, indeed the only text genuinely "read" in the course of the film, is a poster on the wall outside of the dance hall; in addition, a thermometer embedded in a containment wall is read just before the explosion occurs. The location of reading on exterior walls is indicative of the dissolution of traditional bourgeois notions of privacy (a development underscored by the single shot of a domestic interior in the center of which one sees the gaping speaker of a victrola for the reproduction of sound). The insistence on the writing on the wall is moreover evidence of the proximity of an impending catastrophe, since *Kameradschaft* is so much about the tumbling down of walls and, therefore, the obsolescence of an older media culture.

The catastrophe is the explosion of the masses: the masses of commodities in the shop window, the masses of the crowd, and the masses of a threatening nature. *Kameradschaft* describes an inadequate response by tracing the journey of the grandfather who sneaks into the mine and searches on his own for his beloved grandson. With little equipment, he signifies a technologically backward mode of operation; with his tiny lamp in the cavernous darkness, all he can do is light up the imagery, take shots, so to speak, but his abilities, a metaphor for the silent film, prove insufficient for the task at hand. Only with the successful and collective repression of nature, the conquest of fire, and its metamorphosis into the electricity of the telephone can the project of retrieval be completed.

The success of that project and the recognition of the potentially progressive use of technology do not fully obscure the simultaneous regressive potential, i.e., the manipulative use of the new technology. Nevertheless *Kameradschaft*, with its unbroken historical optimism, indisputably emphasizes the positive developments, just as it fully conceals the pain and suffering of the *via dolorosa* of progress. As an analysis of a profound restructuring of the organization of the media, it therefore too naively insists on the beneficial role of the electric reproduction of sound. The telephone as a tram to heaven does not only anticipate the role of sound in subsequent cinematic realism, including Pabst's own; it also prefigures the use of sound in propaganda and the function of the radio in National Socialist Germany. *Kameradschaft*, like much of the contemporary workers' movement, fails to understand that a solidarity based on repression cannot be progressive and that technology as a blind domination of nature is bound to prevent solidarity.

Chapter 8

The Masses and Margarita

Faust at the Movies

A recent study of Faust films includes more than forty entries, and even this surprisingly long list is incomplete. The most obvious examples are literary films, cinematic adaptations of canonic plays and novels: *Faust*, directed by Peter Gorski and Gustaf Gründgens, based on Goethe's play (1950); *Doctor Faustus*, directed by Nevill Coghill and Richard Burton, who stars with Elizabeth Taylor in a version of Marlowe's drama (1967); and Aleksander Petrovic's treatment of Bulgakov's novel, *The Master and Margarita* (1973). Others retell the Faust story in contemporary settings: *L'homme qui vendit son âme* by Jean-Paul Paulin (1943) and John Farrow's *Alias Nick Beal* with Ray Milland as the Devil (1949). Still others focus on the central female figure, like Claude Autant-Lara's *Marguerite de la nuit* (1955), or transform Faust into a woman: *Faustina* by Jose Luis Saenz de Heredia (1958); *Faustina* by Luigi Magni (1968); and *Faustine et le bel été* by Nina Companeez (1975).[1]

Interestingly nearly half of the recorded Faust films were produced before the First World War during the earliest period of cinematic history. The Lumière catalogue of 1897 lists a *Faust* by Georges Hatot which lasted little more than a minute and included two shots: the appearance of Mephistopheles and the transformation of Faust with the image of Gretchen. The first Méliès version, *Le cabinet de Méphistophélès*, was made in the same year, and three more followed by 1904. Clearly the Faust material fascinated the first generation of filmmakers and has continued to attract the attention of directors ever since.

In "The Work of Art in the Age of Mechanical Reproduction," Benjamin remarks how Faust films necessarily surrender the literary-historical specificity that adheres to even the worst performances on stage.[2] This loss of aura, however, sheds light on the character of the cinematic process as well as on the ramifications of the Faust theme. Three issues are especially crucial: mass culture and the masses, whose role Benjamin underscores; the role of Margarita or the representation of women in narrative cinema; and the aesthetic specificity of the movies, the wish-filled illusions, which is set in relation to the diabolical power to produce images. I want to discuss these issues in five Faust films, each of which transforms the material both in terms of its own historical context and within the institutionalization of commercial mass culture.

After his successes with *Nosferatu* in 1922 and *Der letzte Mann* (*The Last Laugh*) in 1924, Friedrich Murnau had considerably less luck with *Faust: eine deutsche Volkssage* in 1926. On the eve of his move to Hollywood, the project, which, as the subtitle indicates, was understood as a cinematic rendering of the German national epic, turned into a financial flop, grossing only half of its two million mark production costs. Conservative critics, who measured the film against its literary models, resented the eclectic mixture of elements from the sixteenth-century chapbook and Goethe's drama. Others, like Herbert Ihering, pointed to the insipid performance of Gösta Ekman in the title role, upstaged by Emil Jannings as Mephisto and Camilla Horn as Gretchen (a role initially planned for Lilian Gish). In this atmosphere of critical hostility, the Prussian Interior Ministry was able to declare the film unfit for minors in 1927, a strange echo of an earlier conservative antipathy for Goethe's alleged immorality.[3]

Murnau's *Faust* found a somewhat warmer reception abroad but there too a negative tone prevailed. A critic for the *National Board of Review Magazine* bemoaned that "we find ourselves descending from the masculine version of Marlowe and the philosophical concept of Goethe to the level of the libretto which inspired Gounod to write his opera." Siegfried Kracauer, who cites this remark in *From Caligari to Hitler*, concurs and continues,

> *Faust* was not so much a cultural monument as a monumental display of artifices capitalizing on the prestige of national culture. The obsolete theatrical poses to which the actors resorted betrayed the falsity of the whole. . . . The Germans of the time did not take to Faustian problems, and moreover resented any interference with their traditional notions of the classics.[4]

Without adopting these critical judgments, one can recognize them as evidence of the early reception history, in which two allegations predominate: a feminization of the Faust material, and the triviality of cinematic renditions contrasted with traditional high culture. These claims are based on broad sexual political and cultural conservative assumptions, which could serve as evidence for a general cultural history of the period. However, they also indicate features of the cinematic culture industry during the twenties and of Murnau's film in particular.

The accusation of a feminized Faust is not adequately explained by pointing to the unequal performances of Ekman and Horn. Consider instead the structure of the narrative: the initial prologue, in which the battle between good and evil is announced; the medieval city, beset by Mephisto's plague that forces Faust to sign the fateful pact; the brief erotic episode with the Duchess of Parma; and finally the lengthy vicissitudes of love played out between Faust and Gretchen. After the first three sections, which, no matter how richly detailed, amount to fragmentary vignettes, it is through the Gretchen material that the film develops suspense and cohesion, and the victimized female lover is indisputably the center of attention. In this sense, Murnau's *Faust* is no exception: commercial narrative cinema generally involves a love story which, as feminist critics like Laura Mulvey and Teresa de Lauretis argue, demands the sacrifice of the woman.[5] When Faust goes to the movies, Gretchen comes to the fore, if only to go up in flames.

This shift in the sexual economy of the narrative, resulting in the relative dwindling of the Faust figure, is compounded by an additional factor. Three years after the era of astronomical inflation and the profound political crises that nearly toppled the Weimar Republic, the first German democracy had achieved a relative stability. Murnau presents his *Faust* as a German *Volkssage*, a legend of the people, and while it is hardly a democratic *Faust*, it is definitely a *Faust* of the *demos*. Excluding for a moment the dialogue between Satan and the heavenly forces at the beginning and end of the film, one notes that the popular masses frame the film and define the action: the crowds at the fair, the victims of the plague, the throngs at the Easter mass, and the irate populace, outraged by Gretchen's crimes, swarming forward to watch her burn at the stake. The mass culture industry mobilizes the masses in representation in order to march them in reality past the ticket counter. Poor Faust, the individual, is nearly forgotten. Instead of attributing his willingness to enter the diabolic pact to his singular crisis of faith or knowledge, as in earlier accounts, Murnau's version ascribes priority to the needs of the people suffering from the scourge of the plague, while Faust's decision assumes a secondary, derivative status. It is almost as if sovereignty derived from the people, but the democratization of the culture industry remains inauthentic insofar as ultimate authority is located in the metaphysical debate and celestial power, Murnau's popular counterpart to the fundamental ontology of his philosophical contemporaries.

The ideological context of the Weimar Republic explains why Murnau could try to sell his film by foregrounding the masses, which in turn erodes the centrality of the Faust figure, one of his critics' major complaints. Their other complaint, the negligible quality of the cinema when compared with the Goethean legacy, also strikes right to the heart of the legitimation problem of the film industry. Murnau's film itself incorporates the tension between a high culture of verbal literacy and a popular culture of visual imagery. The simple masses at the fair are entertained by acrobats and a shadow theater, while the isolated scholar Faust, looking like an Old Testament patriarch, is surrounded by books and words. When he is overcome by despair, he casts his books into the fire, forsaking the word of God. Mephisto, characteristically, approves of this transition, when he later asserts that Faust's earlier life had been only "Bücherstaub und Moder," the dust of books and mold. In place of verbality, Mephisto offers illusions, the deceptive imagery of youth, wealth, and eros, and he can generate these images thanks to his control over fire, the power of light, the same force that produced the initial shadow theater.

Faust succumbs to Mephisto because he rejects books, and he is saved at the end by love, designated as "the one word," an obvious reference to Luther's "ein Wörtlein." Mephisto can enact compelling visual images, but they are always deceptive. This line of argument suggests that the message has to do with the victory of the divine word over the sensuous illusions of diabolical pleasure, a plausible if unoriginal homily. Yet that is indeed a strange message for a film, and especially a silent film, that depends so centrally on the montage of images. But perhaps it had strategic value: when conservative critics attacked the film by referring to traditional high culture, they were already caught in the logic of the film, which denounced images in the name of books. Mephisto, as the master of illusions, is Murnau's cinematic principle, which, however, always subverts itself, since Murnau, as director, never questions the priority of the word. The culture industry attempts to legitimate itself by pledging allegiance to the same high culture it opposes: clearly a case of Mephistophelean legerdemain.

This self-critique of the film medium is thematized in the double courtship between Faust and Gretchen and between Mephisto and Marthe. The affairs are initiated in similar manners. Mephisto hides a box in Gretchen's dresser, and he carries another one with him to Marthe. Each metaphoric camera obscura contains a chain on which the illusions of love are spun, a constellation of images repeated in the chains of children and the chains of flowers. When Gretchen counts petals to determine Faust's love, Mephisto acts out a parodic inversion, plucking at a sunflower, in order to play with Marthe's fantasies and, implicitly, to reveal the hopelessness of Gretchen's dreams. Yet his own machinations sparked those dreams; it is his mise-en-scène that stages the delusions. In Murnau's cinematic Faust, Mephisto's prestidigitation becomes a self-critique of the magic of the silver screen.

After his death in the role of Valentin in Murnau's film, Wilhelm Dieterle turns up in Hollywood in 1941 as the director of *All That Money Can Buy*, also known as *Here Is a Man* and, more generally, as *Daniel and the Devil*, based on Stephen Vincent Benét's story, *The Devil and Daniel Webster*, published in 1937. The history of American Faust films begins with Edison's *Faust and Marguerite* of 1900 and includes at least one *Faust* in 1909, a film of Gounod's opera in 1910, a parody of Gounod, entitled *Bill Bumper's Bargain*, in 1911, and *Faust and the Lily* in 1913. Charles Hackett's 1929 *Faust* drew on Gounod's music and treated the hero as a businessman, and for the Goethe centennial in 1932 Howard Higgins presented a twenty-minute educational film, *Walpurgis Night*.[6] Interestingly, this tradition is much longer and more varied than the German lineage, which does not begin until 1926 with Murnau, unless one counts the integration of certain Faustian elements in *Der Student von Prag* of 1913, remade in 1926 and 1935.

Dieterle's film borrows from the American tradition by maintaining a humorous tone and, in the wake of Higgins, by using the Faust material to examine the business ethics of capitalism. On both these points he follows his literary model closely; in fact Benét, who had already transformed his story into a play, collaborated on the script. In the original version, Jabez Stone, a poor New Hampshire farmer, is constantly beset by bad luck. When he cries out that enough is enough and offers to sell his soul to the devil, a stranger shows up and a contract is signed, replete with the obligatory spot of blood and the seven-year term. Jabez prospers, of course, but as the due date of the mortgage draws near, he begins to worry and appeals to the popular hero Daniel Webster, who, as an accomplished rhetorician and skilled lawyer, agrees to represent the worried farmer.

But the devil, Mr. Scratch, has an ironclad contract, and Webster is forced to leave civil law and torts behind him and invoke constitutional grounds: "Mr. Stone is an American citizen, and no American citizen may be forced into the service of a foreign prince. We fought England for that in '12 and we'll fight all hell for it again." Scratch can counter, however, that no one has a better right to American citizenship than he himself: "When the first wrong was done to the first Indian, I was there. When the first slaver put out for the Congo, I stood on her deck." Faced with this state of affairs, Webster calls for a trial by jury. Scratch quickly complies and conjures up quite a hellish crew: "there was Walter Butler, the loyalist, who spread fire and horror through the Mohawk Valley in the times of the Revolution; and there was Simon Girty, the renegade, who saw white men burned at the stake and whooped with the Indians to see them burn. . . . There was Teach, the bloody pirate, with his black beard curling on his breast." And so on—the judge, Justice Hathorne, presided at the Salem witch trials.[7]

Things look bad for Daniel and worse for Jabez Stone, but Webster's words work wonders. Beginning with descriptions of simple human experiences, he goes on to talk of American history and its promise, and then of Stone as an example of a man who has had bad luck and made a wrong choice but now wants to change. He convinces the jury, which acquits Stone, and Webster can banish Scratch.

Although Dieterle's version follows this plot line closely, different sorts of changes are evident. Some have to do with the specificity of the film medium.

For example, the populist language of the story disappears—there is no voiceover narration—but a similar effect is achieved through a plethora of shots displaying the details of rural life: farm animals, wagon wheels, a barn dance, and the like. This cinematic realism is compounded by an expressionist use of lighting, evidence of Dieterle's training with Murnau. In the opening shot, Webster sits at his desk, while behind him, a giant shadow of the devil looms ominously, whispering: "Don't write that speech." In addition, the visual potential of the film allows for the direct representation of supernatural phenomena, generally omitted in the story: Scratch can suddenly appear out of nothing, bags of gold coins can pop out of the ground, and ghostlike visitors besiege Jabez.

A more significant change involves the age of the farmer; in the story he is an older man, while the film presents him in his mid-twenties. This transformation may seem curious because it prevents the devil from granting his victim youth, the cinematic representation of which had worked so well for Murnau. However, given the character of the culture industry, the change from Benét's senior citizen to Dieterle's young man is crucial, since it makes room for three female roles grouped around Jabez: his mother, played by Jane Darwell, remembered for her remarkable performance as the matriarch in *Grapes of Wrath*, his wife, Mary, and the maid Belle, a demonic temptress who provides Jabez with Faustian pleasure while introducing discord into the Stone household. Only the wife is mentioned in the story (and she remains nameless there); the other two women are cinematic innovations. As with Murnau's *Faust*, it appears that the cinematic appropriation of the narrative leads to a feminization of the material.

More generally, Dieterle transforms Benét's terse legend through the addition of background details, minor figures, and subplots. The initial story simply recounted the origins of the pact, Stone's despair, and Webster's plea to the jury. The film traces the character of Stone's affluence: his sudden wealth, his success at farming, his growing importance in the village, and his increasingly luxurious life-style. This expansion was undoubtedly necessary to magnify the short story into a feature-length film. It also conforms to an additional imperative of the commercial cinema, the possibility of audience identification. Benét's story of an exemplary case employed distancing with a didactic intent, reminiscent of Benjamin's comments on epic narration. The film invites an empathetic reception from its first title: "This is a story they tell in New Hampshire, but it could happen anywhere. Yes, it could even happen to you."

Yet the major consequence of the integration of the new material involves the political substance of the film. The story vaguely invokes a progressive American tradition. It designates the treatment of Indians and the slave trade as evil, while invoking as a normative ideal the inalienable right to the pursuit of happiness, the grounds on which Stone is acquitted. References to Webster's political horizon—his antagonist John C. Calhoun, the Missouri Compromise, and the impending threat of the Civil War—are never fleshed out and ultimately only provide local color. Dieterle maintains the historical setting, even dating it specifically as the period 1840–47, but his treatment of the Faust material clearly displays the tensions in progressive American politics on the eve of the Second World War.

While the individual Jabez Stone is as unlucky in the film as he was in the story, Dieterle transforms his financial crisis into a typical case of rural life during the Depression. All the farmers are impoverished; all suffer from loan sharks and the banks. Mary and Stone's neighbors repeatedly implore him to join the grange, but after concluding his deal with Scratch, he insists that he will "take care of himself" and separates himself from community solidarity. As he grows increasingly wealthy, the other farmers become his debtors and, later, his wage laborers. When Mary begs Webster for help, she describes how her husband turns the poor away from their door, despite his own past. As Jabez pursues an upward social mobility, he loses all his initial rural social virtues.

In Benét's story, Webster's politics remain unclear, despite loose references to antebellum debates. In contrast, Dieterle makes him an explicit opponent of the banks and an advocate of the debtor farmers. This characterization of Webster as a New Deal reformer runs throughout the film and culminates in the speech to the jury. Because its members were greedy, Webster asserts, they believed in Scratch and lost their freedom. Jabez did so too, but he has recognized his error. Every man has a right to rebel against his fate, and Stone therefore deserves another a chance. Webster concludes with a ringing exhortation: "You can't be on his [Scratch's] side, the side of the oppressor. Don't let this country go to the Devil. Free Jabez Stone." Dieterle turns the struggle for Faust's soul into a political trial with social implications. For the Devil represents the principle of unfettered capitalist accumulation, the law of contracts, which the liberal Webster wants to modify, if not abolish. The line from the story regarding Stone's American citizenship is expanded in the film to include Webster's apodictic assertion: "A man is not a piece of property." The rhetoric of the politician articulates the objective goals of the populist grange, which Jabez joins at the conclusion of the film.

Dieterle's Webster may be a Roosevelt reformist, but the historical problem of American populism is its proximity to nativism. The film treads a thin line here. The coins which Scratch kicks up out of the ground are described as "Hessian gold," lost by an ambushed convoy on its way to Saratoga during the Revolutionary War. Is lucre thereby associated with counterrevolutionary forces, the mercenary soldiers whose origin is described parenthetically in Schiller's *Intrigue and Love?* Or is the designation of wealth as "Hessian" an attempt to mobilize anti-German sentiment in 1941? A similar semiotic ambivalence recurs in the case of the devilish lady, Belle, who speaks with a French accent but who describes her home simply as "over the mountain," or later, as "I am not anything."

Both story and film are thick with Americana, and the emigré director has included signs of foreignness that may be negatively charged. Recall, by the way, how Murnau treated his *Faust* as a specifically German legend and how his hero, after the erotic vacation in Parma, yearns to return to his *Heimat*. The question of national identity is inherent in the Faust material, while presenting a specific problem for progressive politics, especially at the historical juncture where the New Deal is about to become the war effort. Dieterle may not have an answer, but he at least poses the question in a clever way. The story ends with Scratch's exile. The film ends with Scratch, sitting on a fence, pondering where next to ensnare a gullible soul. He looks to the left and to the right and then straight forward. As the camera zooms in for a close-up shot, he points his finger at the viewer and grins. He is of course the ever-present Devil, waiting for the spectator, as indicated at the outset of the film. Yet with his hat, scruffy beard, bushy eyebrows, and the pointed finger, the resemblance to the Uncle Sam of recruitment and war bonds posters is unmistakable. Or is the military Uncle Sam the mechanism with which the Devil will put an end to Webster's reformism? For Dieterle, cinematic representation simultaneously critiques and reproduces a vernacular American iconography. The ambiguous signification is indicative of the political paradoxes of 1941.

Both *Faust: eine deutsche Volkssage* and *Daniel and the Devil* locate the Faustian hero within a social collective. After the experiences of the Second World War, this characteristically modernist faith in community loses its credibility, and cinematic renditions of Faust turn to explorations of individual autonomy. This transition reflects the privatization of public culture in the consumer society of advanced capitalism as well as the growing intellectualization of the cinema, due in part to the competition with the new mass medium, television. An early example of this neo-individualist Faust is provided by René Clair's *La beauté du diable* of 1949, where the masses appear only briefly as a threat and the heroic scientist insists on severing his ties to the state. Against the background of contemporary existentialism, Clair uses the Faust material to demonstrate an irreducible human freedom and the priority of immediate experience over conceptual knowledge.

Attempting to emancipate the narrative from religion and metaphysics, Clair shifts attention away from the consequences of the pact and toward the initial duel between a rationalist Faust and Mephisto. The Gretchen material consequently loses importance and becomes little more than a plotty embellishment. An aging professor in a small Italian principality in the seventeenth century,

Henri Faust is besieged by the "second-class demon," who cannot convince him to relinquish his soul. In order to accelerate the negotiations, Mephisto rejuvenates Faust, while himself taking on Faust's old body. Henri learns about the long-forsaken pleasures of life and continues to resist Mephisto's entreaties. Inspired by his master, Lucifer, Mephisto sets out on a new course: he grants Henri fame and success, attributing to him the alchemistic discovery of a method to transform sand into gold. The court adores him, the Princess loves him, and Henri exclaims: "I'm the happiest man in the world."[8] At this point Mephisto whisks him away; believing all his happiness was an illusion, Henri signs the pact on the understanding that he will regain what was lost. But it was never lost; Mephisto has succeeded on the basis of a ruse.

Although all his wishes are granted, Henri grows melancholy and insists that Mephisto show him the future. In images conjured up in a mirror, he sees his undying love for the Princess rapidly giving way to other amorous affairs; his political leadership leads to war; and the scientific progress in which he places so much faith ends in mass destruction. He commands Mephisto to undo all he has done; in the ensuing crisis, Mephisto tries to ensnare Marguerite, the innocent gypsy girl who loves Henri, by showing her the pact with Faust's signature. She grabs it and throws it to the angry mob that responds by chasing Mephisto—remember, he has exchanged bodies with Faust—who must jump to his death from a window, a victim of mistaken identity. As the film ends, a gypsy caravan moves off through an idyllic countryside, and one can only assume that Henri and Marguerite will live happily ever after.

In an afterword to the screenplay, Clair explains that Henri's exclamation, "It's never too late," sums up the message of the play: an emphatically human "refusal to accept the yoke of destiny."[9] Although the scientist has spent decades in ascetic self-denial, the rejuvenation permits him to rediscover the joys of physical existence. Unlike Murnau in the Parma episode or Dieterle with the temptress Belle, who both present sensuality negatively as diabolical pleasure, Clair treats the physical experience of sense certainty as an authentic reality superior to all abstract claims. Because the world is perpetually open and indeterminate, no material necessity compels Faust to enter the pact. On the contrary, Mephisto must deceive him at the turning point in the plot with the assertion that the world is a place of suffering and joy only imaginary, and precisely that claim turns out to be mendacious. For Clair existence precedes essence and no necessity binds human creativity. Accidentality is therefore an ever-present grace, and the illogical defeat of Mephisto and Faust's salvation make sense precisely as nonsense or aleatory play.

The Heisenbergian critique of determinacy is articulated specifically by the rejuvenated Faust as a denunciation of institutionalized science:

> Plato used to close men inside a cavern in order to explain to them the secrets of the earth . . . Later . . . the astronomer Newton flew off among the stars

to explain to men the secrets of the sky. Well, the philosopher and the astronomer were wrong. It's a third sage who is telling you. I, Henri! Because there is only one secret to know. It's the secret of youth! It's the secret of happiness. It's the secret of joy. It will be revealed to you inside. Come in, ladies and gentlemen![10]

Attacking science and idealist philosophy in the name of experiential immediacy, Henri stands in front of the gypsies' circus tent, suggesting that aesthetic representation too provides an alternative to deterministic knowledge and the authoritarian state. That aesthetic dimension certainly includes the cinema as well, the medium which Clair employs in order to elaborate his critique of a system of domination based on an alliance between government and the universities. In a film made four years after the attacks on Hiroshima and Nagasaki, the most vivid accounts of the destructive potential in scientific progress are consequently found in the cinemorphic images provided by Mephisto when Faust inquires into the future. Like Murnau, Clair uses the diabolical production of illusions as a metaphor for his own medium of representation.

Multifold contradictions beset Clair's oeuvre. The director insists on the rationality of an irreligious Faust but denigrates philosophical reason. He scorns the Gretchen material but preserves Marguerite for the conclusion. He attacks Newtonian mechanics from the advanced standpoint of indeterminacy but constructs a plot organized in terms of the conservation of matter: for Faust to grow young, Mephisto must become old; sand turned into gold must return to its original state; everything must be paid for; and all supernatural elements in the tradition are reduced to a clumsy realism. A mythic eternal return of the same coexists with a faith in freedom raised to the level of dogma. The political passions of the previous decades have receded, and the privatized consumer retreats into the creativity of a world of do-it-yourself accumulation. The postwar Faust renounces the Faustian projects of universal emancipation, but his postmodern quietism cannot disempower a hellish objectivity simply by denying it.

Clair's secularization of the Faust story continues in Louis Pauwels' *President Faust* of 1974. Because of the hero's atheism, the Devil, whose classical proposal makes no sense, complains, "Now it's up to me to convince men that they have a soul before I can seize it. You just have to do everything yourself. God has abandoned me." A ruthless industrialist, President Henry Faust is locked in combat with Boucard, a left-wing leader. Marguerite and Valentin are Boucard's children. Faust advocates unlimited technological modernization, while Boucard insists on social welfare and organizes strikes. A scientific invention promises a utopian reduction of oil dependency. Although Faust initially opposes utilization of the discovery, he falls in love with Marguerite who tempers his avarice and teaches him humanity. He breaks up his monopoly and concludes by telling the disappointed Devil that he has no desire but to become "un homme parmi les hommes," as he disappears into the crowd.[11]

Against the background of the energy crisis, the spread of environmental-
ism, and an increasing hostility toward traditional models of economic growth,
Pauwels emphasizes the problematic character of Faustian progress. In contrast to Clair's private escapism, however, his rendition at least touches on some
possible political and economic reforms. The theological component has all
but disappeared, and Marguerite, the traditional vehicle of grace, operates as
a metaphor for human love rather than as a catalyst for divine intervention.
Freedom depends on a dismantling of hypertrophic political, economic, and
scientific structures. Moreover, Pauwels thematizes the debilitating effects of
the culture industry; the Devil's dwelling is full of television sets. The mass
media thoroughly control the conditioned reflexes of the manipulated viewer.
With its episodic structure, *President Faust* attempts to counteract this reception process by underscoring the necessity of choice and creativity. [12]

The examination of the culture industry and aesthetic representation in Faustian terms, evident in the works of Murnau, Dieterle, Clair, and Pauwels, occu-
pies the thematic center of Istvan Szabo's film *Mephisto* (1981), based on Klaus
Mann's 1936 novel of the same name. As in the case of *Daniel and the Devil*,
the film follows its literary referent closely but also makes extensive changes.
It is always crucial to examine such changes, but not in order to determine
whether a film accurately adapts the prior text; the notion of accuracy is here
methodologically untenable. The terms of the transformation can, however,
tell us something about the alternative media and the differing concepts of
author and director.

The novel begins in 1936 with a festive celebration of the Nazi elite, in which
the actor Hendrik Höfgen plays a central role. The subsequent narrative begins
by returning to the early years of the Weimar Republic and proceeds to trace
the rise of Höfgen's career, i.e., his personal history constitutes the main concern of the novel, a roman-à-clef in which Mann attacks his former colleague,
Gustaf Gründgens, for collaborating in the Third Reich. While Szabo cannot
omit the Gründgens material, his film redirects attention to another issue. The
party, with which the novel commences, is transported to its appropriate chronological place near the end of the cinematic narrative. Instead the film opens
with an aesthetic spectacle, an operatic performance in the Hamburg Arts Theater during the twenties. The film cuts to a dressing room where Höfgen is
crying. In the novel, the corollary performance is described as a "successful
middle-brow drama," and the actor's tears are shed because of an unrequited
love. [13] By reorganizing this material, Szabo foregrounds the triviality of the
traditional theater and suggests that Höfgen's despair refers to the low quality
of the stage. In place of Mann's opportunist careerist, Szabo presents the actor
as an aesthetic innovator, anxious to modernize the theater, no matter what
the cost. This Faustian pursuit of progress leads him to his success as Mephisto
and his alliance with the diabolical powers of the state.

The differing perspectives of novel and film become particularly evident in the alternative treatments of Höfgen's aesthetic leftism during the Weimar Republic. In the novel, he promises to join a revolutionary theater project but constantly postpones actual participation. When he finally does appear on stage, he merely utters a pro forma declaration of solidarity. The narrator quickly points out the perfunctory character of this engagement: "The day is approaching. That blazing conviction drives [the fascist and communist activists] Hans Miklas and Otto Ulrichs forward, consuming them and millions of other young people. But for what day is Hendrik Höfgen waiting? He never waits for anything but a new part."[14] In contrast, the film shows Höfgen as actor and director attempting to institute a new aesthetic practice grounded in left-wing thought; in a passionate speech he calls for a "total theater" for the working class, described in terms reminiscent of Brecht.

Disappointed by Gründgens' collaboration, Mann presents a vacillating Höfgen ready to sacrifice all political integrity. In 1936 the author wishes the actor had been as much of a leftist as he had once promised. In 1981 Szabo has a very different position, intimately tied to the postwar Eastern European experience. He not only distrusts any politicization of art, which apparently always threatens to lead to totalitarian results. He also scrutinizes the manner in which the aesthetic avant-garde easily mobilized revolutionary political ideologies in order to demolish traditional modes of aesthetic representation—the operatic performance at the opening of the film, which the avant-gardist Gründgens so detests. Therefore Szabo himself presents a traditional narrative film, a standard period piece, concerned with the dangers of aesthetic modernism.

Consider also the alternative conclusions. Mann confronts Höfgen with a mysterious revolutionary emissary, the harbinger of a better day. Needless to say, that figure is absent in the film. More important, the two versions culminate in radically divergent treatments of *Hamlet*. In Mann's account, fascist aesthetics push Höfgen to Shakespeare as a purportedly Aryan genius, and the Danish prince represents Nordic profundity and the exigency of action. At the close of the film, the Goering figure drags the actor in the middle of the night to the Olympic stadium and, blinding him with a spotlight, calls out his name again and again. Höfgen is the Hamlet who has no identity and can no longer act, because, in the course of aesthetic modernization, he has destroyed all substantive values and traditional legitimacy. He is Faust, Mephisto, and Philemon and Baucis all at the same time.

The hostility to the aesthetic avant-garde ends up close to a neoconservative nostalgia for traditional art and bourgeois individualism. Yet Szabo fails to comprehend how individualism initially emerges as a protest against a reified traditionalism, Höfgen's Faustian despair, even if the erosion of that tradition also undermines the possibility of subjectivity. This dialectic of individuation runs like a red thread through all Faust films, cinematic narratives of the autonomous subject in the age of a culture industry that produces the collective mass of consumerist recipients. "The work of art in the age of mechanical repro- duction," Benjamin's optimistic circumlocution for the capitalist moderniza- tion of culture, promises stories of individuals—Faust is a case in point—in order to prevent them. It is almost as if the notion of Faust films were always a contradiction in terms. But the immanently contradictory character of aes- thetic representation is the esoteric trace of contradictions present in society: "Am farbigen Abglanz haben wir das Leben."

Chapter 9

The Rhetoric of Citation and the Ideology of War in Heinrich Böll's Short Fiction

It is useful to treat some literary texts as if they were constructed as elaborations on a single figure of speech.[1] In a similar vein, other texts invite readings that focus on citations or familiar quotations that occupy positions of greater or lesser prominence in them. If standard critical practice relegates quoted material to a secondary status as a passing allusion or a vehicle to characterize individual fictional figures, an alternative approach might judge the citation to be of genuinely central importance and consequently evaluate the full text, in which the citation is embedded, as a sort of commentary on the citation.

It is of course most tempting to test this critical hypothesis, with its presumption of some considerable rhetorical sophistication, in the case of texts that appear to be least self-conscious with regard to their formal construction. Early short stories by Heinrich Böll provide particularly useful examples. Generally read as naively realistic, both "Wanderer, kommst du nach Spa . . . " ("Stranger, Bear Word to the Spartans We . . . ", 1950) and "Als der Krieg ausbrach" ("When the War began", 1961) operate with citations: the former with a classical epitaph in the title, the latter with a verse from a popular song mentioned in the body of the text. By scrutinizing these operations, one not only achieves a more complex understanding of Böll's subject matter, the experience of war, but also comes to recognize that rhetorical and ideology-critical approaches, commonly treated as alternative interpretive strategies, are far from incompatible.

The Epitaphic Moment and National Identity

The poet Simonides provided the laconic epitaph for the Greek dead at Thermopylae: "Against three hundred tens of thousands once fought here / Four thousands from out of the Peloponnese." This verse and the narrative presented by Herodotus in the seventh book of his *Histories* invoke a supraregional national identity that subsumes the local loyalties of the city-states "from out of the Peloponnese"; Leonidas commands not only the Spartans but the armies of Thebes and Thespia as well in order to hold off the countless forces of Xerxes. Simultaneously a supranational Western identity is asserted, for it is Greece as Europe that opposes Persia as Asia in a conflict in which individuality and law confront an evil empire of multitude and might. Thus the poet reserves special praise for the Spartans: "O stranger, bring tidings to the Lacedaemonians / That we lie here obedient to their decrees." W. L. Bowles heightens the rhetorical impact by offering a rhymed translation: "Go tell the Spartans, thou who passest by, / That here, obedient to their laws, we lie." Ruskin is reported to have said that the epitaph belongs among "the noblest groups of words uttered by man." The familiar German rendering is found in Schiller's "Der Spaziergang" of 1795: "Wanderer, kommst du nach Sparta, verkündige dorten, du habest / Uns hier liegen gesehn, wie das Gesetz es befahl."[2] Because Böll's appropriation of the verse constitutes a criticism of its privileged cultural-historical status, it is important first to ponder the specificity of Schiller's modern transformation of the ancient verse. Wandering through nature, the poet contemplates the city below (an elevated perspective foreign to Herodotus) and marvels at its industry and commerce and at the military strength mobilized in their interest: "Fernen Inseln des Meers sandtet ihr Sitten und Kunst, / [. . .] Helden stürzten zum Kampf [. . .]" ("To distant islands of the sea you sent culture and art, / . . . heroes leapt into battle . . . "). The army has a material purpose, the protection of economic prosperity, and this goal can be realized only in victory. Schiller consequently introduces the epitaph with the lines: "Ehre ward euch und Sieg, doch der Ruhm nur kehrte zurücke / Eurer Taten Verdienst meldet der rührende Stein" ("Honor was yours and victory, but only glory returned, / the stone tells with spirit of your valorous deeds"). The eighteenth-century historian knows very well that the battle of 480 B. C., to which Simonides' epitaph in the subsequent verses refer, was hardly a victory for the Greeks, but the logic of the poem forces him to pass off the defeat at Thermopylae as a *Sieg*. He imputes a teleology to battle, an inherent goal orientation within practice, that aims at—and this is the interesting point—not freedom but wealth and property: "Ruhet sanft, ihr Beliebten! Von eurem Blute begossen / Grünet der Ölbaum, es keimt lustig die köstlich Saat. / Munter entbrennt, des Eigentums froh, das freie Gewerbe . . . " ("Rest softly, you loved ones! Wet with your blood / The olive tree grows and precious seed sprouts joyously. / Free industry, happy with property, flourishes with vigor."). Schiller's bourgeois Spartans evidently fought for free trade; in contrast, Herodotus, admirably clear on this point, foregrounds the nexus of freedom, loyalty, and law. When Xerxes asks about the Greeks' readiness to engage an exponentially larger opponent, his adviser Demaratus replies:

So also the Lacedaemonians, fighting singly, are worse than no men; but fighting together, they are of all men the best. For being free, they are not free in all things, but the law is over them for a master, which they dread in their hearts yet much more than thy people dread thee. Assuredly they do whatsoever it biddeth; and it biddeth the same thing ever, not suffering them in battle to flee before any multitude of men, but commanding them to stand fast in their ranks and prevail or perish.[3]

For the ancient nation, political freedom represents the ultimate good, without which life loses its value, and Demaratus therefore contrasts this citizenry with contemporary Persia, treated as a cipher of a debilitating despotism. Where do Schiller's ideals figure in this alternative? The bourgeois nation, organized around the Sisyphean productivity of the *homo laborans*, replaces classical politics with economic progress; hence Schiller's predilection for transfigurative representations of the private *oikos* in the public sphere: "Auf den Mauern erschienen, den Säugling im Arme, die Mütter" ("The mothers appeared on the city walls, infants in their arms"). The bourgeois poet, recoiling from the radicalization of the French Revolution recoils from freedom ("Freiheit ruft die Vernunft, Freiheit die wilde Begierde" ["Reason calls for freedom, but so does wild instinct"]) and invokes law as a regulative guarantor of order. His every vision of emancipation is paid for with the insistence on an even greater restraint.

The differing treatment of the Spartans by Schiller and Herodotus is important for at least two reasons. (1) Even if one imputes to Herodotus something like a "Western metaphysics" and an imperialist antinomy of Europe and Asia, it is crucial to hold onto the historical transformation of the terms of identity and the reification of practical activity as material productivity. The political nation as the agency of freedom in antiquity is replaced by the modern political economy and an always inescapable "Reich der Notwendigkeit," a realm of necessity. While the Spartans at Thermopylae could not imagine life without freedom, Schiller's moderns, for whom meaning has ceased to be immanent in the world, cannot imagine a free life or a life free of a compulsive search for value. (2) To each model of national collectivity corresponds a specific aesthetic practice; Simonides participates in the life of the body politic, while Schiller claims for himself a privileged position, above the city, from which an order is to be projected onto a potentially anarchic and atomized society. His classicism—"Und die Sonne Homers, siehe! sie lächelt auch uns" ("And the sun of Homer, look! It smiles on us too")—ensures stability against freedom. This is the affirmative character of art, especially evident in the ideological inversion of defeat as victory and the conflation of law and commerce. Against this construction of nation, society, and literature Böll directs his short story that cites the Thermopylaean epitaph in its title.

The story is of course vintage early Böll, with its critique of militarism, an exploration of a moment of life in the last months of the war, and the search for traces of human community in accidental encounters. Yet the text provides more, including a concretization of what Adorno meant when he began his *Aesthetic Theory* by claiming that nothing more can be taken for granted with regard to art, even its right to exist.[4] If the general frame of reference for this assertion of an imminent end of art is marked by issues of secularization, the contradictions of modernism, and the legacy of the historical avant-garde, its specific German ramification is the dubiousness of poetry after Auschwitz and the viability of German as a literary language after the war. In "Wanderer, kommst du nach Spa . . . ," Böll demonstrates the illegitimacy of any German writing, but it is paradoxically precisely this demonstration that grounds a central project of West German literature in the thirty years between the end of the war and the neoconservative *Tendenzwende*. Writing becomes an ephemeral reflection on its own impossibility, programmatically renouncing Schillerian solemnity in order to participate in public life; and it describes a politics of individual freedom constantly counterposed to the crude materialism of national or economic interests.

The text is a first-person narrative, that is, the writer speaks, and he does so in the guise of a severely wounded soldier being carried into a makeshift infirmary which he recognizes as a "humanistisches Gymnasium" because of a semiotic display of culture in the corridors: a copy of Feuerbach's "Medea," pictures of the Parthenon and a Greek soldier, busts of Caesar, Cicero, Marcus Aurelius, and a statue of Hermes.[5] This Greek material is mixed with obligatory German signs: portraits of Nietzsche, Prussian rulers, and Hitler. As he begins to suspect that this metaphor for the institutionalization of culture is not just any school but his own, he is pushed into a classroom for art— a *Zeichensaal*, in which one practices *Schriftzeichen*, writing as penmanship in the school of signs—that seems even more familiar, but not until he is stretched out on the operating table, where he will lose both his arms, his writing hands, and one leg, does he see his own handwriting on the blackboard: "There it stood, the saying we had to copy, in that life of despair, only three months ago: wanderer, if you come to Spa . . . " (1:202).

Clearly Böll is not presenting a maudlin account of merely one soldier's fate; if that were the case, one could not explain the proliferation of references to canonized culture and practices of writing. Instead, he scrutinizes the complicity of affirmative culture in fascism and the catastrophe of war, and he suggests that German writing, if it is to be at all, needs henceforth to be wary of any aesthetic projection of Homer's sun onto contemporary reality, the Schillerian project of legitimizing the antirevolutionary poet by invoking the unity of the people. The rejection of the institution of bourgeois culture therefore leads to a denial of the category of "nation" in which it was grounded; collective identity, to the extent that it exists at all for Böll, is a consequence of shared local experience and can certainly not be produced by the invocation of a national name. Hence the rupture of the name in the title: not "Sparta" but "Spa" followed by a three-point ellipsis.

What did the writer see on the blackboard at the moment of amputation? What initial problem grounds the institutionalization of writing in West Germany, while calling both writing and Germany into question? As much as Böll's prose is praised or denounced for its simple clarity, the text remains enticingly obscure. The narrator explains that he had miscalculated, "that I had not planned well, my writing was too big," and that he did not have enough room to finish the sentence, and that the art teacher, the *Zeichenlehrer*, angered by this incompetence, copied the truncated verse six times below the student's misplanned line. What power inheres in an incomplete inscription of the Thermopylaean epitaph that can invert the disciplinary relationship between teacher and student? For it is the punitive teacher who would normally condemn a student to carry out manifold copying on a blackboard. The narrator may give us a clue in the comment, "so I saw the whole saying, only slightly cut off because my writing was too large, too many points" (1:202). "Too many points," the language of printers regarding the size of letters—this rational explanation for the spacing problem on the blackboard simultaneously points, in the ambivalence of the word *Punkte*, to the enigma of what stood on the board. What was the precise written text: Simonides' verse culminating in the incomplete word *Spa* or the verse, ending in *Spa* followed by a three-point ellipsis?—The latter being the version offered in the title and in every rendition in the body of the text. Why does Böll, punning on *Punkte*, draw our attention to the ellipsis? Why does the text include the ellipsis at all, and not simply terminate the verse in mid-word?

The presence of the ellipsis underscores the absence of the name. It is not the case that the stranger might come to "Spa" but only to "Spa . . . ," the ruin of "Sparta," reduced, demolished, existing as fragment, and this ruination is due to a force numerologically encoded in the three points. The truncation of the name indicates the end of classicism, militarism, and national unity. A substantive answer to the Wagnerian query "Was ist deutsch?" is proscribed by the hyperbolic nationalism of the Third Reich, against which the Catholic Böll invokes the triune god, present in the infinite regress of the three points, antithetical to the pagan alliance of Greece and Germany. Böll's antifascist usage of the punctuational rupture inverts the politics of Céline, enthusiast for German fascism, who first inserted the ellipsis in order to explode the ordered syntax of the Third Republic, i.e., the state born at the same moment as the German national unity whose collapse is registered in the diminished name of the title. Meanwhile the writer, wounded in a war which, like the Spartan resistance at Thermopylae, is treated as a conflict between Europe and Asia, recognizes his script in an additional place, the slogan "Long live Togo," scrawled on a photographic representation of German colonialism in Africa: in 1950 the third world intervenes and disrupts European national identity and cultural cohesion. For the writer will become, like his handwriting, "slightly truncated," losing three limbs: the writer as a metaphor for writing as ellipsis, once neither nation nor literature, which bourgeois culture presented as reciprocal alibis, can maintain a unified identity. Simonides' epitaph honored the dead who knew how to live well, and the ancient poet is no antagonist of life. Schiller invokes a nation, "happy with property," for which life is reified as possession; the constant pursuit of commodity accumulation constantly disrupts order, which the poet must replenish through an appeal to newly discovered transcendent values, "the sun of Homer." The citation of Simonides' epitaph in "Der Spaziergang" is deceptive and mendacious, and it is therefore properly set in quotation marks. Böll's story explores this mendacity: the epitaph is truncated not only because Nazi aggression discredited neoclassicism but also because the appropriation of classical ideals by a bourgeois culture that valued wealth more than freedom was always ideological: Böll's ellipsis is contiguous with Schiller's quotation marks.

The wounded narrator comments:

> Then I thought of how many names would stand on the war memorial when they consecrated it again, with an even bigger golden Iron Cross on it and an even bigger stone wreath, and I suddenly knew: if I was really in my old school, my name would be on it, written in stone, and in the yearbook, next to my name, it would say, "left school for the front and fell for . . . " (1:199)

The pursuit of bigger and bigger material objects, the never-ending profit motive, is always oxymoronic—the Iron Cross is golden, the laurel wreath is stone—and that economic acquisitiveness is incompatible with a genuine political culture, an association of free individuals. No reason to die can be articulated, once the only reason to live is material gain. The contradictory structure of German national identity, described by Weber in his study of the East Elbian agrarian question, is realized in the amputated name: "Spa . . ."—national unity and capitalist progress cannot coexist; the name is sundered; Germany divided.

"Wanderer, kommst du nach Spa . . . " can therefore be read as a compelling critique of Schiller's misappropriation of the Thermopylaean epitaph and therefore as a programmatic denunciation of the inherited bourgeois institution of art, organized historically around the complicity of aesthetic autonomy and national identity. Inimical to any version of naturalist identity, Böll's ellipsis points to identity as not-yet-achieved. Proscribing false names, it is the placeholder of a name not written. Postponing a conclusion, it replaces the constraint of periodic closure with a utopian escape. Partitioning Schiller's duplicitous citation, it negates the truncated autonomy promoted by bourgeois culture and anticipates an identity that is less and more than national.

Signs of War: Semiosis and Alienation

Böll's 1961 story presents itself as a personal recollection of a historical moment, linking objective and subjective dimensions by eliding the title—"When the war began" with the initial sentence, "I lay in the window, sleeves rolled up, looking out the window to the telephone office . . . " (4:11). Grand history and individual experience evidently run into each other, collide, and generate the existential scenario typical of much of Böll's work: the living individual in conflict with hierarchies of power, be they political, social, military, or ecclesiastic. Approaching the text in this manner, one ends up asking only whether it should be treated as primarily a subjective, nearly impressionistic remembrance, more than twenty years after the fact, or, on the other hand, as above all an attempt at a definitive, i.e., objective account of the fact itself, the historical moment, "als der Krieg ausbrach."

Yet even if the opening of the text stages the collision of person and history, subject and object, the course of the text demonstrates nothing if not the inadequacy of either account in isolation. For the I who, at the outbreak of the war, is lying at the window never achieves much substantial particularity, and all the purportedly personal memories are strikingly devoid of any nuance or idiosyncrasy that might indicate a concrete individuality. That is, if the text is about personal memory, it is also about the dissolution of personhood. A similar dialectic undermines any naively objectivist reading as well. The title's insistence on temporal specificity is irreparably undercut by the ambiguities of the text: does the war break out at the beginning or the end of the story? The narrator, at least, refuses to accept the notion of the war's having commenced at all, even when he learns of his friend Leo's death, i.e., the moment named by the title remains frustratingly elusive, and the pretext of the story, the promise of chronological accuracy, turns out to be highly labile, with presumably far-reaching consequences for any historiographic project.

If the text is neither purely autobiographical nor naively historiographic, subjective or objective, it is evidently about the relationship—or disjunction—between the two, i.e., it is not an untroubled unity of subject and object but a staging of their separation, their unity as separated, at a specific conjunction in time. The figure who initially lies at the window in a posture of seclusion, recognizably romantic no matter how deflated—indeed he is waiting to call his lover, even if this eroticism is extraordinarily arid—this latter-day romantic ego of the outset is, by the conclusion, marching in a column of soldiers singing "Muss i denn" ("For I must go"), the crucial citation in the text and the announcement of both compulsion (a far cry from "Kein Mensch muss müssen") and separation: the fate of the *Schatz* left behind, never articulated as such in the text but, like the concluding line of the popular song, precisely therefore all the more prominent.[6]

The text records the process by which the prone ego is gotten up out of bed and integrated into the mobilized masses, but this apparent integration of the individual into society remains an unfree and therefore false sublation precisely because it depends on the compulsion and separation named by the citation. Compulsion: at stake is an arbitrary order, the establishment of an arbitrary code that lacks any referential legitimacy vis-à-vis a rapidly vanishing lifeworld. The code depends on the production of differences and, consequently, of separations. To talk about the text as an account of a reorganization of meaning and social structure would be wrong precisely because it investigates something like the enforced organization of meaninglessness and the painfully felt absence of society, i.e., a genuine or adequate human society. A natural order, traditionalism, is present only as memory—what Leo and the narrator used to do; it is replaced by arbitrary signification and the laceration of community, semiotics and alienation (names for the dual absence of meaning and society).

The objection that this relatively simply story cannot support an examination in terms of semiotics and alienation (in other words: structuralism and Marxism) can be easily countered with reference to the frequency with which the text itself foregrounds the problem of signification (and social division as well; more on that later). The point therefore is not to produce a semiotic reading of "Als der Krieg ausbrach" but to note that "Als der Krieg ausbrach" is already a critical reading of semiotics. For the story itself thematizes the status of signs and the proliferation of certain sorts of sign systems as constitutive of the moment of the outbreak of war. Thus the story commences with an account of a sign language: the narrator "waited for my friend Leo to give the agreed-upon sign," and the text proceeds immediately to describe the act of signification: "coming to the window, taking his cap off and putting it on again." This seemingly absurd act is dependent on an arbitrary difference—"Leo alone wore a cap, and only in order to take it off to give me a sign." That is, he is not a lover of caps or a mysteriously formal dresser but rather an element within a system dependent on abstract differentiation.

The initial description of the sign system is surrounded by two questions, each inquiring into the relationship between the system and specific social or political terrains. First we are told that although the system is itself only conventional—what Leo has on his head is meaningful only within the code—it does have an extrasystemic goal: to alert the narrator to the fact that at certain points in time he can use a telephone to call a girlfriend for free. Is there any tighter relationship between the semiotic code and the communicative act (indeed the communication between lovers)? The answer is yes, but it is, counterintuitively, not the relationship suggested by the opening scene. Instead of an elaboration of sign systems augmenting communication, the opposite transpires; as codes proliferate, the connection between the narrator and his lover snaps—their sole conversation is one in which he admonishes her not to come for a visit (as if signifying chains were incompatible with marriage bonds). Yet this marginalization of the woman, or her repression, is itself part of a code of patriarchal separation that is inscribed in the unwritten continuation of the leitmotific citation: "Aber du mein Schatz bleibst hier" ("But you my dear stay here").

If a dimension of communicative authenticity, eros, and woman is left, so to speak, behind the expansion of a semiotic system, does the system—this is the second question—run up against another border too, i.e., what is outside the system? "I suddenly noticed that the rhythm of plugging and unplugging had changed; the arm motions lost their mechanical character, became imprecise, and Leo threw his hands over his head three times: a sign we had not agreed upon but which told me something extraordinary had happened" (4:11). It appears that the system has broken down, that the code has come to an end, and that war amounts to the end of the semiotic order. But the sentence goes on and, in a stunning reversal, keeps the question open. Is war located subsequent to the semiotic scene, or is it, in contrast, the outcome and expansion of semiosis? Is signifying order concluded by the disorder of war, or is the system which produced arbitrary distinction and the repression of communication the sine qua non of war? Thus the text proceeds: "then I saw how one telephone operator took his helmet from the closet and put it on; he looked ridiculous, sitting there, sweating in an undershirt, his tag around his neck and a helmet on his head-but I couldn't laugh, since I recalled that putting on a helmet meant something like 'battle-ready' and I was afraid" (4:12). If the *Stahlhelm* is not the *Mütze*, they are after all both hats, and the difference between them can be accounted for easily within the same binary paradigm of hat-on and hat-off, i.e., the basic system of signification has not changed at all. Is the system itself implicated in the war that is just now breaking out?

Böll's text is centrally concerned with a political critique of the economy of the sign. The initial example of Leo's covered or uncovered head is quickly expanded by a different difference, i.e., the difference between a soldier with or without a helmet. This sort of pattern pervades the story; we read of differentiations between military ranks, discussion topics, and social groups, between Poles and Germans, Protestants and Catholics, open collars and buttoned ones. Meaning constructed in this manner is a function less of reference than of difference, and the production of difference is complicitous in that outbreak of agonistics called war.

Consider a further example: "Once there came a field kitchen. We got lots of goulash and few potatoes, and real coffee and cigarettes we didn't have to pay for. It must have been in the dark, since I remember a voice saying: real coffee and free cigarettes, the surest sign of war; I don't remember the face that went with the voice" (4:15). The "surest sign of war" is therefore identifiable as such not because of any subjective involvement; it is after all a disembodied, faceless voice that speaks, and the agency distributing the wares disappears into the anonymity of the *Feldküche*. Neither sensuous enjoyment nor intentional consciousness is at stake but solely the difference between cigarettes and coffee for free and another state of affairs where one would have to pay for them, i.e., the difference is an absence, costlessness, *umsonst*, in other words, nothing at all, which nevertheless makes all the difference between war and peace. What is the form of social organization that prevails in the bureaucratic context of signification via arbitrary difference?

It is a society of alienation, characterized by an estrangement between groups that is as emphatic as it is absurd: the rank and file soldiers divide into opposing cliques, the foot soldiers face the officers, the Germans confront the Poles, and everyone goes to war. Because of differential semiosis, not only 1939 but also 1949, hot war and cold war ensue, both dependent on the differences. The text suggests a linkage between a specific mode of signification, alienated society, and belligerence. Is this an ontological claim? Does Böll, in his glorious existentialist abstraction, suggest that meaning necessarily means war? Not at all, since the problematic is relativized by a historicizing reference which, on its own, would be rather unconvincing, were it not simultaneously bound to the central question of repression and patriarchy. When Leo reports the news—of full mobilization—he immediately adds that it would be a long time before the two could again bicycle in the countryside, to which the narrator appends the parenthetical comment: "(In our free time, we bicycled through the country, out in the fields, and we had peasant women make us fried eggs with bread)" (4:14). The figure of a utopian return to nature—which is also a return to women—of rustic simplicity and sensuous pleasure, is bracketed between parentheses and relegated to an unretrievable past (although of course even its merely parenthetical presence in the text disrupts the postromantic normalcy of the present). That remembered travel into a gendered world of *Bauersfrauen*, a life-world of preconceptual experience, is now proscribed by a semiotic order that disallows precisely such material experience—subjectivity doesn't count—while it marks women, arbitrarily, as an alterity to be repressed. In place of the journey to the peasant women, the narrator breaks with Marie and moves off from her, represses her, as the repressed verse itself recommends: "Aber du mein Schatz bleibst hier." That is, the world constructed in terms of a proliferation of differentiation is simultaneously both alienated and patriarchal, and it is also a world of universal necessity, general mobilization, and compulsion: "Muss i denn."

Is this world of unfreedom describable as society? Barely, for as the narrator puts it: "I needed company and had none." A stranger in his own land because it is a land of universal estrangement and encoded difference, he finds no society—society, or companionship, sinks into the past of the bicycle trip with Leo. A different mode of organization prevails; instead of society, signifying chains: "this time we loaded detergent cartons, piled in a gym . . . we made a chain, and carton after carton passed through my hands . . . " (4:24).

Significatory order is associated with an authoritarian organization of mechanical labor, i.e., the same principle of compulsion announced by the title of the song. The system of formal difference that excludes subjective consciousness is not just a guarantor of meaning but also a foundational element in the system of domination that depends on an ideology of compulsion. "Sometimes we met or passed soldiers singing 'Muss i denn.' There were three bands and everything was quicker. It was later, after midnight, when we finished the last cartons—and my hands remembered the number of pots and noted little difference between cartons of detergent and cooking pots" (4:24–25). Labor, difference, and intractable necessity are brought into a proximity defining the authoritarian structure at the outbreak of war.

Yet Böll's text does not only delineate this structure and explore the resonance between semiotic order and alienated society; it also articulates a critique in the course of the final scenario of the narrative. The structure of this final scenario is such that it repeats features of the opening; the narrator is again lying on his bed, his comrades are quibbling over minor points, and an interpretive event transpires: the signs of general mobilization in the first scene are paralleled now by the announcement of Leo's death. This death, however, is presented as a consequence of the system of differentiation: only now is the narrator distinguished by being addressed with a formal *Sie*, only in death does Leo become a person with a last name. Death intervenes as the ultimate differentiation, between the living and the dead, and the point where, after all, everything is the same, since nothing matters any longer, which is why the narrator protests and refuses the news. His rejoinder to the report that Leo Siemers had become "der erste Gefallene des Regiments" repeats the congruence of history and individuality evidenced in the first sentence of the story. For Leo cannot have become a *Gefallene*, since there has been no declaration of war— that is the objective argument—and Leo, too, his personal friend, with his disregard for military order, is not one to have sought a hero's death: "Leo doesn't die in battle, not him . . . you know it" (4:26).

The comment on the "surest sign of war," which figured importantly in the investigation of the structure of the sign, was pronounced by an invisible speaker, and the story might well be read as a subtle record of the disappearance of speech: crossed telephone wires giving way to an arbitrary sign system, proceeding finally to the death notice brought, tellingly enough, by a writer, the *Kompanieschreiber*, as if the vocality of the outset (the telephone call) were displaced by the silence and epitaphic writing of the end. The story that records the loss of a life-world and viable communication simultaneously suggests the privileging of writing, a sort of backhanded self-reflection of the author Böll, for whom writing is about its own impossibility or, which is to say the same, will always verge on the obituary.

That a story about the outbreak of the war might be primarily morbid is hardly surprising. Is it only morbid? Preserving Leo's memory, the narrator also rescues him, i.e., the same Leo who enfigured a sort of resistance to division, disregarding the separations of telephone lines and bringing lovers together. The text thereby suggests an alternative to the strategy of difference and control, divide and conquer, the bureaucratic-administrative repression of the life-world whose mode of operation Böll so cogently dissects. "Als der Krieg ausbrach" entails by no means solely a report on the past, the war, and the origins of divided Germany, but something like its redemption and therefore also an imagination of an obliteration of artificial differences and borders: between classes, genders, and states as well.

Chapter 10

Refusal or Denial and the Sky of Europe

Literary Postmodernism in Peter Handke's *Across*

"For a moment, indeed, the sky of all Europe shines blue over the empty bridge."[1] Long before this sentence in the epilogue of Peter Handke's novel *Across*, published in 1983, the careful reader notes the weighty importance of the apparently insignificant adjective *empty*. It has nothing to do with a lack or an absence, and certainly not with the romantic loneliness of an isolated subjectivity, trapped in some infinite suffering and therefore infinitely full. Here emptiness is a capacity that enables both sociability and history. That is why it is precisely the emptiness of the bridge over a small canal on the moors outside of Salzburg that has room for the "sky of all Europe." On the bridge the borders fall: borders between states and between people—without however leading to any sort of passionate, Dionysian erasure of identity. Emptiness leaves room for people to pass and to meet, without pressure and without purpose in a gentle freedom. "An old man is standing on the bridge. His eyes are half closed and he says: 'This canal is so quiet, so unassuming, so modest. This water must conquer'" (133–34). The unmistakable tension between the description of a quiet humility and the insistence on a certain victory underscores the mediating role and liminal position—it is after all a matter of a bridge—that adhere to the image of the half-closed eyes. Refusing the world and nevertheless receptive to it, hermetically sealed and therefore attentive: it is a perception related to blind Homer's whose mimetic repetition of reality depends on the emptiness of sight. This aesthetic autonomy remains free because it is free of both reified facts and tendentious claims. Hence the novel's commencement, an imperative exhortation to a strict artistry: "I shut my eyes and out of the black letters the city lights took shape" (3).

The text is interlaced with an imagery of eyes, especially eye sockets and mountain caves, walled-in spaces—all suggestive of the ivory tower of which the young Handke polemically described himself to be a resident.[2] But the emptiness of the bridge is, as already discussed, not, or no longer, a retreat

159

from society and history but on the contrary their very precondition. The old man is followed by a young girl who lights up a cigarette; a small truck makes the bridge shake; two bicyclists and some pedestrians appear. Only violence is proscribed: "This bridge, he thinks, is so small, there will never be any need to blow it up for strategic reasons. A flag will never be unfurled on it. Under the weight of a tank, it would collapse instantly" (136). Whether it is due to the bridge's function as a guarantor of peace for the "sky of all Europe" or to the work of art, derived from the aesthetic space of the bridge, the bridge elicits history: both as historiography and as narrative. Outside of a degraded political realm, implicitly the precondition of war, the text explores the possibility for stories about history: "Seldom does one of the bridge crossers curse, grumble, or laugh; but once in a while you hear a narrative note: 'When my father . . . ' " (137–38). Yet this historicity stands in marked contrast to Handke's own beginnings; twenty years before *Across*, as part of the group of young authors associated with the journal *manuskripte* in Graz, he shared an explicit antitraditionalism that encompassed a hostility to history as well as to the descriptive realism of the postwar German authors of the "Gruppe 47"; hence also a hostility to stories. The new program dictated that literary language was to be freed from both any extraliterary reality and any communicative responsibilities. Does any bridge lead from those beginnings to the late work? Or conversely: does the narrative solution in *Across* shed any retrospective light on the character of the project in Graz in the sixties?

Once more from the epilogue: in the next-to-last sentence the provisionally last figures appear to cross the empty bridge, staging a self-evident allegorization of art: "After an interval comes a horse-drawn carriage adorned with garlands and crowded with musicians on their way from one performance to another; they have put their clarinets, trumpets, and cymbals aside and look tired; only the accordion player, who is sitting on the back of the shafts with his instrument in the crook of his arm, opens the bellow on the bridge, producing a long-drawn-out tone" (138). Schiller's antinomy of serious life and cheerful art has little to do with this scene. On the contrary, the musicians seem to be refugees from some unnamed disaster that has exhausted and silenced them: an archaic image of the vanquished who, by the rivers of Babylon, refuse song in order precisely to sing this refusal, a sort of negative aesthetics. Is the silence of art resistance or submission, refusal or denial? Does the "long-drawn-out tone" give mournful expression to the cry of the anonymous infant at the beginning of the novel, or is it instead a merely affirmative transfiguration—perhaps in the sense that suffering is taken to be constitutive of unchanging existence? How do rejection and resignation, melancholy and affirmation intertwine in the final, enigmatic sigh?

The last sound is followed by the final word, revealing the paradox without clarifying it and returning again to the question of history, historicity, and life-in-time. "Now from the medieval canal—as from the medieval figures over the doors of the Old City churches—flow peace, mischief, quietness, gravity, slowness, and patience" (138). Obviously this is no case for the historical optimism of progress. Nor is this silence an example of a sudden halt in history, an apocalyptic intervention of the sort described by Walter Benjamin in his "Theses on the Philosophy of History." Nor, furthermore, is it a radical new beginning that might have applied to the young Handke. Art is, on the contrary, relocated in a *longue durée* of a stable order of life, stretching back beyond the Middle Ages into geological time. The patience for survival requires, in Handke's orientalizing metaphor, a Chinese virtue—the literal translation of the German title of the novel, *Der Chinese des Schmerzes*, would be something like "the suffering Chinese"—whereby the fact that the tolerated order remains profoundly painful is not disguised.[3] "Quietness"—as a sign of oppression: but who has denied language to whom? "Quietness"—as a conspiratorial renunciation of a contaminated language: but who can tell stories, who can continue them, who will carry them out? The turn to history in the late Handke, comparable to reexplorations of realist prose elsewhere—one thinks of Marquez, Tournier, and Tom Wolfe—leads not only to an internal dialectical tension. It also leads back to the "Grazer Gruppe" of the sixties, and it is this material which I want to excavate, imitating the archaeological hero of the novel, Andreas Loser.

Yet why inquire into the origins of the Grazer Gruppe and Austrian postmodernism via a relatively late novel of a single author? Is there any methodological justification to explore the position of the literary school of the *manuskripte* through a novel whose author was certainly part of the school but who has also certainly gone far beyond it? One answer is: of course, for reality is understood through its extremes, and the distance of the novel from the beginnings of the movement magnifies its analytic strength, especially because it is a text concerned with history and its own literary history.

There is, however, a more stringent connection. The rich documentation of the first decade of *manuskripte* collected by Elisabeth Wiesmayr allows us to understand and reconstruct the context of the young authors of Graz, in particular their self-understanding as a modernizing opposition to an archconservative environment that—in the eyes of the new rebels—seemed to be implicated in a still fascist aesthetics of blood and soil. That young authors commenced their careers with the assumption that they had to battle a literary Nazism is, of course, not exceptional in postwar German literature. It is certainly possible that this assumption had a heightened validity in Styria. In any case, this adversariality of the *manuskripte* group was less a consequence of a theoretically mature antifascism than of a general, sometimes vague antitotalitarianism: this too no exception in the era of the Cold War. It is therefore important to note that the plot of *Across* depends on a curiously unmotivated deed that can be read as a paradigm of the confrontation with Nazi writing: Loser throws a stone and kills a man whom he finds painting swastikas on a wall along a path on Salzburg's Mönchsberg. This is the primal scene of Grazer authorship: the oedipal dismissal of an obsolete language. That dismissal led the young Handke initially to language criticism and a refusal of history. In the late novel, however, it leads him to a retrieval of language as narration and to a reconstituted historicism. How to account for this differential result? Or, more precisely: Is the alternative consequence of the confrontation with fascist writing to be understood as a self-critical reconsideration of Handke's own past? As a putative self-criticism, a literary-historical Glasnost, the novel itself investigates the origins of recent Austrian literature and its foundational fiction of antifascism.

Given this connection between *Across* and the literary culture of the sixties in Graz, any results of this inquiry require some appropriate framing. The concern is not primarily the development of a single author; such an approach would necessitate a different handling of the text. Nor, however, is the point that this text represents the sole outcome of the Grazer innovation. The issue is solely that the late text may be used as a retrospective spotlight, possibly illuminating the significance of the literary innovation of the sixties: not because Handke was in any way the only relevant member of the group but because *Across* poses the question in an interesting way.

This approach, reading the late novel with reference to the early work, holds for the question of fascist literature, but it also pertains to the relationship of the single author to a cooperative enterprise. Like Alfred Kolleritsch, the longstanding editor of the journal and the virtual center of the group, the novelistic Loser is a high school teacher. As a classicist he participates in local archeological excavations and, in this context, functions like an author: "I obtained a temporary leave of absence from my job. The motive I gave was the urgent need to complete a paper that was to appear next spring in the *Salzburg Yearbook for Regional Studies*. This was an interim report on the excavation of a Roman villa in Loig, a village on the far side of the airfield" (11). Writing is evidently a matter of history, and history entails long structures that outlive any solely current events. This is no new subjectivity—the term used to designate the privatizing prose that proliferated in West Germany and Austria in the seventies—and no epiphanic moment of true feeling: a symptomatic title of a novel by Handke. Evidently a referential language pointing to an extraliterary world is possible; it can also have a communicative character and therefore appeals to possible readers grouped around a journal. The novel is therefore also concerned with how Loser seeks an interlocutor and a witness—it will be his son—to whom he can tell his story, because stories can, again, be told.

Across can be read as an account of how an author, Loser, overcomes a writer's block: the "interim report" is announced at the outset of the novel, but it is finished only at the end, after the murder and the subsequent experiences. "Seated at my desk, I put my manuscript, 'Thresholds of the Roman Villa,' into an envelope, addressed it, and affixed stamps. Only a short while before, I would have looked on without lifting a finger as every page of it burned or flew out the window" (100). What is the social or organizational context of this writing? Does *Across* provide an account of the structure of the literary or cultural public sphere? And is there a connection between the novel's internal model of the public sphere and the social character of the Grazer Gruppe?

Some answers can be excluded immediately. For example, the novel describes no engaged model of popular pedagogy as might have been associated in Austria with the history of Social Democracy. Nor is there any aesthetic revolutionary claim, no avant-gardism which, following Peter Bürger, might have attempted to overcome the distance between the realm of art and philistine reality. Indeed Loser distances himself from the attack on the Salzburg Festival articulated by the figure of the painter. Loser writes neither for a liberal educated middle class, a *Bildungsbürgertum*, from which no one would have been excluded on principle, nor solely for himself—neither an Enlightenment nor a romantic model is useful. In what sense does culture have more than private significance; where is the bridge to a public?

The novel deploys three relevant terrains: archeology, the participation in a group of lay astronomers, and teaching—three sites of objective culture. In each case, Loser's commitment is certainly loose, but it is always important; due only to the social situation does the writer escape a threatening, indeed constantly seductive, propensity for isolation. There will be more to say about the construction of aesthetic autonomy in the text, but the entry into groups establishes a context that renders autonomy historical, in the sense both of belonging to history and the past and being therefore obsolete and passé, and of being oriented toward historical material: if narration is to be possible, culture cannot be solely autonomous and subjective. Nevertheless Loser does not dissolve unproblematically into an objective culture:

Doesn't the public sphere, without which I am incomplete, begin at the school door? Isn't my ride to my public existence the natural thing for me, and doesn't it open up the possibility of a satisfactory way back? In any event, I don't regard myself as a loner, it doesn't suit me to be a freelancer, and certainly not an independent scholar (though early in my studies, someone advised me to become one). I know I should work with others, not just occasionally, but day after day. Only among others does something resembling a world appear to me, if only in the briefly flaring brown of a lichen in the

Antarctic. One day perhaps a stranger from the plains, on his way to a still undiscovered city, will approach our local castle (that forbidding hulk), and the canal at his feet will flow through timeless lowlands, or through the Chinese limestone province of Kwei-lin. Did I, for that, need a kind, my kind of job? (18–19)

"Job" is a pale translation of the German *Amt* that borders on duty, service, and calling. It is this calling that establishes the social world, not through some principle of reason, accessible to all subjects, however, but rather—again Handke's orientalism—through a "Chinese" capacity for patience.

In each of the three cultural terrains, the cooperative world depends on a figure of authority who instills patience and thereby establishes order in a manner portrayed as gentle and nonviolent. "An older archaeologist" reins in Loser's initial curiosity with the admonition, "All you care about is *finding* something," leading Loser to the conclusion "to look less for what was there than for what was missing, for what had vanished irretrievably" (11); the critical problem is to decide whether to treat this as a trace of a repressive denial, or the stifling of an original and instinctive inquisitiveness, or the foundation of the subsequent discourse on "empty forms," "empty places," and "thresholds." In the same sense, the leader of the astronomy group diagnoses, "You're always in such a hurry to identify, instead of just gazing for a while" (36–37). It is, however, in the characterization of the school director that Handke provides an indication of the necessary form of control and power for the successful construction of culture: instead of domination, affective bonding: "[he] had once been my teacher and later became my friend. [I] sat down and wept; not over the praise, but over the salutation, 'Dear Andreas,' for it seemed to me that for years no one had called me by my first name" (100). He is insightful enough to cherish the nonconformism of the outsider Loser, not as an exotic embellishment of an otherwise functional operation but rather as the irreplaceable component of any viable pedagogy. "What enables you to teach is your slight embarrassment, coupled with your total immersion in your subject. There are more than enough competent teachers. But students get the feel of a subject only from those who are at times visibly embarrassed at being teachers, from stutterers and thread-losers. Only such a one remains fixed in the student's memory as 'my teacher'" (100). Is this evidence of Handke's borrowing again from one of his familiar sources, the nineteenth-century Austrian author Adalbert Stifter—in particular his "gentle law" of culture? The cultural public sphere is composed of small groups, devoted to circumscribed areas (the rather conservative selection is noteworthy: archeology, astronomy, and classical languages), and this limitation, excluding any extensive programmatic goals, effectively precludes romantic individualism or revolutionary utopianism: the order is asserted.

Does this model of the cultural public apply to the Grazer Gruppe? It would not be incorrect, if certainly insufficient, to read *Across* as a postrevolutionary, resigned departure from the youthful excitement of the sixties. Yet it is less the difference between Loser's pedagogical calling and the young Handke's attacks on his public that is important than a structural continuity: as if the late, novelistic model were a sort of interpretive extrapolation of the beginning, with all of the external atmospherics of the sixties stripped away in order to get to the core. For the Grazer Gruppe too took part in an ostentatious nonconformism, much like the "stutterers and thread-losers" of Handke's school director. Thus, for example, the spectacular performances in the "Darkroom," literary events designed to provoke the established cultural orthodoxy of the early sixties, as if the success of culture depended on the success of the outsiders: an already recuperated neodadaistic avant-garde. In this sense Wiesmayr quotes from the *Kleine Zeitung* of June 15, 1964:

> "The Darkroom is a literary event,"—this slogan was stretched over the stage on Tuesday at the Forum Stadtpark where, very late at night, a performance took place which was so "eccentric" that the quoted slogan took on a parodic quality. The two authors, Wolfgang Bauer and Gunter Falk, rode into the hall on scooters, played records, smoked, ate and drank, occasionally fed newspaper clippings into a projector, now and then lifted their manuscript pages from the floor and read to the public which was also smoking, drinking, eating and not withholding animated commentaries.[4]

If a dada performance of the early twentieth century had the goal of demolishing the institution of literature, the newspaper report indicates an opposite effect: the gesturing of the young authors, which is described as eccentric only in quotation marks, revives and therefore reasserts the literary sphere: rebellion as resuscitation.

This theatrical nonconformism, claiming to storm barricades but really only breaking down appropriately open doors, did without any theoretical consensus and depended instead on the personal authority of the editor Kolleritsch. Thus Kolleritsch himself: "the notion of a group only indicates constant collaboration but no shared program."[5] Wiesmayr concludes: "It is wrong to treat the Grazer Group as somehow analogous to the Vienna Group. There was no common theoretical concept that might have provided the basis of a collective artistic collaboration. . . . Alfred Kolleritsch was the personal point of crystallization, accepted as an authority not only due to his function as editor but also as a result of his greater access to professional literary information."[6] Thus a personal, not a theoretical authority, tolerant of the individual differences but nevertheless capable of leading individuals to the public—much like the novel's archeologist, astronomer, and school director. If Kolleritsch's great achievement was to lead a group of talented young authors out of the Austrian provinces and to a wider readership—and especially to the attention of West German publishing houses—does *Across* simply repeat the model of the public sphere of the early years in Graz? On the contrary, the novel judges that model of culture and therefore also the beginning of recent Austrian literature. The absence from the novel of any adolescent rebelliousness brushes aside the cultural-revolutionary sloganeering as insignificant and reveals the oppositional antics as a strategy of a young generation attempting to establish itself in the literary market. As a writer, Loser can do without similar gestures. In this light, 1968 appears less as a failed revolution than as a transitional stage for the postwar generation on its way into positions of power in culture and society.

Yet Loser distances himself from this access to society: for him cultural objectivity is to be reached not via a public sphere—not in the *Salzburg Yearbook for Regional Studies* and not in the classroom—but in a refusal of individualism and autonomy aesthetics and in a recollection of an eternal and sacred existence. It is no accident that the novel takes place in the week before Easter. In other words, the continuity between Graz and the novel is evident in the fundamental structure of the public—nonconformism, authority, loose cooperation. The novel, however, takes a new look at this structure and suggests, first, that the collaboration in Graz depended on a false avant-gardism that masked the genuine goal of furthering literary careers (i.e., it was a sort of writers' guild, certainly a legitimate trade enterprise but hardly a cultural program) and, second, that it never overcame a subjectivist autonomy aesthetics. This dialectical verdict of the novel therefore entails a critical statement on the aging of the avant-garde as well as a conservative and postmodern reckoning with the literary revolution; its erstwhile individualism is now accused of incompatibility with the necessity of myth, given the equation: myth = narration.

Handke's grappling with the problem of the social organization of culture makes sense only with reference to a historical background of deep-seated transformations. In his account of a structural transformation of the public sphere, Jürgen Habermas argues that a free space in between the state and intimate privacy—a bourgeois public sphere—developed in the course of the late seventeenth and early eighteenth centuries.[7] In the coffeehouses of London, the salons of Paris, and the reading circles of the German territories, the members of a reasoning public met in order to carry on discussions in the spirit of the Enlightenment: at first of literary topics, and later of increasingly political matters. It was there that the end of the *ancien régime* began. While access was restricted to a small stratum of the population owing to the practical preconditions of property and education, a contrafactual ideal of universal access nevertheless developed, according to which everyone prepared to employ an allegedly universal human capacity to reason would be welcome. In addition, a profoundly consequential reconstruction of aesthetic culture took place. The separation of art from state and religion in the context of a philosophical rationalism meant that the old normative poetics was subverted and gradually replaced by the independence of the internally coherent and therefore original work of art: autonomy.

In the course of the nineteenth century, however, this public sphere slowly dissolved (even if it retained a certain normative value with the discourse of political liberalism). The integration of the majority of the population into the political sphere produced not a transparent democratization but rather an increasingly acclamatory political culture which excluded an authentic participation of the citizens: from Bonapartism to the charismatic leaders of the twentieth century to contemporary media politics. In the aesthetic sphere, literature hardly undergoes a substantive democratization either; instead, commercialized mass culture diverges from an elite culture in which autonomy takes on the character of a hermetic separation from a reality judged to be worthless: low culture and high culture, Ganghofer or George. Any generally accepted literary culture disappears, while this heterogeneity is not experienced as a pluralistic gain. It is taken instead to represent a crisis initiated by an expansive culture industry.

Horkheimer and Adorno described this culture industry as "mass deception." During the early part of the century, several alternatives were available: classical modernism, fundamentally a continuation of autonomy aesthetics, although it tended to foreground the utopia of a transcendence of aesthetic isolation; an avant-garde which, as with dada, attempted to overcome the separation of life and art by introducing everyday elements into literary language in order to explode it; a more political avant-garde which attempted to replace autonomy with an art whose engagement derived from a formal reconstitution (Brecht, Piscator); a realistic writing which claimed to present critical contents in the spirit of the Enlightenment and in a mimetic manner. In this context, there is no reason to play out Mann, Serner, Brecht, and Zweig—or Musil, Hausmann, Horváth, and Roth—against each other or to deny that hybrid forms and overlappings between these ideal types could easily be found The point is rather that the socio-aesthetic lines of the prewar period were received during the fifties and sixties in a very different context: the experience of National Socialism and the Holocaust, the history of Stalinism and the Central European satellites, the disappearance of the radical mass movements and the utopianism of earlier decades, the proliferation of American mass culture, the expansion of an electronic cultural apparatus (radio and television programs as initiators of literary production), and especially the emergence of the postwar generation with changed values and different social interests, leading to youth culture, counterculture, and the student movement.

If one considers this history of literature as a potential agent of opposition—be it in the form of a modern autonomy, an avant-garde, or simply as critical realism—then it comes as no surprise that the founding of the Forum Stadtpark in Graz entailed some confrontation. In fact, it was the small extent of the confrontation that is the real surprise. Because the city fathers did not want to make the park building available for cultural activities, an independent fund-raising drive commenced, with the majoritarian but hardly avant-gardistic name "From everyone, for everyone."[8] The minister of education, Drimmel, chose similarly conciliatory tones in his dedication speech, envisioning a "place of meeting" and, alluding to Hans Sedlmayr's popular cultural conservatism, looked forward to "rewinning the lost center."[9] It would be worth questioning to what extent the Graz authors, despite all evident innovation, also subscribed to this program. Of course, the literary movement depended less on the "Forum Stadtpark" itself than on the journal housed there and its editor. Without privileging any particular literary direction, Kolleritsch was concerned with articulating opposition against "spiritual provincialism."[10] The group was certainly successful in that, and the geographical coordinate could soon be inverted; if it was first a matter of importing contemporary literary culture into the provinces, very quickly the no longer backwoods periphery could conquer the cultural pages of the metropolitan press—hence the victorious march of Austrian authors into the West German publishing industry. With what literary intent?

The celebrated lack of a program in *manuskripte*—an antitheory extension of the ideological skepticism of the antitotalitarian fifties—was modified in the course of the sixties; two delineations were drawn against competing positions, i.e., against the heirs to the two avant-gardes. While Oswald Wiener's *verbesserung von mitteleuropa* was published in *manuskripte* (and the Graz authors, especially Handke, learned a good deal from the language skepticism of the Vienna Group), the journal soon tried to distance itself from Wiener's language experiments which appeared, from the perspective of Graz, as anarchistic. Both Wiener and Kolleritsch of course rejected the literary establishment and, especially, the traditional descriptive realism; yet Wiener's goal was a total rejection of literature as part of a conventionalized reality, Kolleritsch's improved literature.[11] If Wiener's direction is described as "experimental," then the Grazer Gruppe ought to be treated as "postexperimental" literature; for it was characterized by acts of distancing appropriation or, in other words, by "a synthesis of language experiment and literary tradition."[12]

A parallel front developed vis-à-vis the new left avant-garde; Kolleritsch insisted on an independent realm of literature, the political significance of which was fully recognized—"we mobilized critical forces against the extreme right" (Kolleritsch)[13]—but which should not be subsumed into either an operative aesthetics or an authors' union. These issues were fought out with Michael

Scharang, the key Austrian heir of the West German Brecht discussion. In the end, against Wiener and against Scharang, whose own positions were hardly identical, Kolleritsch represented a third position which allowed for traditional narration, greatly modified the then current calls for politicization, and did not dissolve an autonomous aesthetic realm. If one recalls that in 1968 Hans Magnus Enzensberger wrote about the "death of literature" in *Kursbuch*, that consequently West German authors tended to develop toward documentary literature, political journalism, and essayism, and that new talents may have turned away disappointed from literature altogether, the sudden advance of Austrian authors from Graz on the German book market becomes explicable. [14] Not until the seventies, in a relatively "postrevolutionary" period, did West German authors rediscover narration in conjunction with the "new subjectivity," while that same narration had never been thoroughly interrogated in Graz.

Not a linguistic experiment, at best postexperimental, and certainly not part of the political neo-avant-garde, the literature of the sixties in Graz defined itself primarily through such demarcations which always also meant borrowings. The opposition to alleged traditionalism and antimodernism remained central. Thus Kolleritsch polemicized against the conservative cultural hegemony:

> We only want to show that in Graz there are people who are dissatisfied. From now on we will not fail to show that the purple mantle of aesthetic judgment based on the eternal spirit of art is only a lazy excuse. We are amused when modern forms are equated with nihilism or childish stuttering; we are amused when they speak of modernism or modernist epigones. We understand that we can do nothing more for art, but we are nevertheless proud to be epigones of the age. Modernist epigones: the only honorable literary category in this region, so sad for modern art. . . . [15]

A definition through opposition: the movement in Graz defines itself through the negation of whatever it opposes without concrete clarification—it is against the bad and for the good. In the end it is merely an abstract loyalty to literature (hence the subsequent fractional disputes with Wiener and Scharang) and a temporal location: "modernist epigones." That can only mean, however, that modernity has become historical, even in places, such as Graz, where it never succeeded; the young generation of authors, in the wake of modernism, can only mimic it, providing imitations in the age of the simulacrum; original contributions are impossible. "Modernist epigones" means postmodernity—Graz as the Austrian variant of postmodernism?

The category of "postmodernism" alone can help clarify the character of literary innovation in Graz and the relationship between *Across* and the group around *manuskripte*. This is not the place for an intervention in the debate around the term, nor for advocacy or rejection of the material subsumed under the term. Nor is it a matter of arbitrary labeling. The postmodernity of *manuskripte* is, as the last quote demonstrates, a matter of a temporal location, after a modernism which is still defended but can never be recaptured or matched. Kolleritsch glosses this proleptic defeatism with a nod to the backwardness of Graz and, perhaps, Austrian literature in general: "this region, so sad for modern art" is probably a bad interpretation of a correct observation. For in other regions, where the classically modern literature and art did not experience only a history of repression, modernism and the avant-garde were burnt out, and the only concrete goal of *manuskripte*, being modern and up-to-date, already had a strangely grandfatherly tone. The ideology with which the Graz authors armed themselves was modernist, even in its rhetorical turns—for example the constantly repeated attacks on the old-fashioned—but the definitive literary practice was already marked by essential features of postmodernism. *Across* tries to come to grips with this constitutive contradiction.

For Wiener and Scharang, Kolleritsch (whom the young Handke assisted in the theoretical battles) was never radical enough, and his pursuit of an autonomous literature already obsolete. From the standpoint of *Across*, however, even that construction of autonomy was too modern and incompatible with the genuine substance of literature. Instead of the earlier rebelliousness in the name of modernization, the late novelist Handke describes graduality and immaleability, both requiring patience rather than disruption. The difference is apparent in the transformed oedipal structures: for the young Kolleritsch, the epigone can never equal the father—the celebrated success of modernism can never be repeated nor can the threatening antimodernism of the older generation be surpassed: epigonism is weakness. This weakness disappears in the novel, for "this water must conquer." The Nazi can be murdered, but the parricide is atoned for in the sense that every narration represents a sort of festival of resurrection. The erstwhile uprising, which claimed to be modern, was doomed to failure; it was a postmodernism that did not yet understand itself as such. The postmodern literary innovation of Handke, by way of contrast, seeks not the new and the modern but rather the archaic and the permanent: a surpassing of autonomy, quite different of course from Wiener's linguistic anarchism or Scharang's political engagement.

What is postmodernism here? First of all a historical distancing from the canon of classical modernism: the obvious fact that literature continues to be produced even after the accomplishments of Joyce, Proust, and Mann, for example in Graz of the sixties. That, however, implies a dismissal of the modern aesthetics of autonomy and individual originality. Despite the recognition of the impossibility of the undertaking, the *manuskripte* group attempted to rescue the metropolitan aesthetics for the provinces. Twenty years later, in *Across*, this unhappy consciousness is healed through a surpassing of autonomy: subjectivity and secular art are replaced by sacred narration in an ontologized order.

Second, postmodernism means the break with the emancipatory goals of the Enlightenment. In *manuskripte* literary progress is viewed as part of a process of liberation; the distance from Scharang is quantitative, not qualitative. In *Across*, the moderate politics of the past are extended into an existential conservatism: have patience! Third, while genuine modernism thrived in a relationship of tension with a denounced mass culture, postmodernism tends to equalize high and low dimensions (at least on a programmatic level). The claim that postmodernism entails a conservative if not necessarily traditionalist turn follows from the last two points: social hierarchy should no longer be measured against a norm of emancipatory equality, i.e., structural differences in the distribution of wealth are expressed, while indications of such differences are erased in the expressive dimension of art. *Manuskripte* still depended on the tension between mass culture—the allegedly conservative taste of the surrounding culture—and its own advanced position, even when bits and pieces of pop culture were integrated into the literary texts of authors such as Bauer. Handke dissolves the binary opposition of high and low. The concept of narration that emerges from *Across* implies not autonomous artistry nor some cultural elite but much more a constant possibility within the ontological structure of everyday experience for the linguistic transmission of collective provenance and identity. At least on this score, the accusation of conservatism is appropriate: in the context of stable sociohistorical structures, no differentiated expressivity is allowed and certainly no criticism.

This all means that the tension between modernist rhetoric and postmodernist practice at the beginning of the Grazer Group is implicitly thematized in *Across* and, simultaneously, brought to a conclusion. The novel is devoted to articulating a consistently postmodernist aesthetic, different from positions still close to a rebellious modernism. This postmodernism is, despite its conservative nuances, certainly not unbroken; it too can be read against the grain, particularly in the sense that postmodernism is also a resistant variant of modernism itself.

It was noted at the outset that the cry of the nameless child is echoed at the end of the novel by the accordion player, and the question was raised as to how to read this statement on art: as mourning or as resignation. One answer could treat the undecidability, the ambivalence inherent in aesthetic autonomy itself. Another might proceed from the fact that it is precisely folk music, rather than high art, which is mobilized by the text. More important, however, is the much richer structure of the novelistic logic which does not at all lead compulsively to that one solution, however we are to understand the musician; for in addition to the speechlessness of the tone, the text also elaborates the rediscovery of narration: Loser, the father, finds a listener in his son, to whom he can tell his own story. It is, however, solely Loser's own story, not one that lays any claims to a universal validity.

The construction of this postmodernism encompasses the paradox that the *longue durée* of historical stability runs parallel to the narrative privilege of the *petit récit*.[16] At this point, however, the conceptual barriers to the once denigrated descriptive realism disappear, i.e., a writing that claims to be descriptive, narrative, and communicative reappears. In retrospect, however, descriptive realism was once the "modern" position, for there a mimetic reproduction of an extralinguistic reality was linked to a sociocritical agenda. It was there that the past—a definitive chain of historical events—was to be confronted and mastered in the spirit of universal emancipation. In narrative postmodernity, by way of contrast, the goal is instead the preservation of the past in the future, i.e., the uninterrupted linguistic transmission of only local and therefore also arbitrary fictions. Postmodernity surrenders modernity's claim to universal validity and, by extension, to equality: further proof of its substantive conservatism. But by renouncing modernist autonomy—for example, the imagery of self-enclosure that is clustered on Loser's desk—as well as any realistic "mirroring," the postmodernist text gains a capacity to intervene in the social realm. The import of *Across* is therefore more traditional and more radical than Kolleritsch's "modernist epigonism."

The radicalism is by no means limited to the murder, which takes place in the second part of the novel with its Brechtian title: "The Viewer Takes Action." Already in the first part, we find the otherwise contemplative teacher throwing political signs into the canal. Commercial advertisements are similarly destroyed, all part of an effort to save the agrarian *Dasein* from a bad semiotic system. Yet even the fundamental structure of narrating is a rescue mission: for the "sky of all Europe," for peace, for the disappearance of borders. That is why the "empty space" of the "threshold" is always the precondition of the narration that constitutes history. Looking for thresholds in the archeological ruins of Roman villas, Loser notes their absence precisely in the buildings from the period of Italian fascism. "A monstrous picture from Sardinia came into my mind. A colony named Fertilia, built by the dictator's henchmen in the years between the wars: today not a single house has a threshold and the doors to the houses are gaping holes" (123–24). Against Mussolini, who is not even named since fascism is presumably understood to be a system of namelessness, his antipode, Virgil, serves as the example of the descriptive power of language; the Latin teacher Loser visits his place of birth and constantly alludes to the *Georgics*.

Virgil provides a further indication of a European continuity, both as a *longue durée* of tradition and as an antifascist, nonnationalist continental consciousness, nuanced presumably by the frame of the peace movement of the early eighties. It is highly interesting, however, that this archeological rescue of Europe—as immutable fundament, as tradition, and as the open threshold of peace—is carried out with an orientalist metaphoric network. The patient Chinese of the title is only the most obvious example, the corollaries to which include references to the West Bank, Egyptian profiles, Asians selling newspapers, Japan, hibiscus blossoms, a wadi, and, repeatedly, pyramids: alpine pyramids, a pyramid base in Central America, the top of a pyramid, human pyramids, dung pyramids, and a wooden pyramid for the Easter celebration. In addition, Loser is addressed as "Indian" and as "Mr. Chinese." Apparently Europe, both as a space and as a narrative history, is saved only by an escape from Western metaphysics with its emancipatory compulsiveness and through an internalization of the allegedly Asian virtue of patience. Clearly the text is not concerned with a cosmopolitan receptiveness toward non-European cultures or peoples. On the contrary, a rigid image of the Orient with all too familiar elements is being unpacked and deployed: "peace, mischief, quietness, gravity, slowness, and patience" (138). This "Asian deed" is intended to resacralize art and retract the terms of modernity developed in the wake of the Enlightenment: rituals instead of rights. Within postmodernism, everyday life too is aestheticized: in place of the communicative structures of lived life, artificial projections proliferate, in this case in the manner of chinoiserie. If the text succeeds, via the Chinese material in sacrificing the father in order to celebrate his resurrection in narration at Easter, then in fact it is Asia, the emancipation of which postmodernism certainly has no interest in, which is being sacrificed in an ideological exchange for the benefit of an aesthetic project called Europe. The "sky of all Europe" suddenly takes on an exclusive character, and "this water must conquer" sounds threatening.

The Grazer Group understood itself very differently, to be sure: carriers of a cultural opposition, a refusal vis-à-vis an authoritarian hegemony that consistently repressed historical events and aesthetic options. Against various radical fractions, *manuskripte* borrowed some of the arguments of modern autonomy aesthetics, despite a recognition of their obsolescence. That implicit postmodernity comes due in *Across*, particularly in that the norm of hermetic autonomy is conclusively abandoned in the name of a narration of traditions: a Nietzschean aesthetic justification of the world and, simultaneously, the fulfillment of the distant speech opening the Forum Stadtpark. Handke's "bridge" turns out to be the "retrieval of the lost center" to the extent that aesthetic modernism is retracted without any reliance on avant-gardist structures. At that point, however, the basis for any formal polemic against descriptive realism disappears. One consequence might be a revival of the challenge of a political aesthetics; for once again, "intervention" has become crucial. That this post-autonomous political potential is linked in the novel to a disturbingly problematic metaphoric language of Orientalism is indicative of some of the fault lines running through the complexities of literary postmodernism.

Chapter 11

The Gulf War and Cultural Theory in Germany and the United States

Nationhood, Popularity, and Yellow Ribbons

Juxtaposing the political fact of war and the cultural dimension of values, the title alone is deeply problematic. War and culture? An intellectual tradition that commences with eighteenth-century accounts of aesthetic autonomy, especially those of Kant and Schiller, and that retains considerable credibility in both conservative and liberal-centrist camps in contemporary cultural debates, necessarily resists the suggested politicization of cultural objects. Works of art are most successful, so the argument goes, or, phrased more aggressively, works become "great works" when they distance themselves most emphatically from the degraded terrain of politics. Among all the fantastic creatures at home in the delicate world of beauty, there is no room for any tendentious klutz. Should the zones of culture and politics unfortunately overlap, the outcome can only be ideology and propaganda: Nazi painting, parochial kitsch, Rambo instead of Rimbaud. The politicization of culture—or the simultaneous consideration of politics and culture—is then at best a matter of distorted culture, a regression from the structural tendency of modernity to emancipate aesthetic expression from the exigencies of the political system. If, as Auden would have it, poetry makes nothing happen, then, if something does happen, a war, for example, understood as the continuation of politics by other means, then poetry, art, and culture are not significantly involved: metaphors don't shoot.

However, even if one accepts the normative valorization of cultural autonomy—the claim that the best art is the least political—one can still concede an empirical proximity of culture and politics, so that an inquiry into the one somehow entails an inquiry into the other. Perhaps metaphors shouldn't shoot, but they have nevertheless been frequently spotted wandering across the battlefield. Bemoan it, applaud it, or accept it as self-evident, one hardly needs reminding that major cultural debates of recent years have been the locus of

175

intensely political altercation: the Vietnam Memorial, the Mapplethorpe discussion, the controversy over curricula, and so forth. Instead of a neat separation of value spheres—art in this corner, politics in that, and never the twain shall meet—modernity seems to be characterized by their competition, Weber's polytheistic cosmos in which incompatible desiderata make simultaneous demands on our judgments: politics and art, war and culture.

None of that is particularly controversial. Even the most dyed-in-the-wool conservative adherent of cultural autonomy must recognize today that the cultural discussion, especially within the university, is also a political discussion. Yet if this politicization of culture is old hat, what about the aestheticization of politics? Here others, presumably now on the orthodox left side of the spectrum, may find it a more bitter pill to swallow that the political discussion is also a cultural discussion. The suggestion is that the inquiry into a political event, such as a war, can proceed beyond a factual determination of the objective or perceived interests pursued and include as well issues of values, self-understanding, national identity, and experiential significance. In other words, an explanation of the war should not be reduced to the strategic execution of the interests of the state or empowered economic strata but would have to include—and not as an afterthought—the sentiments of all the participants, especially the national populations whose affective mobilization is a precondition for the war. For when soldiers go to war, they do so, presumably, not only owing to the secret decisions of the executive committee of an avaricious bourgeoisie. This line of thought, however, would lead to a surprising and perhaps counterintuitive conclusion. It would imply that the superficially critical practice of the left of revealing one more confidential document, one more hidden conspiracy, one more dangerous liaison is an ultimately pornographic desire to peek through the keyholes of power, rather than a credible mode of explanation, and, furthermore, depends on an elitist privileging of a putatively high domain of politics over a mass culture characterized by an ethics of obligation, loyalty, and community. One would then have to face the cultural contradiction between, on the one hand, the largely antiwar liberalism of relatively privileged and ascendant social strata with their loyalty to the institution of the state (despite opposition to any particular administration) and, on the other hand, the widespread phenomenon of yellow-ribbon populism. At the very least, one has to take note of the disruptive fact that popular culture may not necessarily be politically correct.

This consideration highlights a problem endemic to the cultural studies agenda, the political import of the study of both popular culture and everyday history. To expand a cultural investigation to include a political dimension will seem at least plausible to most, except perhaps for the most rigorous high modernists or old New Critics. To expand a political investigation to include a cultural dimension, however, might well be perceived as a distraction from the allegedly central issues and events, deemed to be the core of the matter. In this sense, one might argue that an *Alltagsgeschichte* of Nazi Germany, focusing on, say, quotidian experience in a small city, would necessarily miss the central matter by missing Auschwitz. Similarly a history of popular culture of early-twentieth-century Russia would tend to deflect our attention from the epoch-making events of the Bolshevik revolution. With regard to the Gulf War, critics of American policy, who understand the war solely in terms of diplomatic machinations and the economics of petrodollars, regard references to values and principles, the ideological need to repel aggression, the subjectively perceived importance of loyalty, or the desire for community, as just so much cultural fog that obscures the allegedly objective interests at stake.

Whether or not one accepts the objections implied by these particular examples, one does well to take note of the asymmetry in the practice of interdisciplinary investigation on the border between politics and culture. There appears to be less resistance to the politicization of the cultural object than to the cultural component of the political object. To account for this status quo of contemporary intellectual life, various strategies are imaginable. One might propose, first, that the different types of objects have fundamentally different structures, as if inherently "soft" works of art allowed for more transgressively disciplinary practices than putatively "harder" political or social scientific facts. Yet this line of argument, not all that different from the assumptions behind autonomy aesthetics, would obviously require a more extensive ontological framing that would probably produce more problems than it would solve and would, furthermore, rob the material of any historical character by essentializing the different object types. Alternatively, one could of course simply historicize the competing discourses by ascribing to the humanities a temporary theoretical advance over the social sciences, i.e., literary scholars go beyond the work of art more than political scientists go beyond the state because of the accelerated theoretical discussion within the humanities disciplines during the past three decades. Yet, if this argument might appear credible with regard to the institutional conservatism of, say, history departments, it could hardly hold for anthropology or some sections of cultural sociology and, in any case, it is an argument that only displaces the problem rather than solving it. For one would still have to explain why methodological change proceeded at different rates within the various fields of study.

In order to present a third and final hypothesis, let me return to the material once more. The tolerance for interdisciplinarity in culture ultimately entails the conceptual dissolution of the work of art, which can be accounted for, following Benjamin, with reference to the proliferation of postauratic forms in the age of mechanical reproduction. Those terms will have to stand in as a shorthand for largely familiar arguments regarding the politicization of art, the contestation of cultural values, and the communitarian involvement in aesthetic processes. The point is that similar transformations are less discernible in the discourse on the state, to which a greater degree of relative autonomy is still ascribed. The political institution is consequently defended as an instrument for the viable pursuit of interests, rights, and social engineering, rather than as a space of democratic participation. The values of the community therefore appear to be solely epiphenomenal to the presumably real agendas of state power. Whether this appearance derives from the institutional conservatism of the state itself or, rather represents a function of the discourse on the state, or even the interests of those intellectuals authorized to carry out the discourse on the state, will remain an open question. However, some of the material on the debates on the Gulf War, to which I now turn, will help us toward formulating an answer.

In order to focus on the relevant cultural issues, I want to bracket explicitly two other sorts of concerns that do not bear directly on my argument. First, the presumably "hard" or "real" facts are not at stake here, the culturally non-mediated stuff of diplomatic historians or political scientists: the truthfulness of April Glaspie, the artificiality of Iraq's borders, the quality of the Kuwaiti state, the authenticity of the alleged nuclear potential, the efficiency of sanctions, etc. Nor will I try to determine the rationale for war, the motivations of the decision-making bodies in the various states involved. Instead I will look at the sorts of cultural-theoretical claims that frequently punctuated the public discussion of these issues. Second, I will not belabor the difference between the quality of public discussion in Germany and that in the United States, the relative dearth of public intellectuals here, a higher standard of debate there. The American discussion has, alas, nothing to match Habermas in *Die Zeit* or Enzensberger in *Der Spiegel*; this is an old story, and, reviewing the material, one can only factor in this difference and hope that one is not just comparing apples and oranges.

Within the public discussion on the politics of the war, the various cultural-theoretical claims and assumptions are of interest, particularly as they relate to their specific national contexts. This is, first of all, a historical context, as Ralf Dahrendorf pointed out, insofar as the American discussion of the Gulf took place in the shadow of Vietnam, while the German perception depended on the memory of the Second World War.[1] Indeed the two discussions are replete with references to these pasts, with complex implications. "No more Vietnams" was inverted in a breathtaking ideological maneuver from an antiwar slogan into an argument for massive intervention rather than gradual escalation, while the antiwar movement was incapacitated by an initial inability to distinguish between the two situations: if Saddam wasn't Hitler, he certainly wasn't Ho Chi Minh. In Germany, the national past generated concern with Israel as well as the reluctance to become involved militarily, not only within the peace movement but far into the circles of conservative power; it was, after all, President Weizsäcker who asserted that "the world doesn't want to discover again what good soldiers Germans can be."[2] These are, of course, some preliminary indications that political actions—American intervention, German reticence—are not solely the consequence of objective interest but also the expression of subjective values and belief structures derived from collective experience. That is not an uncontroversial claim, to imply that American policy may have been driven by the ghosts of Vietnam as much as or even more than it was by oil interests and imperial geopolitics, or that Germany's foreign policy caution was a cultural phenomenon rather than a calculated reliance on American soldiers as mercenary proxies used to protect its own export-oriented economy.

In addition to this diachronic component, the weight of the past, the discursive context also includes the perceived status of the discussants themselves within their synchronic terrains. Who are the presumed addressees of the statements on the politics of the war and its cultural standing? How do the authors imagine their own positions vis-à-vis their readers and the larger public? And how are these two functions, authorized intellectuals and public recipients, configured vis-à-vis the political elite? This implied communicative structure is itself strong evidence of the character of the culture within which the discussion on the war transpires. In both settings, Germany and the United States, the writers tend to claim for themselves a beleaguered status, defending their stance against a presumably widespread alternative position. This is no surprise but rather an example of the standard adversariality of intellectuals, whose metier conventionally includes opposition and criticism. This standpoint for argument is then variously modified to incorporate ambivalence, i.e., the concession that one's own stance is internally conflicted, or to insist on objective certainty, especially when addressing a minority audience presumed to share one's interpretation. An example of the former type is Habermas, the latter, Chomsky, and each implies alternative assumptions regarding the operation of culture in relation both to the mass public and to the political leadership.

If these formalist speculations hold in both Germany and the United States, the situations differ when one begins to examine the content of the material. In Germany, the texts indicate the assumption of either a widespread opposition to the war or, at least, inadequate support, and the key authors arguing for the war are compelled to suggest cultural explanations for this political misjudgment. In contrast, the American texts, by authors opposing the war, have to account for its unmistakable popularity, and they too reach for cultural rationalizations. In both cases, then, and despite the alternative positions on the war, we are dealing with cultural intellectuals who, in the process of making political arguments, mobilize fragments of cultural theory in order to criticize the perceived false consciousness of the body politic. How do German intellectuals, variously defending the war, account for the antiwar sentiment of their compatriots? How do American opponents of the war account for its support? The substance of their arguments may tell us something about their respective cultures as well as about the relationship of intellectuals to the societies within which they operate.

If I have to cite at least one metaphor as proof of the participation of cultural-rhetorical operations in the practice of war, it is the equation of Saddam and Hitler—this poetry did make something happen—and while it may have been authored by George Bush, it was above all in Germany that the memory of the Nazi past played a role in structuring the discourse on the politics of the Gulf. The problem is that metaphors can be wild cards, so it is not immediately obvious who will be cast as the Nazis in the remake; for the peace movement, it was not at all the Iraqis but, on the contrary, the Americans. Hence the comments of Walter Jens, author and literature professor, with regard to his impending prosecution for harboring two American soldiers, absent without leave, reportedly due to their opposition to the war:

> My wife and I lived through the National Socialist period. The risks taken by people who hid others then were thousands of times greater than ours. Naturally we are ready to accept responsibility for what we have done. One can't continually quote Carl von Ossietzky and not be willing to draw the consequences he did in 1933—even if it means going to jail. I don't think it will come to that, but one can expect at least a little consistency from us.[3]

Clearly the argument for civil disobedience is legitimated here through an imitative relationship to historical antifascism. Yet it is also equally clear that the metaphor is strained, insofar as it is unlikely that Professor Jens will suffer the same fate in a concentration camp as did von Ossietzky, whom he claims to emulate. Nevertheless Jens's stance exemplifies what one might call the belated antifascism that can structure German political debate: because of the failure of the German left to defeat Hitler in the forties, it opposes Hitler subsequently in the guise of the Americans: during the Vietnam era, in the context of the missiles discussion of the early eighties, and again with regard to the Gulf.

The play of this metaphor is, however, more complex, since it was after all to a large extent American forces who defeated German fascism. On one level, one suspects a submerged jealousy on the part of antifascist Germans of the American success where they themselves failed. On a deeper level, the German anti-Americanism may still draw precisely on a resentment of the American defeat of Hitler, superficially hidden by a partially pretextuous antifascism. Hence an identification with the Iraqis who, like the Germans, are the victims of an American bombing campaign, perhaps even an identification because of Saddam's affinity with Hitler; in any case, the master metaphor of Saddam as Hitler was not, despite Bush's intention, always a univocal argument necessarily for military intervention. The matter is complicated further by the fact that it was, of course, not only Jens's von Ossietzsky who was persecuted by the Nazis. Given the legacy of the Holocaust, the issue of Israeli security plays a significantly larger role in Germany than in the United States (where it is, for reasons worth pursuing, rather suppressed).[4] Hence the disappointment of the Israeli author Yoram Kaniuk with Günter Grass's antiwar stance or, more vitriolically, Henryk Broder's accusations of de facto anti-Semitism within the German peace movement.[5]

So in Germany, the equation of Saddam and Hitler is translated into a recollection of the Second World War as a model for understanding the Gulf, and the results are, to say the least, complex. The subtitle of Habermas' essay in *Die Zeit* captures this tension—"a plea for reticence, but not with regard to Israel"—and his commentary explains the historical dimensions of the problem:

> It is true that many citizens of the Federal Republic react ambivalently to the war in the Gulf. There are historical reasons for this. The two strongest sentiments that formed the political consciousness of, for example, my generation derive from the Nazi era and the war; and they are related to what we have retrospectively learned from them. The connection between dictatorship and the genocide on the Jews determines the loyalty toward Israel; the connection between nationalism and the war of conquest determines a skepticism of any power politics that endangers the civil coexistence of nations. The break with the fascist past is expressed nearly instinctively in two reflexes: no more anti-Semitism and the retraction of equal civil rights; no more nationalism and war. The Gulf War leads to a conflict between these affects. Affects can pull us in different directions, but the internal connection of the groundings must not break.[6]

Habermas transforms this ambivalence into what might be described as a moderate position: the recognition of Germany's "special duties" to Israel, hence support for the war, coupled with a cautionary note against the escalation of the "logic of war" into excessive violence or an improper annexationist politics. He can therefore treat the intervention as legitimate but keep the door open for a criticism of the precise character of the use of force or the nature of postwar power arrangements. Thus he rejects the antiwar movement while applauding its antimilitarist values, just as he underscores his opposition to German nationalist militarists, despite his concurring in their support for the United States.

The result is that for Habermas, characteristically, the central political categories are legality and proportionality. It cannot be a "just war," since, within the postmetaphysical context of modernity, an absolute or unquestionable good is not given. It is however a "justifiable war," insofar as there exist adequate grounds to assert international law with conventional military means. The rational limitation on the war involves both the scope of the means employed to reach the end and the legality of the end itself: revoking the annexation of Kuwait, perhaps the destruction of Iraq's nonconventional arms potential, but not an incursion into Iraq's sovereignty or its internal affairs, i.e., the removal of Saddam. For our purposes, however, it is important to recognize that Habermas' motivation is not (or not only) the real politics of the Gulf but rather the political culture of Germany. For the war does not take place solely in the shadow of 1945; it is also—here a further cultural element—post-1989 and implies a debate over the political culture of unified Germany. It is worth noting that commentators across the spectrum complained that the political elite—Kohl and Genscher—failed to articulate clear positions for Germany, and a discussion of values consequently devolves onto cultural intellectuals. In the kindest version, Dahrendorf suggests that the new Germany is simply too young to have developed a clear-cut political agenda. For Habermas, however, as well as for his longtime opponent Karl Heinz Bohrer, there is something bigger at stake that goes to the heart of German culture: what sort of nation is Germany? what traditions determine its political behavior? what does it mean to become a modern state?

Habermas' references to legality and rationality in foreign policy imply their centrality domestically as well: an effectively liberal position that draws its pathos from an always implied critique of German fascism and authoritarian traditions. Thus, despite his approbation of the war, by the end of the essay he defends the German reticence to provide unlimited support to the Americans, and the defense therefore pertains to the peace movement as well, as an indication of a cultural progress beyond the German militarist past. If the assertion of the rule of law means repelling Iraqi aggression, it also means, more importantly, an opposition to the revival of reactionary (for Habermas, antimodern) legacies of war and power politics:

> This reluctance [regarding support for the United States] is neither the result of old *incertitudes allemandes* nor the expression of a new German particularity but at best a reflected understanding of specific German experiences. It is also in the interest of our neighbors and Israel that I hope that the politics of reticence will not be crushed by that terrifying normalcy which would endow reunified Germany with its former aggressiveness and bless us with the long desired amnesia. That would not be pleasant, and not only for us. In terms of the civilized political culture that seemed to be developing in the old Federal Republic, the state unification has hardly meant a liberalization of the expanded Germany: in the East the return of old mentalities,

here [in the West] the burgeoning of a chauvinism of wealth. If the idea of an international order, which the end of the cold war appeared to promise, now gives way to an ongoing state of nature between bellicose states, that would be just fine for the proponents of a fetishized normalcy. Now that they have won anything but laurels for their administratively forced unification politics, are they hoping to shift to a belligerent foreign policy?[7]

To rephrase that densely packed argument: Habermas opposed the relatively administrative rather than democratic process of unification: the annexation of the East German provinces rather than the national plebiscite (and debate) anticipated by the constitution. He can allude to the postunification political turbulence and economic hardships as evidence for the inadequacy of the process. He can critique the conservative constellation of "old mentalities" (i.e., the irrationalism of a political romanticism) and "a chauvinism of wealth" (i.e., the private virtues of accumulation rather than the public virtues of citizenship), to which he counterposes his program of rationality, the more desirable version of German cultural modernization. Germany can become more modern and more Western not through an unquestioned acceptance of the political primacy of the modern West—the United States—but through the development of a rational political culture, even when it leads to a "reticence" vis-à-vis the United States.

Yet when one turns to Bohrer, presumably one of the "advocates of normalcy" intended by Habermas, the arguments in support of the war—or rather, against German opposition to the war—are driven by similar concerns: not rational legality, to be sure, which plays no role in Bohrer's postmodern conservatism, but the character of German culture and the overcoming of political romanticism. How can Germany become modern and Western? By imitating the modern West. Earlier he had contrasted the opportunism of West German politics with what he perceived as the mythic heroism of the British during the Falklands War.[8] Now, in the context of the Gulf War, he views German reticence as a legacy of German "provincialism," an amalgamation of anti-Western sentiment, misidentifications from the Second World War, and traditions of Central European cultural pessimism. If Habermas judged romanticism as the source of an irrational authoritarianism, Bohrer treats political romanticism, following Carl Schmitt, as an inability to make decisions, leading to the same "apathy regarding practical-political morality," that impoverished Wilhelm II and that now generates the German discomfort with the war.[9] Indeed Bohrer criticizes the irrationalism of the German peace movement less for its political tendency (with which he disagrees) than for its inability to express even its own tendency in any politically significant manner: "Who were those teachers," he asks, regarding German antiwar protests, who led little children carrying candles into the street so they could express their "angst" and demonstrate for "peace"? No sense of shame, let alone tact or style. No grasp of the ridiculousness of the ceremony. What was this strangely uncivilized, sentimental language, with undertones of blackmail? I suddenly understood that this was not a matter of different political opinions but different cultural mentalities: an eruption of feelings no longer restrained by a civilizational regulation and which, potentially, could go in a very different direction. At an English or American university there would certainly have been opponents to this language of sentiment, if only to uphold a principle of individualism. . . . As the protest wrapped in "angst" spreads through the universities, one sees that, due to the National Socialist catastrophe, unified Germany cannot, in a moment of crisis, be counted as a Western power with corresponding political mentalities but as a Central European gray zone without the democratic traditions of a politically spontaneous public. American protests against the Gulf War had a concrete goal: their own war-waging government. German protests, by way of contrast, were rituals of sentiment without political argument.[10]

The romanticism of German culture prevents the political elite—for whom Bohrer reserves his most bitter comments—from grasping the imperatives of geopolitics, and it is the same romanticism that even prevents the peace movement from acting in a politically convincing manner. "This appears to be a German peculiarity, for even the mode of argument of the old 68er Noam Chomsky . . . is, despite his deceptively utopian categories, far from the appeal of German polit-kitsch."[11]

Clearly Bohrer is interested less in a critique of Iraq (which Habermas provided in his treatment of the invasion as an infringement of international law) than in a dissection of German culture. Like Habermas, he suggests the need to overcome part of the cultural past. Like Habermas, the experience of National Socialism is of central diagnostic significance. Yet while Habermas presents it as the grounds for a learning process, Enlightenment, leading to liberalization and modernity, Bohrer treats it as an amplification of a long-standing German deficiency in political behavior; instead of progress, only regression has ensued, and the only remaining possibility is an imitative admiration for the health of the West:

Only the Anglo-Saxons can operate normally with the horror scenario (which allowed them to eradicate Dresden in 1944 and later Hiroshima, with nearly no moral scruples). As lords of the history of the twentieth century, they have not developed a sense of pain and guilt, as little as someone who feels well subjectively goes to a psychiatrist. They are so self-assured because their morality is practical, a part of their praxis: their semantics is still covered by a holy cause. Some might be terrified by this, especially when they observe the metaphor of the American commander Schwarzkopf, who promises Hussein to "kick his ass," and apparently means the physical destruction of his army, while George Bush prays to God in pastoral concentration, like England's Henry V on the night of Agincourt. But to denounce this as "false consciousness" entails a naive misunderstanding of an essential structure of the western hemisphere: it is ruled not by cultural critical nihilism but by the hope for meaning in difficult circumstances. One correctly resists the blackmail of the apocalyptic argument. . . . [12]

The prominence of the figures of nihilism and apocalypse within German culture can be confirmed by a brief look at Hans Magnus Enzensberger's essay on Saddam and Hitler. [13] For Habermas, political nihilism produced National Socialism and should be overcome by a program of rationality; for Bohrer, nihilism is a consequence of National Socialism that can be cured only by a Great Power pragmatism; for Enzensberger it was the core of National Socialism but, furthermore, remains an effectively global potential. For Hitler, like Saddam, the goal was not the rational pursuit of power but total destruction, including his own. Therefore, any politics of appeasement or reconciliation are out of place. Second, the affinity between Hitler and Saddam implies that "the Germans were the Iraqis from 1938 to 1945," a claim with considerable consequences. It automatically subverts, at least in Germany, any racist interpretation of the war, and also accounts for the ongoing anti-interventionist sympathies of the Germans: "German industry never had to regret the considerable services it offered Adolf Hitler; that it aids his successor with the same zeal is only consistent. And if a considerable portion of German youth prefer to identify with Palestinians rather than Israelis, if it directs its protests against George Bush rather than Saddam Hussein, this cannot be explained away as innocence." [14]

Yet these aspects of Enzensberger's essay imply relatively limited political claims: that military force and not diplomacy (or sanctions) will be necessary to block Saddam's aspirations; and that the German antiwar movement is marred by some problematic *völkisch* undercurrents. His central point, however, is considerably larger and gives a radically new inflection to the Saddam as Hitler metaphor. Habermas criticized Enzensberger's adoption of the metaphor because it undercuts the uniqueness of the Holocaust, relativizes the judgment on Hitler, and therefore tends to have an exculpatory impact on German history. Indeed in the recent *Historikerstreit*, Habermas went to the barricades against conservative historians who had pursued precisely that agenda. To direct the same criticism at Enzensberger is nevertheless unfair, since he anticipates it anyhow and presents a very different argument: not a reduction of the status of Hitler but an admonition regarding his potential return.

The interesting question is, however, what it is exactly that Enzensberger imagines might be returning.

For Bush, Saddam is Hitler primarily as the aggressor, and the chain of associations leads through Munich, Chamberlain, appeasement, and so forth; the lesson has to do with relationships among states and the respect for international borders. Enzensberger tells a different story. Hitler as well as Saddam is not a normal dictator like "Franco, Batista, Marcos, Pinochet," and others, oppressing their people and oriented toward their own self-preservation, but rather an enemy of the whole world, for whom rational calculation of interests is irrelevant, since "the death wish is his motive, and catastrophe is his mode of rule."[15] Furthermore, the national collective, far from being deceived by such leaders, participates eagerly in precisely this desire for suicidal destruction: "What enthused the Germans was not only the license to kill but much more the prospect of being killed themselves. Today, with similar zeal, millions of Arabs express the desire to die for Saddam."[16] Hence Enzensberger's move from the master metaphor to a claim regarding an anthropological potential for populations to pursue mass destruction, including their own. Such developments will tend to occur when local aspirations appear irrevocably blocked by international arrangements and world orders, leading to hate, resentment, and desperation on the part of the community that perceives itself as disenfranchised.

Enzensberger's essay implies three conclusions. (1) The challenge of a nihilistic community can be met only by force and not by reason. (2) The perpetual disprivileging of population groups within international arrangements will tend to unleash these self-destructive impulses. (3) Saddam will not be the last repetition of Hitler: "Eternal losers are everywhere. Their feeling of abuse and their proclivity to suicide increase every year. The nuclear arsenal for it is available on the Indian subcontinent and in the Soviet Union. Where Hitler and Saddam failed, in the final victory, that is, the final solution—their next follower may succeed."[17] In other words, a new world order designed solely to preserve an unequal organization of legitimate states and that can therefore be regarded as impervious to the appeals of particular communities will face constant threats of disruption.

What sort of general observations does the German material allow? The three authors—Habermas, Bohrer, and Enzensberger—support the war, albeit in different manners and with different arguments. Yet in all three cases, the discussion of the war is, to a greater or lesser extent, subverted by a deeper concern with Germany. There is a pervasive dissatisfaction with the political elite for its inability or unwillingness to clarify a consistent foreign policy. National identity is moreover refracted through at least three historical parameters: the developing character of political culture after the unification of 1989, the conflicted interpretations of the Nazi era, and the deeper legacy of romanticism and cultural pessimism. Furthermore, there is a distancing from the antiwar sentiment of the peace movement, although least emphatically by Habermas, and its deficiencies are accounted for in the terms of the analysis of national identity. The West, understood to be sure in various ways, appears as a desirable model, and the crucial question—the old question—is whether Germany will be able to overcome its past and emulate it.

In the discussion in the United States, the situation is considerably different, although not necessarily different in the same way that Bohrer suggested. The image of Germany presented so far—and it is, of course, an overgeneralization—entails prowar intellectuals facing an antiwar public and a political elite that was, if not antiwar, then certainly extremely ambiguous with regard to the intervention. In the United States, by way of contrast, I want to sketch a scenario of antiwar left intellectuals facing a prowar public and uniquely unable to account for this discrepancy; indeed it is precisely with regard to that discrepancy that some apparently insufficient cultural theory is articulated. This is of course a noteworthy configuration insofar as the left understands itself not only as oppositional vis-à-vis the elite but also as democratic, i.e., allied with the popular will, which in this instance, however, it is evidently incapable of understanding.

If there is a similarity between Germany and the United States, it has to do, strangely enough, with the political leadership. To be sure, Bush's advocacy of the war is a far cry from the ambiguities of Genscherism, but despite the substantive difference, a formal similarity is evident in his inability to provide a clear articulation of the war goals (which certainly contributed to his political difficulties before January 17, and after, as well). If Saddam was Hitler, then why not complete the metaphor and remove him from power? If one calls on the Kurds to rebel, then why not support them? Was the point to end the occupation of Kuwait or destroy the Iraqi arsenal or induce a change in Baghdad? Whatever one's position on the war was, it is likely that Bush said it at some point, since he effectively said every possible position.[18] One implication of this rhetorical confusion is that the motivation behind populist patriotism, the sea of yellow ribbons, was not at all necessarily identical to the motivation of the political elite, even if both supported the war, a point to which I will return in the conclusion.

Bohrer was prepared to extend his crucial distinction between an antipolitical German romanticism and English-speaking pragmatism into the antiwar camps themselves: better a rational American anti-imperialist than an angst-ridden German teacher. Yet if one can do without Bohrer's anglophilia and looks at the material on the war, the picture turns out to be somewhat different: German intellectuals, arguing against perceived public sentiment, operate with historical-hermeneutic means in order to characterize that sentiment, while American opponents of the war can explain the prowar public only instrumentally by invoking charges of secret plans, manipulation, and deception. Thus Michael Emery: "There is now a precedent for wide ranging censorship of U.S. correspondents and for increased use of CIA and psychological operations disinformation—in short, the propagandists won the war."[19] Similarly, Craig Hulet, "We've never had a more censored press in our history since World War Two. . . . So every political objective George Bush has outlined is either false or an outright blatant lie. There can only be one conclusion: There's a political objective he hasn't told us."[20] Or David Bromwich: "A working political democracy does not work like this. But in the conduct of foreign policy, we have gone a long way now to a different system: a plebiscitary despotism, in which the executive is invested with extraordinary powers and contact with a docile public is mediated on television and in newspapers by reports of actions already taken."[21] Or finally, Bohrer's cherished example of the pragmatic and, one supposes, Anglo-Saxon Noam Chomsky:

> You have to remember that this is the post-Orwellian world. When people say "diplomacy," what they mean is "rejection of diplomacy." . . . The reason for the U.S. rejection of diplomacy was also spelled out very clearly from the outset, right on the front page of the *New York Times*. You didn't have to work very hard to find it. There's a position at the *New York Times* called "Chief Diplomatic Correspondent." That's a euphemism meaning "State Department spokesman."[22]

One need not assume that the power elite is composed of paragons of honesty in order to regard the accounts just cited with some skepticism. For their implication is that real politics are always hidden, that the press serves primarily as a vehicle of deception, and that the public is extensively susceptible to the operations of manipulation. Thus public sentiment, i.e., populist support for the war, has absolutely no legitimacy of its own but is solely the intended result of disinformation from on high. It is likely, however, that the production of meaning is somewhat more complex. Indeed one could even concede the dubious claim that politicians are always only liars and still question the insinuation that the public is always only duped, devoid of any intelligence, curiosity, or disbelief, let alone an autonomous capacity for political or cultural will. For if we follow Chomsky et al., then it is only they, the intellectuals, who have access to the truth, while the cognitively impoverished masses make up an infinite field of couch potatoes, always available for harvesting by the mendacious mass media. If this is the only way the left can account for the discrepancy between its opposition to the war and populist support, then one can only say good-by to the past decade of progressivist celebration of popular culture as somehow politically desirable.

Yet this is exactly where Chomsky leads us, back to a cultural theory of mass manipulation.

> A properly functioning system of indoctrination has a variety of tasks, some rather delicate. One of its targets is the stupid and ignorant masses. They must be kept that way, diverted with emotionally potent oversimplifications, marginalized, and isolated. Ideally, each person should be alone in front of the television screen watching sports, soap operas, or comedies, deprived of organizational structures that permit individuals lacking resources to discover what they think and believe in interaction with others, to formulate their own concerns and programs, and to act to realize them. They can then be permitted, even encouraged, to ratify the decisions of their betters in periodic elections. The rascal multitude are the proper targets of the mass media and a public education system geared to obedience and training in needed skills, including the skill of repeating patriotic slogans on timely occasions.[23]

To be sure, Chomsky is critical of this system, and he goes on to make his obligatory anarchist gesture by invoking Bakunin's prediction that in both state socialism and state capitalism, elites of bureaucratic intellectuals would retain power by manipulating degraded masses. The point, however, is that Chomsky himself buys into the paradigm as fully adequate: arcane conspiracies at the top, the deceived populace below. Especially if measured against the diagnoses of antiwar sentiment in Germany, Chomsky's is a sorely inadequate and instrumentalist description of the operation of culture in the United States and one that, in the end, leads directly to the privileging of Chomsky himself as the sole vehicle of enlightenment.

This regression to a cultural theory of mass manipulation sheds an important light on the configuration of American intellectuals vis-à-vis not only the war, politics, popularity, and power but also the much larger *Kulturkampf*, although it was indeed the context of the war that brought underlying problems to the surface. In recent years a good deal of discussion has been devoted to reconsidering the material of cultural representation and, especially, the content of university literary curricula, all of which has been relegated to the rubric of redefining the canon. There is, to be sure, something very natural and unshocking about such an undertaking. Shifting social and political concerns, changing intellectual and scholarly issues, can very understandably lead to an interest in different groups of literary texts. A conservative orthodoxy in cultural matters would quickly lose touch with the lived reality of students and the rest of society and therefore not even provide the sort of stable identity that conservative theoreticians, from T. S. Eliot to Allan Bloom have repeatedly asserted. On the contrary, only through a constant reevaluation of the material of cultural representation, a never terminated reexamination of issues of identity, tradition, and values, can a society undertake an effective self-scrutiny and help clarify the goals it may choose to pursue. Culture—precisely because it is a dimension of freedom—is always involved in a teleological projection, and that telos is never fully or exhaustively articulated.

If, then, canonic rigidity is not socially stabilizing, if cultural conservatism does not translate into social immobility, then neither does canonic reform necessarily imply social reform and, particularly, it does not necessarily imply democratization. This insight goes to the very heart of contemporary cultural debates. For while there are compelling theoretical grounds for an ongoing review of the curriculum, it does not follow that engineering curricular revisions is the same as a democratic or progressive social engineering. Yet this has been the metaphor that has driven much of the discussion within university circles: integrating the erstwhile curriculum with texts authored by minorities and women as a corollary to social integration, or displacing the objects of a denigrated "high culture" with the material of "popular culture," both moves understood as somehow obviously democratic. Getting rid of the elite texts is imagined to be the same as getting rid of the elite.

But every metaphor is always a kind of displacement. Instead of a vague corollary to political change, the culturalist agenda is, at least in part, also a substitute, an alternative, and, in fact, a denial of the very political change that is invoked as a legitimating alibi. Instead of political reform, cultural reform—the victims are given expression rather than power. This sort of aestheticization of politics can be viewed in various ways. In the wake of the collapse of the oppositional movements of the sixties and the perceived irrelevance of the Democratic party, left intellectuals, out of sheer desperation, attempt to hold onto some of their political identity, now displaced into the cultural dimension: cultural studies as the memory of a failed cultural revolution. An alternative—and not incompatible—argument could analyze this culturalist shift as part of a larger transformation in which matters of representation and appearance take precedence over lived experience and material practice. In this account, it is not only the intellectual class that has become transfixed by the wonder of signs but the whole society which, trapped in the structures of ideology that now pervade all of everyday life, accepts the occupation of politics by the media and the occlusion of experience by its representations. In shorthand, the history of this formation runs from the culture industry and the society of the spectacle to a culture of narcissism, where the self is eclipsed by its own image.

Both of these versions have some validity—and some important problems—but a third hypothesis is of greater interest in the present context. It bears especially on the claim that a discrete set of cultural objects labeled "popular culture"—melodrama, harlequin romances, commercial television and cinema, for example—is somehow genuinely "popular," i.e., of the people, and therefore an authentically democratic alternative to other cultural objects, labeled "high culture" and therefore presumably associated with elite social strata. In the rhetorical context of American democracy, any suggestion of illegitimate hierarchy is of course tantamount to a denunciation—and in part rightly so—and this sort of opposition between allegedly high and low terrains is extremely powerful within the public sphere of universities.

My point is not at all to discredit the appropriateness of examining the material of so-called popular culture: intellectual integrity dictates that a scholarly inquiry into the substance of culture examine all possible cases and not only those conventionally and, arguably, arbitrarily recognized as worthwhile. What one wants to test, however, is the claim that this material is in fact "popular," with all the weighty political resonance that the term carries. One line of such questioning picks up with the objection made long ago by Horkheimer and Adorno with their insistence on preferring the term "culture industry" to alternatives such as "mass culture" or "popular culture," a preference implying that this material is commercially produced by a powerful segment of industry whose marketing interests very much depend on the pretense that its products are not its own but of the masses or the people. The more they appear to be popular, the better the sales, and the academic proponents of popular culture turn into little more than the sales agents of the industry. Critical theory's effort to oppose this ideological deception and to defend the de facto consumers against the claims of industry that the commodities of mass culture are somehow substantively a culture of the masses implies, perhaps counterintuitively, that the notorious elitists Horkheimer and Adorno, in their anticapitalist purism, took sides with popular strata against the elites of the corporate boards of the culture industry. The same cannot be said, unfortunately, for the left defenders of popular culture.

There is a second and more germane line of questioning to be pursued regarding the alleged popularity of this material. Reconsider the popular culture argument: in effect, the case is being made for a shift in taste, within the specific zone of the university curriculum. An established taste, not surprisingly associated with members of an older scholarly generation, is denounced as elitist; against it, an alternative set of objects is posed and, furthermore, declared to be popular and democratic. In other words, the first argument for a simple shift in taste is compounded, secondarily, by a political argument, which, however, is not itself necessarily convincing. It is not immediately obvious that the social and political elites constitute the primary recipients of "high culture"—is it really the case that high income means high art, that Ted Kennedy and George Bush prefer Arnold Schoenberg to Wayne Newton? Nor is it self-evident that appreciation of high art is undeniable evidence of high social standing, etc. While there is probably some connection between social status and aesthetic taste, it is simultaneously more flexible and more complex than can be encompassed by a simplistic doubling of the vertical metaphor of high and low from society into art.

One can account for the seductiveness of this doubling—the claim that popular culture means democratic politics—in a number of ways. It may have been the case that in the eighteenth century, in the age of bourgeois revolutions, the class-coding of culture was more precise and the differentiation between aristocratic and bourgeois cultural institutions was easily recognizable. Arnold Hauser's work might be cited in defense of that position, and this paradigm for the interpretation of the social history of culture might lend itself easily to a misapplication in the present when the class lines in culture are considerably more complex. (Or perhaps it was more complex even in the eighteenth century with aristocrats participating in bourgeois culture and vice versa.) In addition, the desire to shuttle back and forth easily between culture and politics is probably a legacy of communism which, during some phases, attempted to articulate cultural policies based on the assumption that certain aesthetic forms corresponded particularly well to particular political positions: hence the search for a politically correct art. One should remember that that historical conflation of politics and art, particularly in the early twentieth century, was extremely murky, with the aesthetic avant-garde mounting political arguments in order to justify artistic innovation and the political vanguardists making cynical aesthetic arguments to carry out political agendas. In addition, other positions within the working-class movement tended to refuse the politicization of culture—as in historical social democracy—arguing instead solely for universal access to the objects of bourgeois culture: a position that probably corresponded to the behavior of working-class strata eager to display the signs of bourgeois taste as an outward indication of upward mobility. That of course would be an example of the decoupling of aesthetic taste from real social status.

Yet if we were to explain the contemporary construction of popular culture as an imitation of either the French or the Russian Revolution—or both—we would still be taking the equation of culture and politics at face value and missing the main point. For the linkage between the contingency of taste (one canon can be replaced with another) and the imperative of politics (popularity is preferable to elitism) is not at all a continuation, metaphoric or otherwise, of a democratic politics into the realm of culture but rather the pursuit of a particular politics—the politics of careerism—within the universities, where the stakes are not demolishing hierarchy, emancipating minorities, freeing political prisoners, peace and freedom, or bread and roses, but rather, more mundanely, tenure and promotion. In other words, a new taste system, labeled arbitrarily (but not uncleverly) "popular," is invented as a tool with which to dislodge the carriers of other taste systems with the help of a high-powered political rhetoric but without any sincere political aspirations. To rally to the cause of what, for example, Julia Kristeva has labeled "the revolution in poetic language" means carrying out the revolution in the English department, and nowhere else, and that revolution turns out to be the next move in the musical chairs—who gets to be chairman—within the academic nomenklatura.

Let me make the provocation clear: instead of simply trying to relativize the conflation of politics and culture inherent in the advocacy of popular culture as a matter of a belated reception of Arnold Hauser or Georg Lukács or whomever, one can query the motives behind certain versions of the discourse on popular culture and therefore treat it, following Bourdieu, as an artificial sign of distinction of a particular variant of homo academicus. Popular culture lends itself to an agenda for professional status—a new-class career strategy— and is not necessarily very much concerned with anything like democracy. To substantiate this offensive claim, I would have to come up with evidence of the weakness of the connection between popular culture and democratic politics, a case where the otherwise rhetorically powerful concatenation collapses and support for popular culture is coupled with contempt for the populace. As luck would have it, I present exhibit A.

In the *New York Times* of March 11, 1991, two professors of English, Constance Penley of the University of Rochester and Andrew Ross of Princeton, introduce themselves modestly: "as scholars of popular culture, we spend a good deal of our time resisting the widespread assumption that people are passive consumers of the mass media." All well and good, here we find the two rhetorical components already discussed. On the one hand, scholarly specialists understandably insist that their embattled field of expertise is interesting and complex, despite an allegedly common misunderstanding that it is solely a realm of a simplistic passive consumption—and what scholar would not be interested in making a similar claim for the wealth of his or her professional specialty? On the other hand, this first claim, in which the demands of intellect and career are necessarily intertwined, is simultaneously lodged within a political rhetoric. For Ross and Penley are not only arguing, they are "resisting," and their resistance entails a defense of "people" whom others misunderstand as "passive consumers." Ross and Penley know otherwise and rush to the defense of the "people," and therefore take up arms against some heavy opponents. Thus they continue: "This myth is expedient for those with an interest in overestimating the media's power—usually media professionals—and for those whose job is to persuade clients and sponsors, commercial or political, that their messages can be delivered." Suddenly the attempt to defend the intellectual viability of the study of popular culture—and, by extension, the canonic legitimacy of its objects—has been expanded into a political program, a defense of popular aesthetic habits against derogatory characterizations, emanating from the boardrooms of the culture industry and, presumably, from cultural elitists as well. The scholars of popular culture turn out to be the vigilant guardians of the people.

Pausing for a moment, one notes the similarity to and difference from the classical position of critical theory: similar because Horkheimer and Adorno, with their terminological choice already discussed, also tried to separate the masses from the ideology of mass culture; different, however, because for Horkheimer and Adorno (and for Guy Debord as well) the culture industry has the tendency to devastate its recipients through effective means of manipulation, while Penley and Ross want to imagine the recipients as more or less immune to the manipulative schemes of the industry, always somehow independent agents and not "passive consumers of the mass media." In fact, on this point, the account of Penley and Ross is more attractive than that of the Frankfurt School, which one has come to read historically, i.e., the culture industry thesis, as part of a description of homogenizing aspects within twentieth-century capitalism, was a probably accurate critique of the conformist and bureaucratizing tendencies during the construction of the welfare state but no longer captures the dynamic of a society in which considerably more negativity and difference are allowed outside of—and as a corrective to—the administrative apparatus. Going beyond the eradicationism inherent in the model of the culture industry, Penley and Ross try to recognize the potentially activist recipient, despite bureaucracy.

Yet just at the point where the advocacy of popular culture might really turn into an appreciation for popular—or populist?—sentiment, Penley and Ross back off, turn out to be as elitist as their colleagues, recoil in horror from the people, and, in their rush back to the safety of scholarship, try to take popular culture—and their careers—with them, leaving the people behind. Why this turnabout? Why does the equation of popular culture and democratic politics break down?

Penley and Ross were writing in the context of the Gulf War and the widespread popular support. This support presented a strong challenge to progressive claims regarding popular culture, because the popularity of the war tended to be attributed to an allegedly propagandistic character of the television reporting. But that is in effect the return to the manipulation thesis already discussed with regard to Chomsky, and this thesis is obviously diametrically opposed to the progressive advocacy of popular culture. If it was television that manipulated the well-meaning but simpleminded people then, alas, popular culture would turn out to involve precisely the sort of passive consumption which Penley and Ross declare to be a myth. But if it is not a story of manipulation, then Penley and Ross would have to take the popular opinion seriously and at least consider the possibility that some people found convincing—and nonmanipulative—grounds to support the war. That, however, would entail a radical critique of canonic political opinion. The irresistible force and the immovable object: how to save popular culture and dump popular opinion? Let's watch.

"For some," the popular culturalists write, "the popular response to the war in the gulf and its aftermath would seem to confirm the couch potato myth, resurrected in the form of the 'war potato' (or 'Scud spud'), haplessly transfixed by the 'CNN effect' of the first video war. . . . The so-called war potato thus seems to be the perfect example of the cultural dupe who is brainwashed by a medium that follows the White House public relations agenda." Again, that is the manipulation thesis, the mortal threat to the legitimacy of popular culture as a field of scholarly or critical inquiry and, especially, as a locus of progressivist values. While the media may have communicated a prowar message, and while the recipients may have supported the war, Penley and Ross will want to deny the causal connection between the two, while they will also—it goes without saying—want to deny the legitimacy of the support. Why did the people support the war, or rather, why did the people wrongly support the war, if they were not manipulated by television? How can popular politics be wrong and popular culture be right?

The answer: "We dispute this [manipulation] thesis, and not because we think the war potato is a non-dupe who came by his or her unconditional support for the war through an independent interpretation of war coverage. [Why not?] On the contrary, we believe that we have a dupe on our hands, but we do not attribute this condition to the 'CNN effect'; rather, we diagnose it as the condition of war itself." Under the pressure of the war and its popularity, the coupling of professional and political rhetorics in the discourse of "popular culture" is apparently loosening up. Manipulation does occur; the people can be duped, which is why, with their self-evidently incorrect political judgments, they so disappoint the popular culturalists. But the popular culturalists refuse to surrender their preferred cultural object, television, to political barbarism, and they invent a different source of cretinization, the "condition of war." Popular culture is saved, popular politics damned; but then the scholars of culture turn out to be just the academic experts specializing in a particular genre (television), trying to argue for its intellectual viability within the canon—(why not?), but all of a sudden jettisoning the erstwhile radical posturing. The study of television is now merely another subfield, like Elizabethan drama or romantic poetry or modernist novels, stripped of the former claims of an illusory democratic privilege. The political agenda turns out to have been only the smokescreen for a professional move; the appeals to democracy, just so much careerism. No blood for oil, but maybe for tenure.

When Penley and Ross denounced the myth "that people are passive consumers of the mass media," the final words are crucial: it is not the mass media—the topic of popular culture studies—that make the people passive consumers, for "it is war that makes people stupid, not TV"—a phrase worth savoring. Does the popular cultural critique of canonic hierarchy actually rest on sentiments like this? Here our friends scramble to cover their tracks: "War, most fully embodied in the command and control structure of the military, is the most undemocratic of all activities. In this light, war requires that citizens be less than citizens." Having just demonstrated their contempt for popular opinion, the authors still want to come out smelling like democratic roses: if the people support war, they are stupid, but if they watch television, they are smart. At this point, at the very latest, the ideological duplicity and confusion inherent in the discourse on popular culture, the confusion of culture and politics, have come to a dead end. For while Penley and Ross use the most sophisticated and interesting arguments regarding television, separating the practices of mass media spectatorship from the ideology of the mass media industry, they accept the crudest and most militaristic argument regarding war. Why be poststructuralists for television but traditionalists on war? Is war truly "most fully embodied in the command and control structure of the military?" Are not other practices, beliefs, sentiments and sacrifices involved which precisely scholars of popular culture might take seriously? Is it absolutely impossible that some supporters of the war might have minds at least as independent as those of Professor Penley and Professor Ross? Are war and democracy as fundamentally incompatible as they insist? Or should one not, alternatively, question the sincerity of their democratic pretenses and the political valency of their fundamentalist pacifism?

It goes without saying that there are strong scholarly and intellectual grounds to recognize television and other previously understudied materials of cultural representation as legitimate topics of research and teaching. Yet because the resources of the academy are always necessarily limited, the advocates of individual specialties engage in conflicts to defend their particular niches. It is imaginable that some of these conflicts might sometimes be carried out through the conventions of sincere intellectual argument. The problem is that the proponents of certain fields, to which the label of popular culture has been ascribed, have opted for a rhetoric of class struggle, counterposing the popular to the purported elitism of other material. In addition, as we have just seen, when push comes to shove, the sincerity of those political claims turns out to be less than unbroken. One is forced to the conclusion that, despite the democratic gestures of the popular culturalist discourse, it is no less elitist than that of its opponents, which it has tried to cast as a sort of cultural ancien régime. In fact, the popular culturalists may well be more elitist, since they have pushed their case by making claims in the name of the "people" and they have consequently been forced to denounce the "people" as "stupid" when the "people" have transgressed against the precepts of the political orthodoxy, a gesture which traditionalist colleagues, relatively oblivious to popular opinion, would never have been forced to make.

The suggestion that the discourse on popular culture might in fact entail an elitist agenda is surprising only if one is prepared to accept as genuine the flaunted democratizing gestures of the proponents. On closer examination, however, those gestures have turned out to be mendacious; the culture of the people is invoked, with egalitarian pathos, only in order to wage a campaign for the redivision of academic positions, and the people are junked as soon as popular sentiment diverges from that of the liberal elite. Yet this is nothing new and certainly not merely a post-new-left phenomenon. On the contrary, it has long been a strategy of upwardly mobile social and political groups to operate in the name of the people and, particularly, to invoke a fictionally constructed popular culture, in order to pursue an effectively elitist agenda; the new elite battles the old elite by conjuring up images of the popular nation: the Ossian controversy, the ballad collections of the 1770s, the folksongs and fairy tales of German romanticism, the emergence of nationalistic folklorism in the nineteenth century, avant-gardist primitivism, the search for the proletarian aesthetic, Latin American indigenism, the *völkisch* fictions of fascism, and now the institutionalization of popular culture, all of which could be grouped under Benjamin's term as examples of an aestheticization of politics.

The historical scope of the phenomenon indicates how popular culturalism is a constant potential in bourgeois society, a result of several separate structural features. Owing to the dynamic character of the modernizing economies, a constant social revolution is under way—vide the Communist Manifesto— with a new elite always on the rise; in this context of perpetual conflict, the egalitarian and universalizing rhetoric of national citizenship means that the more democratic position will tend to carry greater legitimacy; and the institutionalization of an aesthetic of autonomy separates taste from status, so that an emergent elite is never tied to inherited aesthetic codes and will tend to choose the taste most effective in the pursuit of its political goals.

Within this dynamic process, the discourse on popular culture is therefore directed not only against an entrenched elite; it is additionally a matter of cultural class warfare against nonelite groups with their own populist cultures. Hence the effort of Penley and Ross to preserve the democratic cachet of a commitment to popular culture while arrogantly denouncing the "stupid" values of popular politics. Populist culture: shared structures of meaning in local settings, barred from the optimism of progress and mobility and, more than likely, resistant to the concomitant disruption of community values and traditions. From the standpoint of any dynamic elite—including popular culturalism—it will appear conservative, rough, sedentary, and insular. Yet precisely because its central concern is community and the mediation of the concrete experience of everyday life, its potential for intersubjectivity will always be greater than that of elite culture. Similarly because of its proximity to lived experience and its limits—birth and death—its involvement with transcendence and religion will be more emphatic, if never unproblematic in secular modernity. But since intersubjectivity and transcendence are component elements of any viable culture, populist culture always tends to have more substance and tenacity than any elite culture, including the elite discourse of popular culture, which, in turn, will always try to lay claim to its populist competitor, to colonize it, and to destroy it through its greater access to the systems of education and the mass media. The discourse on popular culture, in other words, entails the structures which the ideologues of the new class attempt to project and impose on the cultural meanings and practices of the organic and self-constituting communities that survive despite the bureaucratic state, corporate capitalism, and the culture industry. Indeed, "popular culture" ends up as little more than the academic extension of the culture industry—public relations for the industry—a phenomenon that can often be traced even into the modes of debate, self-presentation, and academic style.

The War and Culture: in Germany the discussion slid quickly into a debate over the character of the newly unified state, while in the United States the hidden anxiety concerned the mechanism of cultural cohesion. Still, the differences between Germany and the United States are, obviously, immense. The Hitler metaphor has divergent implications, and the situation in post-1989 Germany, entailing a reorganization of the cultural-political landscape, has little in common with contemporary America. There may have been a latent similarity with regard to popular support which, according to some accounts, may have been extensive in Germany outside of the peace movement, even if the political leadership failed to mobilize it. Yet here my data are too slim to permit any conclusions, and, in any case, the American material is in need of further conceptualization, precisely owing to the collapse of any viable left cultural theory. The problem is to do better than Chomsky and Penley and Ross and account for the discrepancy between prowar populism and antiwar intellectuals. If American culture is not just a Pentagon conspiracy, what is it?

Let me underscore two qualifications before proceeding. First, it is of course certain that not all intellectuals opposed the war, as a glance at the *New Republic, Commentary*, or even *Dissent* quickly shows. Many accept the neo-Wilsonian arguments for a new world order based on the formal principles of international law and unqualified respect for the sovereignty of states. Needless to say, however, this same statism operates on the left as the grounds for an anti-imperialist critique of American interventionism in the sovereign affairs of other nations, while, for Bush, it immediately led to a series of political fiascos: upholding the sovereignty of the Kuwaiti state held him back from supporting the rebels against the Iraqi state, the Lithuanians against the Soviet state, or the Slovenians and Croatians against the Yugoslav state. Second, it is precisely this contradiction which separates the administration's interventionism from populist prowar support; in other words, the public approved of the war and soldiers could be mobilized to fight it not for the overt reasons of the administration (Penley and Ross were right before they retreated to the manipulation thesis: the public is not made up of passive consumers) but for reasons of their own. At stake was less a Wilsonian new world order, a pax americana rationalized as international law, but a desire for community, which bears domestically the name of patriotism, and which, abroad, implies a fundamental sympathy for and sense of obligation to other communities correctly or incorrectly perceived as being victimized by oppressive states. Support for the war dropped with the betrayal of the Kurds, for at that point the public, not at all as manipulated as media critics would have it, could perceive that the war had become one for state sovereignty and not communitarian autonomy, and it therefore carried considerably less populist appeal.

This is a provocative analysis, which I still want to take one step further, but first let me retrace the key steps of the argument. The popularity of the war produces a crisis for the cultural left, which is forced to renounce much of its erstwhile popular culture agenda and retreat to a theory of state manipulation. But if the older arguments against manipulation are treated as valid, then the prowar populism is, in effect, unexplained. The course of that populism in the winter and spring of 1991 proceeds from an initial congruence with aspects of administration policy to a definitive break over the Kurds and, hence, declining support. This observation allows for the articulation of the difference between a statist paradigm and a communitarian paradigm of political culture, amounting to a central contradiction in the United States and, perhaps, in Germany (where, however, the configuration may be somewhat different). Neither paradigm corresponds uniquely to prowar or antiwar positions. Thus, both Bush, despite his principles, and Chomsky, despite his anarchism, place the state in the center of their analyses; neoconservative support for the war was statist—defending sovereignty and law—but populist support was communitarian, as was, by the way, the paleoconservative opposition of the antiwar isolationists on the right. In fact, I would argue that for a while during the war, this tension found expression in a slightly skewed semiotic relationship between the two objects of display of prowar sentiment: the yellow ribbon, indicating support for the troops, and the flag as the sign of allegiance to the state. The oxymoronic relationship between ribbon and flag collapsed at that point when administration policy finally showed its colors and its ultimate loyalty to the flag, the Iraqi flag that is, and the sovereignty of the state; for it is the sovereign, even if he is Saddam Hussein, to whom the new world order ascribes legitimacy, and not the popular insurrection.

It is precisely this contradiction between ribbons and flags, the troops and the state, which are not the same thing (although the state certainly wishes they were), that leads to the conclusion of a deep-seated conflict between two competing ethics: on the one hand, an ethics of obligation, sacrifice, and duty, lodged within a yearning for community that is, however, regularly disappointed; on the other hand, an ethics of rights, interest, and law that appeals to the state—rather than to community—as the appropriate vehicle for the pursuit of a possessive individualism, necessarily antagonistic to sacrifice, including the sacrifice that military service might require. Further argument would be necessary to identify the former option with lower-middle- and working-class strata, and the latter with the ascendant new class, for which state and progress are nearly interchangeable. This could, in any case, shed light on the methodological problem posed earlier regarding the resistance to cultural inquiries into politics, a phenomenon which can now be accounted for as a discursive consequence of the defense of the sovereignty of the state against any incursion of a communitarian dimension of values. Phrased more abrasively, the left retreats to a cultural theory of manipulation not because of an inability to provide an alternative conceptualization but in order to avoid recognizing the potential for populist communitarianism that erupted during the war. For precisely this communitarianism challenges entrenched positions of the left that has largely abandoned the participatory-democratic models of the sixties and accepted the welfare statism of the bureaucracy.

To conclude with two questions: what are the prospects for populism in the United States? why is there no (or less) populism in Germany? The answers would have to address issues like the specific status of the state, different relations between regional units and central power (the question of federalism), alternative notions of national culture, shifting evaluations of the distinction between high and low culture, values of individualism and community, and so on. The inquiries would necessarily break down the border between politics and culture, returning us again to the methodological outset. The point is not at all to politicize culture, certainly not in the sense of expanding state-political intervention into the terrain of aesthetic expression, or its equally obnoxious corollary, making judgments on political correctness. Rather, by insisting on the accessibility of politics to culture, i.e., collective action to collective values, one begins to imagine a collective action informed by collective values rather than a politics derived solely from the instrumental exigencies of the administrative state. The advantage to this account is that the interdisciplinarity of such a cultural-studies agenda ceases to be just another methodology but participates instead directly in a profound social transformation. For insofar as it abrogates the conventional distinction between political fact and cultural value, it tends to facilitate the communitarian revision of the bureaucratic state and the reinvigoration of public life.

Notes

Index

Notes

Introduction: Marking Time

1. Cf. David Gross, *The Past in Ruins: Tradition and the Critique of Modernity* (Amherst: University of Massachusetts Press, 1992); Jean-François Lyotard, *The Postmodern Condition: A Report on Knowledge* (Minneapolis: University of Minnesota Press, 1984).

2. Cf. Carl Schmitt, *Die geistesgeschichtliche Lage des heutigen Parlamentarismus* (Berlin: Duncker und Humblot, 1985).

3. Cf. Russell Berman, "The Peace Movement Debate," *Telos* 57 (Fall 1983): 129–44.

4. Peter Schneider, *Extreme Mittellage* (Reinbek: Rowohlt, 1990), 34.

5. Ibid., 50.

6. Hans Jürgen Syberberg, *Vom Unglück und Glück der Kunst in Deutschland nach dem letzten Kriege* (Munich: Matthes u. Seitz, 1990), 115.

7. Ibid., 116.

8. Ibid.

Chapter 1. Cultural Criticism and Cultural Studies: Reconsidering the Frankfurt School

1. Theodor W. Adorno, *Ästhetische Theorie* (Frankfurt: Suhrkamp, 1974), 9.

2. Theodor W. Adorno, *Philosophy of Modern Music* (New York: Continuum, 1973), 30.

3. Theodor W. Adorno, *Prisms* (Cambridge: MIT Press, 1982), 19.

4. Ibid., 34.

5. Ibid.

6. Ibid.

7. Theodor Adorno, "On the Question: What is German," in *German Mosaic: An Album for Today* (Frankfurt: Suhrkamp, 1972), 333.

8. Theodor W. Adorno, *Noten zur Literatur* I (Frankfurt: Suhrkamp, 1971), 92.

9. Adorno, *Prisms*, 34.

10. Theodor W. Adorno, *Noten zur Literatur* II (Frankfurt: Suhrkamp, 1970), 152.

11. Theodor W. Adorno, *Aesthetics and Politics*, ed. Rodney Taylor (London: New Left Books, 1977), 123.

12. Adorno, *Prisms*, 30.

Chapter 2. Poetry for the Republic: Heine and Whitman

1. Thomas Mann, *Gesammelte Werke*, Vol. 10 (Oldenburg: S. Fischer, 1960), 843.

2. Ibid., 835.

3. Ibid., 839.

4. Ibid., 824.

5. F. O. Matthiessen, *American Renaissance* (New York: Oxford University Press, 1941), 532.

6. Ibid., 531–32.

7. Theodor W. Adorno, *Noten zur Literatur* I (Frankfurt: Suhrkamp, 1971), 151.

8. Heinrich Heine, *Historisch-Kritische Gesamtausgabe der Werke* I, ed. Manfred Windfuhr (Hamburg: Hoffman und Campe, 1983), 111. For English, see *The Complete Poems of Heinrich Heine*, trans. Hal Draper (Boston: Suhrkamp/Insel, 1982), 393.

9. Matthiessen, *American Renaissance*, 540.

10. Ibid., 540–41.

11. Paul Zweig, *Walt Whitman: The Making of the Poet* (New York: Basic Books, 1984), 8.

12. Walt Whitman, *Prose Works 1892*, Vol. 2, ed. Floyd Stovall (New York: New York University Press, 1964), 365.

13. Ibid., 364–65.

14. Walt Whitman, *Leaves of Grass*, ed. Harold W. Blodgett and Sculley Bradley (New York: New York University Press, 1965), 283–84; Heine, *Historisch-Kritische Gesamtausgabe*, 2:109.

15. Heine, *Historisch-Kritische Gesamtausgabe*, 2:109; *Complete Poems*, 392.

16. Whitman, *Leaves of Grass*, 337–38; *Historisch-Kritische Gesamtausgabe*, I/1:207–8; *Complete Poems*, 76.

17. Whitman, *Leaves of Grass*, 371.

18. Heine, *Historisch-Kritische Gesamtausgabe*, 4:109; *Complete Poems*, 498.

19. Whitman, *Leaves of Grass*, 337.

20. Heine, *Historisch-Kritische Gesamtausgabe*, I/1:208–9; *Complete Poems*, 77.

21. Whitman, *Leaves of Grass*, 334.

22. Ibid., 336.

23. See Kurt Hamsun, "Walt Whitman," *Die Gesellschaft* 26 (1900): I/24–35; Ezra Pound, "What I Feel about Walt Whitman," in *Selected Prose, 1909–1965*, ed. William Cookson (New York: New Directions, 1973), 145–46.

24. Heine, *Historisch-Kritische Gesamtausgabe*, 4:92; *Complete Poems*, 484.

25. Whitman, *Prose Works 1892*, 2:376–77.

26. Jonathan Culler, letter to the editor, *London Review of Books*, April 21, 1988, 4.

27. Geoffrey Hartman, "Blindness and Insight," *New Republic*, March 7, 1988, 31.

Chapter 3. Citizenship, Conversion, and Representation:
Moritz Oppenheim's *Return of the Volunteer*

1. Wilhelm Christian Dohm, *Über die bürgerliche Verbesserung der Juden* (1781); cf. David Bronson, ed., *Jews and Germans from 1860 to 1933: The Problematic Symbiosis* (Heidelberg: Carl Winter Verlag, 1979); Max Horkheimer and Theodor W. Adorno, "Elements of Anti-Semitism," in *Dialectic of Enlightenment* (New York: Seabury Press, 1972), 168–208.

2. Fritz Stern, *The Politics of Cultural Despair* (Berkeley: University of California Press, 1974); Walter Boehlich, ed., *Der Berliner Antisemitismusstreit* (Frankfurt: Insel Verlag, 1965).

3. "The KRISIS passes through all the self-assertiveness, all the sense of freedom, all the attainments, claims, and orthodoxies, in our faith." Karl Barth, *The Epistle to the Romans* (Oxford: Oxford University Press, 1968), 524.

4. Hermann Cohen, *Die Religion der Vernunft aus den Quellen des Judentums* (Leipzig: G. Fock, 1919); Eugen Rosenstock-Huessy, *Judaism despite Christianity* (University: University of Alabama Press, 1969); Hans-Joachim Schoeps, *Urgemeinde, Judentum, Gnosis* (Tübingen: Mohn, 1956); *Paulus: die Theologie des Apostels im Lichte der jüdischen Religionsgeschichte* (Tübingen: Mohr, 1959); *Barocke Juden, Christen, Judenchristen* (Bern and Munich: Francke Verlag, 1956).

5. A. McCaul, *Stimmen über Jerusalem* (Berlin: Wilhelm Besser, 1842), especially 15–16.

6. W. T. Gidney, *At Home and Abroad: A Description of the English and Continental Missions of the London Society for Promoting Christianity amongst the Jews* (London: Operative Jewish Converts' Institution, 1900).

7. Cf. Albert Augustus Isaacs, *Biography of the Rev. Henry Aaron Stern, D.D.* (London: James Nisbet, 1886).

8. Constantin Frantz, *Ahasverus oder die Judenfrage* (Berlin: Wilhelm Hermes, 1844).

9. Interestingly, the chapbook of 1602 was republished in the popular Reclam series in 1879.

10. Michael A. Meyer, *German Political Pressure and Jewish Religious Response in the Nineteenth Century*, Leo Baeck Memorial Lecture, 25 (New York: Leo Baeck Institute, 1981), 8.

11. Norman Kleeblatt and Vivian B. Mann, *Treasures of the Jewish Museum* (New York: Jewish Museum, 1968), 148.

12. Rudolf M. Heilbrunn, "Leben und Werk des Malers Moritz Oppenheim," *Bulletin des Leo Baeck Instituts,* 9, no. 36 (1966):286–87.

13. Ibid., 287.

14. Theodor W. Adorno, *Ästhetische Theorie* (Frankfurt: Suhrkamp, 1974), 106.

15. Russell A. Berman, "Avantgarde und Bilderverbot," in *Kunst und Politik der Avantgarde,* ed. syndicat anonym (Frankfurt: Künstlerhaus Mousonturm, 1989), 49–64.

16. Heilbrunn, "Leben und Werk," 288.

17. For biography, in addition to Heilbrunn, cf. Cecil Roth, *Jewish Art* (Greenwich, 1971), 554–56; Elisheva Cohen, "Moritz Daniel Oppenheim," *Bulletin des Leo Baeck Instituts* 16/17, nos. 53–54 (1977/78), 42–74 (hereafter *LBI*); and Elisheva Cohen, "Moritz Daniel Oppenheim: His Life and Art," in *Moritz Oppenheim: The First Jewish Painter* (Jerusalem: Israel Museum, 1983), 7–29. The key source is Oppenheim's *Erinnerungen,* ed. Alfred Oppenheim (Frankfurt: Frankfurter Verlagsanstalt, 1924).

18. E. Cohen, "His Life and Art," 8.

19. Oppenheim, *Erinnerungen,* 20–31.

20. "But Oppenheim derived the greatest satisfaction from his relationship with the much-respected Danish sculptor Bertel Thorvaldsen, in whom he found a patron. Many of his friends, whose names are hardly remembered today—Emil Wolff, Christian Lotsch, Schmidt von der Launitz (whose studio in Frankfurt he painted many years later)—belonged to Thorvaldsen's circle, either as students or assistants. . . . Next to Thorvaldsen, Oppenheim most greatly admired Friedrich Overbeck, the revered leader of the Nazarenes." E. Cohen, "His Life and Art," 15.

21. Oppenheim, *Erinnerungen,* 75.

22. E. Cohen, "His Life and Art," 19.

23. Oppenheim, *Erinnerungen,* 99.

24. Ibid., 33–36, 40–41, 55–57.

25. Ibid., 89–90.

26. E. Cohen, *LBI,* 60.

27. Oppenheim, *Erinnerungen,* 91.

28. Ibid., 92.

29. Cohen, *LBI,* 61.

30. Cf. I. Kracauer, *Geschichte der Juden in Frankfurt a.M.* (Frankfurt: Kaufmann Verlag, 1927), 2:491–95.

31. *Erinnerungen,* 73. On the visit to Weimar, see ibid., 81–84.

32. Ismar Schorsh, "Art as Social History: Oppenheim and the German-Jewish Vision of Emancipation," in *Moritz Oppenheim: The First Jewish Painter,* 33–34.

33. Ibid., 36.

34. For a general description, see ibid., 31. Cf. Vivian B. Mann, *A Tale of Two Cities: Jewish Life in Frankfurt and Istanbul, 1750–1870* (New York: Jewish Museum, 1982) 109–110. Cf. the reprint, Moritz Daniel Oppenheim, *Pictures of Traditional Jewish Family Life* (New York: Ktav Publishing House, 1976).

35. Alfred Werner, *Families and Feasts: Paintings by Oppenheim and Kaufmann* (New York: Yeshiva University, 1977), 9.

36. Schorsch, "Art as Social History," 31.

37. Ibid., 45–51.

38. Ibid., 31.

39. Ibid., 51–52.

40. Ibid., 52.

41. Ibid.

42. Ibid.

43. Cf. Eckart Kehr, "The Social System of Reaction in Prussia under the Puttkamer Ministry," in *Economic Interests, Militarism, and Foreign Policy*, ed. Gordon A. Craig (Berkeley: University of California Press, 1977), 109–31.

44. *New York Times*, Dec. 15, 1989, A20.

45. Russell A. Berman, *The Rise of the Modern German Novel* (Cambridge: Harvard University Press, 1986), 60–63.

46. E. Cohen, *LBI*, 63. "What made the gift appropriate is that it epitomized Riesser's political ideology: loyalties to faith and fatherland were not in conflict." Schorsch, "Art as Social History," 32.

47. Gabriel Riesser, *Schriften über Literatur und literarische Verhältnisse, Gesammelte Schriften*, ed. Comite der Riesser-Stiftung von M. Isler (Frankfurt: Riesser-Stiftung, 1868), 4:720–21.

48. Ibid., 717.

49. Ibid., 714–15.

50. G. W. F. Hegel, *Phänomenologie des Geistes* (Hamburg: Felix Meiner, 1952), 330–42 (*die sittliche Handlung*).

51. Ernst Randak, *Peter Altenberg oder das Genie ohne Fähigkeiten* (Graz and Vienna: Stiasny Verlag, 1961), 207.

52. Cf. Rudolph Sohm, *Wesen und Ursprung des Katholizismus* (Leipzig and Berlin: B. G. Teubner, 1912).

53. Cf. Ernst Robert Curtius, *Europäische Literatur und Lateinisches Mittelalter* (Bern: A. Francke Verlag, 1948), 75–76, and George Kurman, "Ecphrasis in Epic Poetry," *Comparative Literature* 25, no. 1 (Winter 1974):1.

54. Peter Bürger, *Theory of the Avantgarde* (Minneapolis: University of Minnesota Press, 1984).

55. E. P. Thompson, *The Making of the English Working Class* (New York: Vintage Books, 1966), 370–71.

56. Sigmund Freud, "Analyse der Phobie eines fünfjährigen Knaben," in *Stu-*

dienausgabe (Frankfurt: S. Fischer Verlag, 1969), 7:36, n. 2. As for Weininger, so too for Public Enemy; see *New York Times*, December 26, 1989, B1-B2.

57. Richard Wagner, "Judaism in Music," *Stories and Essays*, ed. Charles Osborne (London: Peter Owens, 1973), 27.

**Chapter 4. Piedmont as Prussia: The Italian Model
and German Unification**

1. Cited in Theodor Schieder, "Das Italienbild der deutschen Einheitsbewegung," in *Studien zur deutsch-italienischen Geistesgeschichte*, ed. Istituto italiano di cultura and the Petrarca-Institut of the University of Cologne (Cologne and Graz: Böhlau Verlag, 1959), 141.

2. Heinrich Heine, *Reise von München nach Genua* in *Historisch-Kritische Gesamtausgabe*, Vol. 7/1, ed. Alfred Opitz (Hamburg: Hoffman und Campe, 1986), 48.

3. Ibid.

4. Ibid., 49.

5. Ibid.

6. Ibid., 69.

7. Regarding the Frankfurt parliament's claim on northern Italy and, more generally, German attitudes to the risorgimento, cf. Robert Michels, *Italien von Heute: Politische und Wirtschaftliche Kulturgeschichte von 1860 bis 1930* (Zürich and Leipzig: Orell Füssli Verlag, 1930), 13–19.

8. Annie Mittelstaedt, *Der Krieg von 1859: Bismark und die öffentliche Meinung in Deutschland* (Stuttgart: Union Deutsche Verlagsgesellschaft, 1904), 21; cf. Rudolf Margraff, *Vor und nach dem Frieden von Villafranca: Studien zur Geschichte und Kritik der politischen Entwicklung des letzten Zeitdramas* (Leipzig: Adolph Lehmann, 1860), and especially Ernst Portner, *Die Einigung Italiens im Urteil liberaler deutscher Zeitgenossen: Studien zur inneren Geschichte des kleindeutschen Liberalismus*. Bonner Historische Forschungen, No. 13 (Bonn: Ludwig Röhrscheid Verlag, 1959).

9. Theodor von Bernhardi, "Frankreich, Österreich und der Krieg in Italien," *Vermischte Schriften* (Berlin: G. Reimer, 1879), 2:236–37. Reprinted from *Preussische Jahrbücher* (1859).

10. Ibid., 349.

11. Hermann Baumgarten, "Der deutsche Liberalismus: Eine Selbstkritik," in *Preussische Jahrbücher* 18 (1866):485.

12. Ibid., 489.

13. Ibid., 600.

14. Ibid., 482.

15. Ibid.

16. Ibid.

17. Ibid., 600.

18. Ibid.

19. Wilhelm Lang, "Deutsche und italienische Einheit," in *Preussische Jahrbücher* 27 (1871):208.

20. Ibid.

21. Ibid., 220–21.

22. Ibid., 210–11.

23. Ibid., 212.

24. Ibid., 215.

25. Ibid., 217.

26. On the importance of anti-Catholicism for German literary discourse and popular representations of national identity, see Günther Hirschmann, *Kulturkampf im historischen Roman der Gründerzeit: 1859–1878* (Munich: Wilhelm Fink Verlag, 1978).

27. P.-J. Proudhon, *La Fédération et l'unité en Italie*, in *Œuvres complètes* (Paris: Marcel Rivière, 1959), 18:105.

28. Cf. Max Nettlau, *Der Anarchismus: Von Proudhon zu Kropotkin. Seine historische Entwicklung in den Jahren 1859–1880* (Berlin: Verlag Der Syndikalist, 1927), 5–34.

Chapter 5. Literary History and the Politics of Deconstruction: Rousseau in Weimar

1. Jean-Jacques Rousseau, *The First and Second Discourses* (New York: St. Martin's Press, 1964), 103–4.

2. Ibid., 104.

3. Jean-Jacques Rousseau, *Œuvres complètes*, Vol. 3 (Paris: Editions Galli-mard, 1964), li.

4. Ibid., lvii–lviii.

5. Paul de Man, *Allegories of Reading: Figural Language in Rousseau, Nietzsche, Rilke, and Proust* (New Haven and London: Yale University Press, 1979), 141.

6. Rousseau, *First and Second Discourses*, 149.

7. Rousseau, *Œuvres complètes*, 1327.

8. De Man, *Allegories of Reading*, 143–44.

9. Ibid., 152–53.

10. Ibid., 153.

11. Ibid., 155.

12. Heinrich Mann, *Essays* (Hamburg: Claassens, 1960), 7.

13. Ibid., 8–9.

14. Ibid., 14.

15. Ibid., 9, 11.

16. Heinrich Mann, *Ein Zeitalter wird besichtigt* (Stockholm: S. Fischer, 1944), 344.

17. Robert Darnton, *The Great Cat Massacre and Other Episodes in French Cultural History* (New York: Vintage Press, 1985), 215–52.

18. Carl Schmitt, *Die geistesgeschichtliche Lage des heutigen Parlamentarismus* (Berlin: Duncker und Humblot, 1985), 18–19.

19. Carl Schmitt, *Political Theology: Four Chapters on the Concept of Sovereignty* (Cambridge, Mass., and London: MIT Press, 1985), 59.

20. Walter Benjamin, *Illustrations* (New York: Schocken Press, 1969), 242.

21. Walter Benjamin, *Reflections: Essays, Aphorisms, Autobiographical Writings* (New York and London: Harcourt Brace Jovanovich, 1978), 225.

22. Paul de Man, *Wartime Journalism* (Lincoln and London: University of Nebraska Press, 1988), 45.

23. Rousseau, *First and Second Discourses*, 141.

24. Ibid., 144; de Man, *Allegories of Reading*, 156.

25. Geoffrey Hartman, "Blindness and Insight, *New Republic*, March 7, 1988, 31.

26. Werner Hamacher, "Fortgesetzte Trauerarbeit," *Frankfurter Allgemeine Zeitung*, February 24, 1986, 35.

27. Jeffrey Mehlman, "Writing and Deference: The Politics of Literary Adulation," *Representations* 15 (Summer 1986):1–2.

28. Jürgen Habermas, "Modernity versus Postmodernity," *New German Critique* 22 (Winter 1981):13.

29. Anne McClintock and Rob Nixon, "No Names Apart: The Separation of Word and History in Derrida's 'Le dernier mot du racisme'," in *"Race," Writing, and Difference*, ed. Henry Louis Gates, Jr. (Chicago and London: University of Chicago Press, 1986), 352–53.

30. Jacques Derrida, "Racism's Last Word," trans. Peggy Kamuf, in *"Race," Writing, and Difference*, 331.

31. Ibid., 333; *New York Times*, June 27, 1990, A8.

32. Michel Foucault, *The Order of Things: An Archaeology of the Human Sciences* (New York: Random House, 1973), 387.

Chapter 6. German Primitivism/Primitive Germany: The Case of Emil Nolde

1. Hellmut Lehmann-Haupt, *Art under a Dictatorship* (New York: Oxford University Press, 1954), 79–81.

2. Theda Shapiro, *Painters and Politics: The European Avant-Garde and Society, 1900–1925* (New York, Oxford, Amsterdam: Elsevier, 1976), 265.

3. *Meyers Neues Lexikon* (Leipzig: VEB Bibliographisches Institut, 1974), 10:141–42.

4. Shapiro, *Painters and Politics*, 114, 212.

5. Cf. Georg Lukács, *Essays on Realism*, ed. Rodney Livingstone (Cambridge: MIT Press, 1980), 76–113.

6. Lehmann-Haupt, *Art under a Dictatorship*, 73.

7. Joseph Wulf, *Die bildenden Künste im Dritten Reich: eine Dokumentation* (Gütersloh: Sigbert Mohn Verlag, 1963), 50–51.

8. Emil Nolde, *Jahre der Kämpfe: 1902–1914*, 2d ed. (Flensburg: Christian Wolff Verlag, 1958), 125–26.

9. Max Sauerlandt, *Die Kunst der letzten 30 Jahre: eine Vorlesung aus dem Jahre 1933* (Hamburg: Harmann Laatzen Verlag, 1948), 72.

10. Ibid., 80.

11. Nolde, *Jahre der Kämpfe*, 177, 181.

12. Nolde, *Welt und Heimat: die Südseereise, 1913–1918* (Cologne: Verlag M. DuMont-Schauberg, 1965), 58.

13. Ibid.

14. Ibid., 106.

15. Shapiro, *Painter and Politics*, 10.

16. Renato Rosaldo, *Culture and Truth: The Remaking of Social Analysis* (Boston: Beacon Press, 1989), 68–87.

17. Nolde, *Welt und Heimat*, 145.

18. Cf. Jean Laude, *La peinture française (1905–1914) et 'l'art nègre' : contribution à l'étude des sources du fauvisme et du cubisme* (Paris: Editions Klincksieck, 1968), 402–526.

19. Carl Einstein, *Die Kunst des 20. Jahrhunderts* (1926), cit. in Reinhard Wegner, *Der Exotismus-Streit in Deutschland: Zur Auseinandersetzung mit primitiven Formen in der bildenden Kunst des 20. Jahrhunderts*, European University Studies Series 28, Vol. 27 (Frankfurt, Bern, New York: Peter Lang, 1973), 101.

20. Paul de Man, *Wartime Journalism: 1939–1943*, ed. Werner Hamacher, Neil Hertz, and Thomas Keenan (Lincoln and London: University of Nebraska Press, 1988), 216–17.

Chapter 7. A Solidarity of Repression: Pabst and the Proletariat

1. "A Mine Disaster," *New York Times*, November 9, 1932; Lee Atwell, *G. W. Pabst* (Boston: Twayne, 1977), 101; Siegfried Kracauer, *From Caligari to Hitler: A Psychological History of the German Film* (Princeton: Princeton University Press, 1971) 240.

2. "As the film stands now, to accept the accord which effected the rescue as permanent in proletarian fraternity would be a delusive irony, especially when we recall that the actual event at Courrières did not prevent that war of 1914." Harry Alan Potamkin, "Pabst and the Social Film," in *Horn and Hounds*, January/March, 1933, 303. Cf. "Kameradschaft," in *Deutsche Filmzeitung*, no. 51/52 (1931):

14–16, rpt. in *Erobert den Film!* (Berlin: Neue Gesellschaft für bildende Kunst, 1977), 171.

3. Cf. the discussion of politics and language in Ernesto Laclau and Chantal Mouffe, *Hegemony and Socialist Strategy: Towards a Radical Democratic Politics* (London: Verso, 1985).

4. Cf. Nancy Webb-Kelly, *Homo Ludens, Homo Aestheticus: The Transformation of "Free Play" in the Rise of Literary Criticism*, Diss., Stanford University, 1988.

5. Cf. Michael Rohrwasser, *Saubere Mädel, Starke Genossen: Proletarische Massenliteratur?* (Frankfurt: Roter Stern, 1977); Klaus Theweleit, *Male Fantasies* (Minneapolis: University of Minnesota Press, 1987).

6. Sigmund Freud, *The Interpretation of Dreams*, in *The Standard Edition of the Complete Psychological Works*, Vol. 5 (London: Hogarth Press, 1953), 354.

7. Cf. Alice Yaeger Kaplan, *Reproductions of Banality: Fascism, Literature, and French Intellectual Life* (Minneapolis: University of Minnesota Press, 1986), and Peter Brückner et al., "Perspectives on the Fascist Public Sphere," *New German Critique*, no. 11 (Spring 1977):94–132.

8. Cf. Rosa Luxemburg, *Selected Political Writings*, ed. Dick Howard (New York: Monthly Review Press, 1971).

9. Sigmund Freud, "The Acquisition and Control of Fire," *Standard Edition*, Vol. 22 (London: Hogarth Press, 1964), 188, 190.

10. "It is as though primal man had the habit, when he came in contact with fire, of satisfying an infantile desire connected with it, by putting it out with a stream of his urine. The legends that we possess leave no doubt about the originally phallic view taken of tongues of flames as they shoot upwards. Putting out fire by micturating—a theme to which modern giants, Gulliver in Liliput and Rabelais' Gargantua, still hark back—was therefore a kind of sexual act with a male, an enjoyment of sexual potency in a homosexual competition. The first person to renounce this desire and spare the fire was able to carry it off with him and subdue it to his own use. By damping down the fire of his own sexual excitation, he had tamed the natural force of fire. This great cultural conquest was thus the reward for his renunciation of instinct." Sigmund Freud, *Civilization and Its Discontents*, *Standard Edition*, Vol. 21 (London: Hogarth Press, 1921), 90.

11. Noel Carroll, "Lang, Pabst, and Sound," *Cine-Tracte* 2, no. 1 (1978):22.

Chapter 8. The Masses and Margarita: Faust at the Movies

1. Ernest Prodolliet, *Faust im Kino: Die Geschichte des Faustfilms von den Anfängen bis zur Gegenwart*, Arbeiten aus dem Institut für Journalistik an der Universität Freiburg Schweiz, ed. Florian H. Fleck (Freiburg, Switzerland: Universitätsverlag, 1978), 83–91.

2. Walter Benjamin, *Das Kunstwerk im Zeitalter seiner technischen Reprodu- zierbarkeit* (Frankfurt: Suhrkamp Verlag, 1969), 52.

3. Prodolliet, *Faust im Kino*, 49–52. Ludwig Greve et al., *Hätte ich das Kino! Die Schriftsteller und der Stummfilm*, catalogue of the Deutsches Literaturarchiv (Stuttgart: Ernst Klett Verlag, 1976), 260–61.

4. Siegfried Kracauer, *From Caligari to Hitler: A Psychological History of the German Film* (Princeton: Princeton University Press, 1971), p. 148–49.

5. Teresa de Lauretis, *Alice Doesn't: Feminism, Semiotics, Cinema* (Bloom- ington: University of Indiana Press, 1984).

6. Prodolliet, *Faust im Kino*, 53–54.

7. Stephen Vincent Benét, "The Devil and Daniel Webster," in *Thirteen O'Clock: Stories of Several Worlds* (New York and Toronto: Farrar and Rinehart, 1932), 172–74.

8. René Clair, *Four Screenplays*, trans. Pierguiseppe Bozzetti (New York: Orion Press, 1970), 174.

9. Ibid., 213.

10. Ibid., 145.

11. Louis Pauwels, *President Faust* (Paris: Albin Michel, 1974), 46, 168.

12. Jean Kerchbron, "La réalisation militante," in Pauwels, *President Faust*, 15–17.

13. Klaus Mann, *Mephisto*, trans. Robin Smyth (New York: Penguin Books, 1983), 22.

14. Ibid., 151.

Chapter 9. The Rhetoric of Citation and the Ideology of War in Heinrich Böll's Short Fiction

1. Clayton Koelb, *Inventions of Readings: Rhetoric and the Literary Imagina- tion* (Ithaca and London: Cornell University Press, 1988).

2. *Herodotus*, trans. J. Enoch Powell (Oxford: Clarendon Press, 1949), 2:564; cf. Georg Büchmann, *Geflügelte Worte: Der Zitatenschatz des deutschen Volkes* (Frankfurt, Berlin, and Vienna: Ullstein Verlag, 1981), 252; Friedrich Schiller, *Sämtliche Werke in zehn Bänden*, Berliner Ausgabe, ed. Hans-Günther Thalheim et al. (Berlin: Aufbau-Verlag, 1980), 1:269–274.

3. *Herodotus*, 510.

4. Theodor W. Adorno, *Ästhetische Theorie, Gesammelte Schriften*, Vol. 7, ed. Gretel Adorno and Rolf Tiedemann (Frankfurt: Suhrkamp, 1970), 9.

5. Heinrich Böll, *Werke: Romane und Erzählungen*, ed. Bernd Balzer (Cologne: Gertraud Middelhauve Verlag and Kiepenheuer und Witsch, 1977), 1:194–97. Sub- sequent references to this edition will be placed in the main text.

6. Gotthold Ephraim Lessing, *Werke* (Darmstadt: Wissenschaftliche Buchge- sellschaft, 1971), 2:219 (*Nathan der Weise*, act 1, scene 3).

Chapter 10. Refusal or Denial and the Sky of Europe: Literary Postmodernism in Peter Handke's *Across*

1. Peter Handke, *Across*, trans. Ralph Mannheim (New York: Farrar, Straus, and Giroux, 1986), p. 134.
2. Peter Handke, *Ich bin ein Bewohner des Elfenbeinturms* (Frankfurt a.M.: Suhrkamp, 1972).
3. Cf. Edward Said, *Orientalism* (New York: Pantheon Books, 1978).
4. Elisabeth Wiesmayr, *Die Zeitschrift "manuskripte," 1960–1970* (Königstein i Ts.:Hain, 1980), 21.
5. Ibid., 16.
6. Ibid.
7. Cf. Jürgen Habermas, *The Structural Transformation of the Public Sphere: An Inquiry into a Category of Bourgeois Society*, trans. Thomas Burger (Cambridge, Mass.: MIT Press, 1991).
8. Wiesmayr, *Die Zeitschrift "manuskripte,"* 3.
9. Ibid., 4; cf. Hans Sedlmayr, *Verlust der Mitte: die bildende Kunst des 19. und 20. Jahrhunderts* (Salzburg: O. Müller, 1948).
10. Wiesmayr, *Die Zeitschrift "manuskripte."*
11. Ibid., 74.
12. Reinhard Priessnitz and Mechtild Rausch, cit. in ibid., 79.
13. Ibid., 45.
14. Hans Magnus Enzensberger, "Gemeinplätze, die neueste Literatur betreffend," in *Kursbuch*, no. 15 (1968):187–97.
15. Wiesmayr, *Die Zeitschrift "manuskripte,"* 19.
16. Cf. Jean-François Lyotard, *The Postmodern Condition: A Report on Knowledge* (Minneapolis: University of Minnesota Press, 1984).

Chapter 11. The Gulf War and Cultural Theory in Germany and the United States: Nationhood, Popularity, and Yellow Ribbons

1. Ralf Dahrendorf, "Nachdenkliches zum Krieg am Golf," *Merkur* 45, no. 3 (March 1991):234–35.
2. Cited in Jürgen Habermas, "Wider die Logik des Krieges: ein Plädoyer für Zurückhaltung, aber nicht gegenüber Israel," *Die Zeit*, February 22, 1991, 16.
3. "Ich hoffe, daß unsere Politiker dem Druck von außen standhalten." Interview in *die tageszeitung*, February 11, 1991.
4. The special section of the *New York Times* of June 9, 1991, entitled "Operation Welcome Home," celebrating the victory parade on June 10, includes selected articles reporting the course of the war. None address the SCUD attacks on Israel; one treats of a "retaliation plan that the Israelis abandoned" (19). What for other states would be regarded as a matter of self-defense is, in the case of the Jewish state, imagined to be vengeful "retaliation."

5. Yoram Kaniuk, "Dreieinhalb Stunden und fünfzig Jahre mit Günter Grass in Berlin," *Die Zeit*, June 28, 1991, 17; Henryk M. Broder, "Unser Kampf," *Der Spiegel*, April 29, 1991, 255–67; Alice Schwarzer, "Bornierte Freund-Feind Muster," *Der Spiegel*, May 20, 1991, 248–51; Hans-Christian Ströbele, "Broders Spiegelfechtereien," ibid., 251–55; Brigitte Erler, "Ein Schreckgespenst," ibid., 255.

6. Habermas, "Wider die Logik des Krieges."

7. Ibid.

8. Karl Heinz Bohrer, "Falkland und die Deutschen," *Frankfurter Allgemeine Zeitung*, May 15, 1982.

9. Karl Heinz Bohrer, "Provinzialismus (II): ein Psychogramm," *Merkur* 45, no. 3 (March 1991):261.

10. Ibid., 255–56.

11. Ibid., 257.

12. Ibid., 257–58.

13. "Hitlers Wiedergänger," *Der Spiegel*, February 4, 1991, 26–28; trans. in *Telos*, no. 86 (Winter 1991).

14. Ibid., 27.

15. Ibid., 26.

16. Ibid., 27.

17. Ibid., 28.

18. On Bush's uncontrolled rhetoric, see Bob Woodward, *The Commanders* (New York: Simon and Schuster, 1991), 260f., 282, 302, 323.

19. Michael Emery, *How Mr. Bush Got His War: Deceptions, Double-Standards & Disinformation* (Westfield, N.J.: Open Magazine, 1991), 1.

20. Craig Hulet, *The Secret U.S. Agenda in the Gulf War* (Westfield, N.J.: Open Magazine, 1991), 5, 7.

21. "The Gulf War—Taking Positions," *Dissent*, spring 1991, 155.

22. Noam Chomsky, *The New World Order* (Westfield, N.J.: Open Magazine, 1991), 9, 10.

23. Noam Chomsky, *Deterring Democracy* (London and New York: Verso, 1991), 369–70.

Index